EARLY SETTLERS MECKLENBURG COUNTY VIRGINIA VOLUME I

COMPILED
BY
KATHERINE B. ELLIOTT
SOUTH HILL
VIRGINIA

Copyright 1964
By: Katherine B. Elliott

Copyright Transferred 1983

All rights reserved. No part of this publication may be reproduced, stored in a retrieval system, transmitted in any form, posted on to the web in any form or by any means without the prior written permission of the publisher.

Please direct all correspondence and orders to:

www.southernhistoricalpress.com
or
SOUTHERN HISTORICAL PRESS, Inc.
PO BOX 1267
375 West Broad Street Greenville,
SC 29601
southernhistoricalpress@gmail.com

ISBN #0-89308-379-8

TABLE OF CONTENTS
Volume I

	Page
Introduction	5
Formation of County Government	11
Land Grants	15
Mecklenburg County Creeks	73
Early Brunswick County Deeds	77
Tithe Lists - 1748	96
Tithe Lists - 1752	100
Early Lunenburg County Deeds	105
Land Processioning - 1759	141
St. James Parish Tithe Lists - 1764	151
Notes on Tithe Lists for 1764	169
Notes from Bristol Parish Register	172
Brunswick County Notes	175
Colonial Soldiers	184
Notes on Some Early Settlers	185
Some People who went to Other States	200
Index	205

INTRODUCTION

It has been the purpose of the compiler to present the names of all of the early people who settled in the area now Mecklenburg County which can now be documented by extant records. It has not been the purpose of the compiler to write a history of the area, but to present basic source material. This material is presented as a supplement to Mecklenburg County records - "Eary Wills", "Marriage Records 1765-1810", "Marriage Records 1811-1853" and "Revolutionary War Records" - which have been published.

Since Lunenburg County was cut from Brunswick County, and Mecklenburg County was in turn cut from Lunenburg, it is necessary to search records of all three counties for names of the early settlers in Mecklenburg County.

The first court for Mecklenburg County was held on the 11th day of March 1765. The first court for Lunenburg County was held on the 5th day of May 1746; and the first court for Brunswick County was held on the 2nd day of May 1732.

Brunswick County was created in 1720 from Prince George County, but the area was so sparsely settled it was ordered that jurisdiction over the county be retained by the Court of Prince George County until a county government was established. The first county government for Brunswick County was not established until 1732. The records of Brunswick County were recorded in Prince George County prior to that date. Unfortunately many of the Prince George County records for this period have been lost. In extant Prince George records, there are references to Brunswick County in recorded deeds and in land surveys.

The eastern and northern boundaries of Brunswick County were fixed by the Act creating the county. The western boundary was theoretically the crest of the Blue Ridge Mountains but in fact nebulous. The southern boundary was the line dividing the Colony of Virginia from the Province of North Carolina. On its face, this seemed a settled boundary but as a matter of fact the actual boundary line had never been settled. After the creation of Brunswick County in 1720, patents were issued for grants of land on both the north and south side of the Roanoke River. But the exact point at which the river crossed the boundary line into North Carolina had never been established. It was questionable as to whether such grants were in Virginia or in North Carolina. Constant disputes brought about the surveying of the boundary in 1728 which fixed the line between the two colonies permanently.

The running of the dividing line brought to light a number of problems that had developed. John Banister of Prince George County patented 560 acres of land on the south side of the Roanoke River on 13 of October 1727 in the area now Mecklenburg County. John Banister lived in that part of Prince George County which became Dinwiddie County in 1752. John Banister of Dinwiddie County sold 250 acres of land to Samuel Jones in 1753 "being all of the land that falls within the dividing line between Virginia and North Carolina". This deed refers to the patent of 13 October 1727. Virginia had granted John Banister 310 acres of land in North Carolina in error.

The earliest settlers in Brunswick County came from Prince George and adjoining Surry County. Many of these settlers, or their descendants, moved into the area later to become Mecklenburg County. The earliest settlers in the Mecklenburg area came from Prince George County. Many of the early patentees of land in Mecklenburg were from Prince George County, but they did not move to the area. They sold the land later to others who settled in the county.

The earliest patent for land in Mecklenburg County was a grant of 2811 acres to Robert Munford and John Anderson of Prince George County on 15 May 1722. This land lay on both sides of the present boundary line between Mecklenburg and Brunswick Counties. Edward and Mary Munford of Dinwiddie County sold the 811 acres on 25 November 1752 to Frederick Jones of Dinwiddie County. The deed describes the land as "beginning at Cocke's Creek" and "devised to Edward Munford by Robert Munford by his will dated 20 April 1734". The deed states also that it was part of 2811 acres granted to Robert Munford and John Anderson 15 May 1722.

The "Cocke's Creek" referred to in the deed is now known as Poplar Creek, and has often been confused with Cox Creek farther west between Miles and Allens Creeks.

Robert Hicks, Senior, of Prince George County, who settled later in that part of Surry County which was added to Brunswick County in 1732, patented 580 acres on the north side of the Roanoke River adjoining the land patented by Robert Munford and John Anderson. Robert Hicks gave 100 acres of this tract to Cornelius Keith in 1734 "for seating and cultivating" a part of the land. Robert Hicks gave the remaining 480 acres in 1735 to Samuel Clark, Junr., "for true love and natural affection". This tract of land on the north side of the Roanoke River was opposite the tract of land patented by John Alexander in 1727.

Between these tracts of land was the famous "Horseford". Captain Hicks, noted as an Indian Trader, undoubtedly had selected this tract of land on one of his many trading trips to trade with the Southern Indians. The Trading Path into the Carolinas crossed the Roanoke River at this point. Near this point, Cornelius Keith was granted a license in 1739 "to keep a ferry over the Roanoke River from his own landing below the Horseford to Alexander's landing".

Cornelius Keith apparently discontinued the operation of the ferry, however, for in 1741 Martha Alexander, widow of John Alexander, petitioned the Brunswick Court for a license to "keep a ferry from her landing over the River to Cornelius Keith's landing" which was granted. Cornelius Keith sold his land in 1742 to Thomas Twitty.

Cornelius Keith was undoubtedly a first generation immigrant for in a deposition 3 May 1739, in the Brunswick County Court, he stated that "he has resided 30 years in this Colony since his importation". He had apparently come to Virginia as an immigrant in 1709.

Drury Stith, Henry Morris and Michael Cadet Young appear many times in Brunswick records pertaining to Mecklenburg County. They jointly patented many hundreds of acres of land in Mecklenburg County which they later sold. Drury Stith, of Prince George County, was a surveyor, and his survey discloses that he surveyed many tracts of land in the area which became Mecklenburg, Halifax and Pittsylvania Counties.

In making surveys in Halifax and the area now Pittsylvania County, Drury Stith was probably working as an assistant to Peter Fontaine, Junr. Peter Fontaine, Junr., had been appointed surveyor for Halifax County when it was created in 1752. Peter Fontaine, Junr., in a letter to his uncle, John Fontaine, which appears in "Memoirs of a Huguenot Family", states that "by means of the indulgence granted me, of having assistants, I do not go at all in the woods, which indeed my weakly constitution is not fit for". If Peter Fontaine, Junr., kept a book of surveys, its present location is unknown to the compiler. The survey book of Drury Stith is in the Clerk's Office of Pittsylvania County, but when it was deposited in this office is unknown.

Many later surveys were made in Halifax County by Robert Wooding. These surveys are recorded in the deed books of Halifax County. The business of a surveyor, while hard work, was a lucrative one. Any patentee seeking a grant of land had first to select the land, and then have it surveyed. With a copy of the survey, he then applied for a patent or grant of the land. When the grant was approved, he then "sued out" the patent. That is, he cleared the patent out of the office of the Secretary by payment of the proscribed fees which were usually ten shillings for each 100 acres granted. Records of the grants were kept by the Secretary of the Colony.

When patented land was sold it was frequently surveyed again. Large grants were usually cut into smaller tracts which required the services of a surveyor. Many of the early sales of land were made by lease with a nominal payment of five shillings, and later confirmed by a deed of release stating the full purchase price. Sometimes a considerable period of time passed before such transactions were completed.

Since most patents required that the land be "seated and a minimum acreage be cleared", the grantee frequently hired someone to clear the necessary acreage and make any required improvements on the premises. The Court many times appointed commissioners to view and value such improvements. Armistead Burwell, a large patentee in Mecklenburg County, employed John Cox, Senr., of Finneywood to make improvements on the land patented. Armistead Burwell conveyed to John Cox on 2 January 1749 100 acres "for sundry work, labor and services by Cox in improving a tract of land & for 5 shillings" as compensation for his work.

It was not necessary for a wife to sign a deed in the sale of land, but if the purchaser subsequently sold the land the wife had to release her dower right before the seller could give a valid deed. Sometimes the release of dower was not recorded until years later. In most county records, the release of dower right was recorded when executed, and in many cases long after the deed was recorded. In Mecklenburg County, the clerk left a margin under the deed for recording the release if executed at a later date.

Henry Morris and Michael Cadet Young were first generation immigrants. At a Court held for Brunswick County on 3 May 1739, Henry Morris stated that "he had been imported from Great Britain 21 years". At the same court, Michael Cadet Young stated that "it is now 17 years since his importation into the Colony". It appears that Henry Morris came to Virginia in 1718, and that Michael Cadet Young came from Great Britain to Virginia in 1722. The Brunswick and Lunenburg records disclose that many of the early settlers were first generation immigrants.

It has been thought that all of the early records of both Brunswick and Lunenburg Counties, with the exception of the early marriage records, have been preserved; but this does not seem to be so. Order Book 2 of Brunswick County begins 4 June 1741 and ends on Friday, 4 June 1742. Order Book 3 begins on 2 January 1745. There does not appear to be any extant order book records between these dates. There appears to be a number of deeds which were never recorded also. At a Court held for Brunswick County 3 July 1735, Thomas Wilson acknowledged lease and release of 52 deeds, but these deeds are not recorded in the deed books.

Many of the very earliest settlers in Mecklenburg County came from Prince George County, but by the 1730's many came from that part of Henrico County which became Chesterfield in 1749. By midcentury, settlers were coming into the area from New Kent, Hanover and Louisa Counties; and a little later from King and Queen, Essex, Caroline and Richmond Counties.

Many of the landmarks referred to in early deeds are now unknown or cannot now be identified. The partial and only extant land processioning record lists roads now unknown, and which cannot now be located.

The names of some early creeks have been changed, but some of these are now known. Avents Creek is now Evans and Cocke's Creek is now Poplar Creek. Both of these are near the present Brunswick County line. Stiths Creek is now called Smith Creek.

Before the beginning of the Revolutionary War, many Mecklenburg County people had begun to move to other states. This movement of people to other states continued well into the nineteenth century. Mecklenburg County contributed many settlers to North and South Carolina, Georgia, Kentucky and Tennessee whose descendants are now scattered throughout the western and southwestern states.

The largest patentees of land in Mecklenburg County, Col. John Baker and Col. John Ruffin of Surry County, never resided in the county. Unlike the area which became Halifax, Bedford and Charlotte Counties, there was no other large grant acquired for speculation. Col. William Byrd of Charles City County was a comparatively large land owner in Mecklenburg County, but his grants were relatively small and a part of his holdings were acquired by purchase.

James Daniel, who was Sheriff of Albemarle County in 1750, acquired a number of tracts of land in Mecklenburg which he left by will to his sons. Chesley Daniel, one of his sons, died soon after his father, and administration on his estate is recorded in Lunenburg County. Josiah Daniel sold his land and removed to Granville County, N. C.

Theophilus Feild and Hugh Miller, merchants of Prince George County, and Lewis Parham, merchant of Brunswick County, acquired land in Mecklenburg County which they owned for many years. Later Roger Atkinson, merchant of Dinwiddie County, bought considerable land in the county. The Rev. William Willie of Surry County and the Rev. James Maury of Albemarle County owned land in Mecklenburg County.

MECKLENBURG COUNTY

Mecklenburg County, to-wit:

    At a Dwelling House of Richard Swepson on Monday the eleventh day of March 1765, A Commission of the Peace for the said County and Dedimus for administering the Oaths and Tests, therein mentioned, under the hand of Francis Fauquier, Esquire, his Majesty's Lt. Gov. and Commander in Chief of the Colony and Dominion of Va., bearing date the first day of March 1765, and in the fifth year of the reign of our Sov. Lord King George the third, directed to Robert Munford, Richard Witton, John Speed, Henry Delony, Edmund Taylor, Benjamin Baird, John Camp, Thomas Erskine, John Potter, John Cox, Thomas Anderson, John Speed, Jr. and Samuel Hopkins, Gentleman, being produced and read -

    Thomas Erskine and John Potter, Gents, administered the said Oaths and Tests to Robert Munford, Gent, who took and subscribed the oaths to the government, subscribed the abjuration oath and repeated oaths and tests, and then took the Oaths of a Justice of the Peace and for the County Court in Chancery - and then the said Robert Munford administered all the aforesaid - to Thomas Erskine, John Potter, John Cox Thomas Anderson, John Speed, Jr., and Samuel Hopkins, Gentlemen - who subscribed and repeated the aforesaid oaths and tests.

Order Book 1, Page 1

    At a Court held for Mecklenburg County on Monday the 11 day of March 1765:
                          Present:

Robert Munford	Thomas Anderson	)	
John Camp	John Cox	)	Gentlemen
Thomas Erskine	John Speed, Junr.	)	Justices
John Potter	Samuel Hopkins	)	

    John Tabb produced a commission under the hand & seal of Thos. Nelson, Esq., deputy Secretary of Va. bearing date the 22nd day of December 1764 and in the fifth year of the reign of our Sovereign Lord King George the third, appointing him, the said John Tabb, Clerk of this County Court, which being read, the said John Tabb took the usual oaths to his Majesty's personal government and subscribed the same and also took the Oath of Clerk and repeated and subscribed the Test, and is admitted Clerk of this Court accordingly.

    Richard Witton, Gent. produced a commission under the hand of Francis Fauquier, Lt. Gov. and Commander of the Colony, bearing date of the 2nd day of March 1765, appointing him Sheriff of this County, which being read, Richard Witton entered into and acknowledged three several bonds together with Robert Munford, Edmund Taylor, Thomas Anderson, William Taylor and Joseph Taylor, his securities according to law - which bonds were ordered to be recorded - whereas the said Richard Witton took the oaths appointed by Act of Parliament so to be taken instead of the Oaths of Allegiance and Supremacy and subscribed the said and repeated and subscribed the Test and then had the Oath of Sheriff administered to him.

On the motion of Richard Witton, Gent. Sheriff of this County, William Taylor, John Ballard, Junr. and Joseph Taylor are admitted his undersheriffs, and whereupon took the oaths of undersheriff.

Gray Briggs and Philip Taylor, Gents. produced licenses to practice (law), took the Oaths and Tests, and took the oath of attorney to practice as attorneys in this County.

Edmund Taylor, Gent. produced a commision from the Masters of William & Mary College appointing him Surveyor of this County, which being read, the said Edmund Taylor entered into and acknowledged bond with Robert Munford, his security, according to law, and then took the oath and subscribed the Tests, and had the oath of surveyor administered him.

Robert Munford, Esquire, Lieut. Colonel,
Edmund Taylor & Robert Alexander, Gents. Colonels,
Benjamin Baird, Major,
John Tabb, Quartermaster,
Jacob Royster, Tignal Jones, Sr., John Potter,
Samuel Bugg and Dennis Lark, Captains,

severally produced commissions from his Honor the Governor (as Militia Officers), and took the oaths to his Majesty's personal government, and repeated and subscribed the Tests.

(The foregoing entries are recorded in the first Order Book of Mecklenburg County, beginning on page one, establishing the first government for the new county.)

OATH OF ABJURATION

"I, Robert Munford, do swear that I do from my heart abhor, detest, and abjure, as impious and heretical, that damnable doctrine and position that Princes excommunicated, or deprived by the Pope, or any authority of the See of Rome, may be deposed or murdered by their subjects or any other whatsoever. And I do declare that no foreign Prince, Prelate, Person, State, or Potentate, hath, or ought to have, any jurisdiction, power, superiorty, pre-eminence, or authority, ecclesiastical or spiritual, within this realm. So help me God".

OATH OF ALLEGIANCE

"I, Thomas Erskine, do sincerely promise and swear that I will be faithful and bear true allegiance to his Majesty King George, the Third, so help me God".

St. JAMES PARISH

At a Court held for Lunenburg County
June 1761

John Potter, Joseph Truman (Tureman ?), Thomas Lanier, John Speed, Thomas Moon, John Camp, William Hunt and Richard Swepson were elected Vestrymen of the new Parish of St. James, and took the oath of Vestrymen.
Lunenburg County O.B. 7, p. 49

The foregoing constituted the first Vestry of St. James Parish. The loss of the records of St. James Parish makes it infeasible to attempt to list subsequent Vestrymen although there are scattered entries in the order books of Mecklenburg County naming some of the later Vestrymen who took the oath of office.

OATH OF A VESTRYMAN

"I, John Potter, as I do acknowledge myself a true son of the Church of England, so I do believe the articles of faith therein professed, and do oblige myself to be conformable to the doctrine and discipline therein taught and established; and that, as Vestryman of St. James Parish, I will well and truly perform my duty therein, being directed by the laws and customs of this country and the canons of the Church of England, so far as they will suit our present capacity; and this I shall sincerely do, according to the best of my knowledge, skill, cunning, without fear, favor, or partiality; so help me God".

LAND PATENTS AND GRANTS

The land grant records, now at the Virginia State Library, are divided into two sections as they pertain to Mecklenburg County. They are the Colonial Patents covering all grants by the Colonial Government, and the Commonwealth Grants made by the Commonwealth of Virginia beginning in 1779.

These invaluable land records are little known to the public since they are not recorded in the county in which granted. The first grants of land in the area now Mecklenburg County were made soon after the creation of Brunswick County in 1720.

During the first two decades after 1720, the number of patents issued were few and the grants widely separated. The population in 1748 of the area now Mecklenburg County, based on the extant Cumberland Parish tithe lists, was less than eight hundred people. Hundreds of patents were issued during the next twenty years for land in the area, however, and the population of the area had increased to more than 5,000 when the act to divide Lunenburg County was passed in 1764.

The largest grant of land in the area totaled 13,912 acres. This patent was issued jointly to Col. John Ruffin and Col. John Baker of Surry County in 1755. The smallest grant was for a little more than one acre consisting of an island in the Roanoke River. The last grant of land was for two and one-half acres in 1918. This was an island in the Roanoke River which had not been included in grants along the river, but is now under the waters of Buggs Island Lake.

Many of the larger grants were patented by people who never resided in the area now Mecklenburg County. Some of the patentees established "quarters" on their grants, while others sold the land granted to them after having the land surveyed into smaller tracts.

Among those who patented land in the area, but did not move to the county, were John Allen, Col. John Baker, John Banister, Major John Bolling, John Bolling, Junr., Colonel William Byrd, Thomas Cocke, Alexander Erskine, Theophilus Feild, Memucan Hunt, Peter Johnston, Peter Jones, Robert Langley, Henry Morris, James, Robert and William Munford, John, Robert and Thomas Ravenscroft, Col. John Ruffin, Wm. Starke, Drury Stith, George Walton and Michael Cadet Young.

Armistead Burwell and Lewis Burwell, Sr., acquired large tracts of land in the area that was to become Mecklenburg County. They established quarters on the land with overseers in charge, but did not reside in the county.

Lewis Burwell, Jr. and Thacker Burwell, subsequently, moved to Mecklenburg County where they lived on land which had been patented by Armistead Burwell and Lewis Burwell, Sr.

Armistead Burwell died before 1764. The only extant tithe list for St. James Parish, Mecklenburg County, is that for the year 1764. This lists the estate of Armistead Burwell with John Oliver, George Tureman and John Westbrook as overseers. Thomas Carleton, Hugh Franklin and John Jeffries, Junr., were listed as overseers for Colonel Lewis Burwell.

At Colonel William Byrd's plantations in the area now Mecklenburg County in 1752, Thomas Pool, Jacob Royster, William Royster and Thomas Anderson were listed as overseers.

There were still many tracts of unpatented land in Mecklenburg County at the end of the Colonial Period, and grants were made by the Commonwealth of Virginia for many years after the end of the Revolutionary War. Sir Peyton Skipwith was granted 1,026 acres on Bluestone Creek in 1799.

Many of the streams in Mecklenburg County were named for members of early survey parties and for patentees of land. William Smith patented 790 acres on the south side of the Roanoke River on October 13, 1727. This land was located on a creek in the extreme south eastern part of the county. This creek now known as Smith's Creek was undoubtedly named for him. Butchers Creek was named for John Butcher who had patented 632 acres on the north side of the Roanoke River on September 28, 1728.

Aarons Creek, the present boundary line between Halifax and Mecklenburg Counties, was named for Aaron Pinson a very early settler. This creek was known by its Indian name, however, for many years as Tewayhomony Creek, and appears in some early deeds under such name rather than as Aarons Creek.

The location on many early patents can be pinpointed, or approximated, by reference to the map following these pages.

The reference in some patents to the "county line" is to the line dividing Mecklenburg County from Granville County N. C. Many of the early settlers in that area owned land in both counties. They had obtained grants in Colonial Granvill County from Lord Granville in additions to grants in Virginia.

LAND GRANTS - MECKLENBURG COUNTY

AKIN, Joseph   Patent Book 36, Page 1070

    218 acres on the Mine Branch and Long Branch of Little Creek, beginning at Jesse Bugg.
        7-10-1766

ALEXANDER, John   Patent Book 13, Page 184

    900 acres on south side of Roanoke River.
        10-13-1727

ALLEN, John   Patent Book 14, Page 302

    1780 acres on north side of Roanoke River.
        8-25-1731

ARNOLD, James   Patent Book 21, Page 609

    250 acres on west side of Mountain Creek.
        11-25-1743

        Patent Book 30, Page 97

    520 acres on both sides of Mountain Creek, adjoining Vaughan, et als.
        6-1-1750

        Patent Book 32, Page 624

    440 acres on Mountain Creek and adjoining Edward Broadnax.
        9-10-1755

    725 acres on both sides of Mountain Creek, adjoining Wilson, Williams, et als.
        12-15-1755

        Patent Book 32, Page 72

    480 acres at the head of Mountain Creek, adjoining Wilson and Gordon.
        8-16-1756

AVENT, John   Patent Book 13, Page 179

    500 acres on north side of Roanoke River.
        10-13-1727

AVENT, Thomas   Patent Book 29, Page 30

    304 acres on Dockery Creek, adjoining Gilbert Gordon.
        12-15-1749

AVENT, Thomas   Patent Book 32, Page 708

    390 acres at the head of Dockery Creek, adjoining
        Ballard.
                                               3-10-1756

                                   Patent Book 34, Page 1046

    404 acres on a branch of Butchers Creek.
                                               3-25-1762

AVENT, William   Patent Book 13, Page 180

    630 acres on south side of Meherrin River.
                                           10-17-1727

BAIRD, Benjamin   Patent Book 32, Page 635

    534 acres on the upper side of Dockery Creek, adjoining
        John Lett, Holmes, et als.
                                             9-10-1755

                                   Patent Book 38, Page 648

    400 acres on Cox Creek, adjoining Adams, Atkinson, et
        als.
                                             7-14-1769

BAIRD, Benjamin and   Patent Book 38, Page 647
    Richard Pemberton

    400 acres on Buckhorn Creek, adjoining Coleman, Keeton,
        et als.
                                             7-14-1769

BAKER, Jerman   Patent Book 38, Page 564

    434 acres on a branch of the south fork of Allen's
        Creek, adjoining Daniel and Gorry (Gorre)
                                               4-6-1769

                                   Patent Book 38, Page 576

    446 acres on Mine Creek, adjoining Stith, Blackwell, et
        als.
                                             4-6-1769

BAKER, Josias   Patent Book 23, Page 964

    153 acres on both sides of Butchers Creek
                                               8-1-1745

BAKER, Thomas   Patent Book 22, Page 200

    516 acres on the south side of the great branch of Butchers Creek.   8-30-1744

BALLARD, John   Patent Book 30, Page 193

    1403 acres on the upper side of Miles Creek, adjoining Speed, Malone and Lark   7-12-1750

BALLARD, William   Patent Book 34, Page 659

    360 acres on a branch of Allens Creek, adjoining Mallett, et als.   8-20-1760

    Patent Book 34, Page 991

    400 acres on the east side of Allens Creek, adjoining Delony, et als.   3-25-1762

BANISTER, John   Patent Book 13, Page 204

    560 acres on south side of Roanoke River.   10-13-1727

BASKERVILL, George   Patent Book 33, Page 411

    82 acres on Miles Creek and Roanoke River.   11-10-1757

BEDDINGFIELD, John   Patent Book 13, Page 180

    588 acres on north side of Roanoke River.   10-13-1727

BENNETT, Joseph   Patent Book 27, Page 280

    785 acres on both sides of Parhams Creek, adjoining Amos Timms.   7-25-1749

    298 acres on both sides of Parhams Creek, adjoining Tanner's lower line.   7-25-1749

BILBO, John Peter   Patent Book 29, Page 205

    1626 acres on both sides of Allens Creek.   6-1-1750

BILLUPS, Joseph   Patent Book 33, Page 25

      700 acres on both sides of Dry Creek, adjoining
          Christopher.
                                         8-16-1756

BLACKSTONE, John   Patent Book 23, Page 631

      187 acres on both sides of Stiths Creek.
                                             11-25-1743

                                  Patent Book 26, Page 49

      254 acres adjoining his own lines.
                                               6-25-1747

BLALOCK, Richard   Patent Book 32, Page 126

      400 acres on east side of Butchers Creek, adjoining
          Thomerson, Hawkins, et als.
                                              6-5-1753

BLANKS, Joseph   Patent Book 17, Page 375

      414 acres on north side of Flatt Creek.
                                             7-9-1737

BLANTON, James   Patent Book 39, Page 33

      400 acres on a fork of Great Creek, adjoining Jones,
          Harwell, et als.
                                                    Page 37

      400 acres on a fork of Great Creek, adjoining Douglas,
          Jones, et als.
                                               5-12-1770

BOLLING, Major John   Patent Book 19, Page 907

      473 acres on north side of Roanoke River.
                                               12-1-1740

BOLLING, John   Patent Book 22, Page 608

      818 acres on north side of Roanoke River.
                                             3-20-1745

BOLLING, Col. John   Patent Book 27, Page 174

      988 acres on north side of Roanoke River at the mouth
          of Butchers Creek.
                                             5-20-1749

BOLLING, John, Junr.   Patent Book 14, Page 445

473 acres on north side of Roanoke River.
5-4-1732

BOWEN, Drury and   Patent Book 37, Page 350
    Robert Bowen

425 acres on south side of Meherrin River and on Eagles Nest Creek.
7-20-1768

BRACEY, Francis   Patent Book 33, Page 21

4681 acres on a branch of Butchers Creek.
6-16-1756

BRACEY, Randall   Patent Book 28, Page 665

273 acres on Cox Creek.
9-5-1749

BRAY, John   Patent Book 33, Page 627

1000 acres on south side of Roanoke River on Island Creek, adjoining Feild, Mitchell, et als.
9-20-1759

BROADNAX, Edward   Patent Book 19, Page 710

1414 acres on both sides of Miles Creek.
8-20-1740

BROADNAX, Stephen Edward   Patent Book 34, Page 76

413 acres on head branches of Miles Creek.
8-16-1756

BROOKS, Robert   Patent Book 28, Page 76

630 acres on both sides of Meherrin River.
6-25-1747

BROWN, Henry   Patent Book 14, Page 88

671 acres on lower side of Great Creek.
9-28-1728

BROWN, John and   Patent Book 13, Page 181
    Richard Brown

230 acres on south side of Roanoke River.
10-13-1727

BUGG, Anselm   Patent Book 39, Page 27

    350 acres on south side of Roanoke River.
                                                    5-12-1770

BUGG, Edmond   Patent Book 37, Page 9

    400 acres on his own line, and adjoining Howard, et als
                                                    7-10-1767

BUGG, John   Patent Book 34, Page 1076

    400 acres on south side of Taylors Creek, adjoining
       Mize, Bates, et als.
                                                   9-25-1762

BUGG, Sherwood   Patent Book 32, Page 116

    125 acres on south side of Roanoke River.
                                                 5-31-1753

                                     Patent Book 33, Page 352

    1193 acres on Cotton Creek.   4-16-1757

                                     Patent Book 33, Page 440

    904 acres on north side of Roanoke River, adjoining
       Hyde, Abbott, et als.
                                                 6-2-1758

BURTON, Allen   Patent Book 37, Page 254

    75 acres on Mine Creek and Long Branch, adjoining Akin,
       Hatsell, et als.
                                               7-20-1768

BURTON, Hutchins   Patent Book 34, Page 248

    404 acres on Miles Creek, adjoining Morgan.
                                               5-12-1759

BURTON, Robert   Patent Book 40, Page 847

    375 acres adjoining Donathon, Hester, Avory, et als.
                                               8-1-1772

BURWELL, Armistead   Patent Book 28, Page 27

    3404 acres on Finneywood Creek, and on branches of said
       creek.
                                               1-12-1744

BURWELL, Lewis   Patent Book 22, Page 270

    4300 acres on both sides of Butchers Creek, adjoining
        Thomas Ravenscroft.
7-10-1745

Patent Book 29, Page 313

    1740 acres on both sides of Butchers Creek.
11-3-1750

Patent Book 34, Page 336

    4650 acres on west side of Butchers Creek, adjoining
        Bracey, Harris, Evans, et als.
8-10-1759

BUSBY, John   Patent Book 33, Page 683

    400 acres on both sides of Mitchell's Mill Creek.
3-3-1760

BUTCHER, John   Patent Book 14, Page 129

    632 acres on north side of Roanoke River.
9-28-1728

BUTLER, William   Patent Book 34, Page 338

    420 acres on a branch of Laytons Creek/
8-10-1759

BYRD, William   Patent Book 13, Page 504

    1550 acres on north side of Roanoke River, including
        two islands.

    379 acres on north side of Roanoke River.
9-28-1728

Patent Book 17, Page 461

    200 acres on Roanoke River.   2-9-1737

Patent Book 17, Page 465

    580 acres on south side of Roanoke River.

    1480 acres on north side of Roanoke River.
2-9-1737

Patent Book 29, Page 435

    3821 acres on both sides of Bluestone Creek, adjoining
        Robertson.
7-5-1751

CAMPBELL, Robert   Patent Book 34, Page 82

    300 acres on south side of Dockery Creek.
                                                           8-16-1756

CARDWELL, John   Patent Book 33, Page 52

    294 acres on lower side of Miles Creek.
                                                           12-15-1758

CARGILL, Cornelius   Patent Book 14, Page 65

    365 acres on north side of Roanoke River.
                                                           9-28-1728

                                            Patent Book 14, Page 307

    662 acres between Hicks Creek and Jeneto Creek.
                                                           8-25-1731

                                            Patent Book 15, Page 434

    450 acres on north side of Roanoke River.
                                                           2-27-1734

                                                                  Page 504

    100 acres on north side of Roanoke River.
                                                                  Page 505

    150 acres on north side of Roanoke River.
                                                           6-9-1735

CARTER, James   Patent Book 26, Page 554

    83 acres on both sides of Allens Creek, adjoining
        Holmes land.
                                                           8-20-1748

CHAMBERLAYNE, Thomas   Patent Book 33, Page 931

    262 acres on a branch of the south fork of Allens
        Creek.
                                                           9-26-1760

CHANDLER, Joseph   Patent Book 34, Page 510

    1850 acres on both sides of Meherrin River, adjoining
        Poindexter, et als.
                                                           6-10-1760

CHAVIS, Jacob   Patent Book 41, Page 315

  287 acres at head of Reedy Branch, adjoining Burwell,
  Enroughty, et als.
6-15-1773

CLACK, John   Patent Book 34, Page 509

  330 acres on south side of Meherrin River.
6-10-1760

CLARK, Bolling   Patent Book 32, Page 693

  180 acres on east side of Butchers Creek.
3-10-1756

CLARK, Edward   Patent Book 27, Page 527

  154 acres on Butchers Creek, adjoining John Bolling.
12-15-1749

CLARK, John   Patent Book 33, Page 33

  400 acres on a ridge between Roanoke River and
  Bluestone Creek, adjoining Byrd, Harris, et als.
8-16-1756

CLARKE, James   Patent Book 33, Page 927

  400 acres between Allens and Laytons Creeks.
9-26-1760

CLAUNCH, Jeremiah   Patent Book 34, Page 81

  200 acres on south fork of Allens Creek.
8-16-1756

COCKE, Thomas   Patent Book 13, Page 347

  790 acres on north side of Roanoke River.
9-28-1728

COLEMAN, James   Patent Book 23, Page 1102

  400 acres on north side of Roanoke River.
8-20-1745

Patent Book 24, Page 88

  274 acres on both sides of south fork of Allens Creek
  Note: South Fork now called Coleman's Creek.
9-20-1745

Patent Book 34, Page 501

380 acres on both sides of a branch of Allens Creek, adjoining, Mallett, Coleman, et als.
6-10-1760

COLEMAN, John   Patent Book 38, Page 625

230 acres on south side of south fork of Allens Creek, adjoining Miller.
4-6-1769

COLLIER, William   Patent Book 18, Page 206

350 acres on north side of Miles Creek.
2-1-1738

Patent Book 20, Page 112

390 acres on a branch of Miles Creek.
1-30-1741

COOK, Abraham   Patent Book 23, Page 720

289 acres on north side of Roanoke River.
8-30-1744

COOK, John   Patent Book 18, Page 347

278 acres on north side of Roanoke River.
6-29-1739

COOK, John Lett   Patent Book 33, Page 1042

400 acres adjoining Holmes, Clack, Watson, et als.
7-1-1761

COURTNEY, Clack   Patent Book 41, Page 288

62 acres on Dockery Creek, adjoining his own land.
3-1-1773

COX, John   Patent Book 26, Page 86

404 acres on both sides of Blackstone Creek.
8-20-1747

Patent Book 28, Page 494

404 acres on south side of Meherrin River at the mouth of Finneywood Creek.
1-10-1748

Patent Book 27, Page 523

302 acres adjoining Henry Robertson.
12-15-1749

Patent Book 34, Book 628

1190 acres on both sides of Meherrin River, adjoining Evans, et als.
6-10-1760

COX, John   Patent Book 36, Page 576

1545 acres on both sides of Bluestone Creek - 435 acres formerly granted to Thomas Williams 20 May 1749 and 1110 acres never before granted.
8-4-1764

CRAWLEY, Robert   Patent Book 40, Page 725

400 acres on south side of Roanoke River on Taylor's Mill Creek.
6-20-1772

CROWDER, Abraham   Patent Book 38, Page 653

145 acres on north side of Peckerwood Creek, adjoining the land where he now lives.
7-14-1769

CROWDER, Jeremiah   Patent Book 39, Page 125

400 acres on branches of Cox and Laytons Creeks, adjoining Moore.
8-27-1770

CULBREATH, Edward   Patent Book 34, Page 360

400 acres on Grassy Creek, adjoining grant of Stith, Morris and Young.
8-10-1759

CULBREATH, John and   Patent Book 39, Page 234
    Mary Culbreath

400 acres on Grassy Creek, adjoining the grant of Stith, Morris and Young.
2-16-1771

CULBREATH, Peter   Patent Book 34, Page 80

250 acres on Grassy Creek, adjoining John King.
8-16-1756

CUNNINGHAM, Robert   Patent Book 39, Page 3

245 acres on Taylors and Flatt Creeks, adjoining Wood and Duke.

5-12-1770

DANIEL, Elizabeth   Patent Book 14, Page 305

466 acres on south side of Jeneto Creek.

8-25-1731

DANIEL, Hugh   Patent Book 20, Page 506

392 acres on both sides of Poplar Creek.

3-30-1743

DANIEL, James   Patent Book 29, Page 349

469 acres on south side of Roanoke River, adjoining land of Smith, Nobles, et als.

11-3-1750

DAVIS, Baxter   Patent Book 15, Page 349

240 acres on south side of Roanoke River, beginning at the mouth of Smith Creek.

10-3-1734

Patent Book 17, Page 376

187 acres on south side of Roanoke River.

7-9-1737

Patent Book 30, Page 119

827 acres on south side of Roanoke River, adjoining Edward Davis.

6-1-1750

DAVIS, John   Patent Book 14, Page 66

554 acres on north side of Roanoke River.

9-28-1728

Patent Book 29, Page 346

2443 acres on south side of Roanoke River, adjoining Richard Fox.

11-3-1750

DAVIS, William   Patent Book 13, Page 185

836 acres on south side of Roanoke River.

10-13-1727

DAVIS, William   Patent Book 39, Page 140

    400 acres on Reedy Branch, adjoining land where he now
        lives.   8-27-1770

DECKER, Henry   Patent Book 32, Page 711

    435 acres on south fork of Allens Creek, adjoining
        Coleman.   3-10-1756

DELONY, Lewis   Patent Book 21, Page 577

    7197 acres on both sides of Flatt Creek, and on north
        side of Allens Creek.
                                              10-31-1743

                              Patent Book 29, Page 325

    450 acres adjoining William Humphry.
                                              11-3-1750

DELONY, Lewis, Junr.   Patent Book 28, Page 465

    300 acres on east side of Cox Creek at the mouth of
        School Branch.   1-10-1748

DICKSON, Thomas   Patent Book 34, Page 83

    1025 acres on both sides of Miles Creek, adjoining
        Munford's line.   8-16-1756

DONALD, Alexander   Patent Book 41, Page 198

    410 acres on Great Creek adjoining his own land, and
        adjoining Gabriel Hardin.
                                               3-1-1773

DORTCH, David   Patent Book 28, Page 520

    160 acres on north side of Miles Creek, adjoining
        Collier's line.
                                              1-10-1748

                              Patent Book 33, Page 409

    82 acres on Dockery Creek, adjoining land of Lucas.
                                              11-10-1757

DORTCH, John, Junr.   Patent Book 27, Page 294

384 acres on Miles Creek, adjoining Dennis Lark.

9-5-1749

DOUGLAS, John   Patent Book 26, Page 612

351 acres on south side of Meherrin River.

8-20-1748

DREW, Newer(?)   Patent Book 21, Page 488

197 acres on north side of Miles Creek.

8-30-1743

DUKE, John Taylor   Patent Book 32, Page 387

400 acres on a branch of Jeneto Creek and Wolfpitt Fork of Flatt Creek.   8-14-1754

Patent Book 34, Page 661

245 acres on heads of Taylors and Flatt Creeks.

8-20-1760

DUPREE, Lewis and   Patent Book 34, Page 703
Stephen Wiles

382 acres on lower side of Buffalo Creek at mouth of the creek.   9-10-1760

EASTLAND, Thomas   Patent Book 25, Page 132

238 acres on both sides of Mitchells Creek.

7-25-1745

Patent Book 40, Page 742

1039 acres on north side of Roanoke River on both sides of Mitchells Creek, adjoining Hill, Lanier, et als

6-20-1772

EDMUNDS, Nicholas   Patent Book 33, Page 221

676 acres on both sides of east fork of Bluestone Creek

8-16-1756

EDWARDS, William   Patent Book 23, Page 1129

372 acres on both sides of Allens Creek.

8-20-1745

ELLIDGE, Francis   Patent Book 28, Book 136

    331 acres on north fork of Allens Creek and adjoining his own land.
                                                 8-20-1747

EPPS, John   Patent Book 34, Page 568

    444 acres on a branch of Buffalo Creek, adjoining Josiah Seat and William Byrd.
                                                 7-15-1760

ERSKINE, Alexander   Patent Book 33, Page 453

    400 acres on a branch of Middle Bluestone, adjoining William Harris.
                                                 8-19-1758

                                                       Page 454

    400 acres on Mitchells Creek, adjoining Miller.
                                                 8-19-1758

EVANS, Robert   Patent Book 34, Page 88

    420 acres on Woodpecker Fork of Bluestone Creek.
                                                 8-10-1756

EVANS, Stephen   Patent Book 28, Page 74

    804 acres on a branch of Bluestone Creek.
                                                 6-25-1747
                                Patent Book 32, Page 376

    400 acres on the Great Branch of Middle Bluestone Creek
                                                 7-2-1754
                                Patent Book 33, Page 612

    2635 acres on both sides of Middle Fork of Bluestone Creek, adjoining James Murray and William Evans.
                                               7-4-1759

EVANS, William   Patent Book 32, Page 392

    400 acres on a branch of the middle fork of Bluestone Creek.
                                               8-24-1754

                                Patent Book 33, Page 696

    1201 acres on Bluestone Creek, adjoining James Murray.
                                               3-3-1760

EZARD, John					Patent Book 28, Page 458

    620 acres on Finneywood Creek, adjoining Munford.
						9-20-1748

FARRAR, Feild					Patent Book 31, Page 184

    447 acres on both sides of west fork of Cox Creek.
						8-19-1752

FARRAR, John					Patent Book 40, Page 895

    400 acres on both sides of the Long Branch of Allens Creek, adjoining Delony.
						8-1-1772

						Patent Book E, Page 18

    95 acres on branches of Allens Creek, adjoining Lundy, Hawkins, et als.
						5-1-1775

FARRAR, Thomas					Patent Book 34, Page 389

    400 acres on a branch of Laytons Creek, adjoining Lanier's line.
						8-10-1759

						Patent Book 40, Page 895

    450 acres on a branch of Laytons Creek, adjoining land of Ellidge.
						8-1-1772

FEARIS, Jacob (Ferris)				Patent Book 34, Page 387

    165 acres on north fork of Allens Creek.
						8-10-1759

FEILD, Theophilus				Patent Book 28, Page 517

    1304 acres on south side of Parhams Creek.   1-10-1748

						Patent Book 31, Page 443

    1004 acres on south side of Roanoke River on Nutbush Creek.
						6-26-1755

						Patent Book 34, Page 85

    400 acres on south side of Roanoke River.
						8-16-1756

FEILD, Theophilus   Patent Book 34, Page 85

    404 acres on lower side of Grassy Creek, adjoining Lettice Owen.
                                              8-16-1756

                              Patent Book 37, Page 282

    1900 acres on south side of Roanoke River on a branch of Cotton Creek.
                                            7-20-1768

FERRELL, Hubbard (Hubert)   Patent Book 28, Page 222

    223 acres on south side of upper fork of Miles Creek.
                                             10-1-1747

                                            Page 204

    230 acres on both sides of Cox Creek, adjoining his own land.
                                             8-20-1747

FINNEY, Alexander   Patent Book 15, Page 500

    220 acres on west side of Jeneto Creek.
                                             5-20-1735

FLOYD, Josiah   Patent Book 23, Page 1143

    398 acres between the lines of George Hix and Eldridge.
                                             8-20-1745

FLOYD, Richard   Patent Book 39, Page 94

    400 acres on Poplar Branch and on north side of Grassy Creek, adjoining Culbreath, et als.
                                             8-27-1770

FOWLER, John   Patent Book 34, Page 663

    366 acres on north side of Smiths Creek.
                                             8-20-1760

FRANKLIN, Owen   Patent Book 34, Page 637

    134 acres on both sides of Grassy Creek.
                                             7-15-1760

GARLAND, David   Patent Book 40, Page 623

    400 acres at the head of Allens Creek and on a branch

of the Meherrin River, adjoining Stith, et als.

8-3-1771

GILLIAM, John   Patent Book 33, Page 62

343 acres on south side of Roanoke River, adjoining his old line.

8-16-1756

Patent Book 33, Page 364

185 acres on a branch adjoining his own line, and adjoining Robertson's line.

4-19-1757

GORDON, John   Patent Book 34, Page 221

234 acres on both sides of the head branch of Dockery Creek, adjoining Brewer and Ward.

5-22-1759

GOREY, Daniel (GORRE)   Patent Book 32, Page 659

550 acres on both sides of Allens Creek, adjoining Humphries.

3-11-1755

GREEN, Henry   Patent Book 28, Page 635

331 acres on both sides of Buffalo Creek, adjoining his upper line.

8-20-1748

Page 637

404 acres on both sides of Buffalo Creek, adjoining his own land.

8-20-1748

GREEN, John   Patent Book 39, Page 324

380 acres on both sides of Buffalo Creek, adjoining Griffin.

2-16-1771

GREER, Joseph   Patent Book 32, Page 412

870 acres on branches of Allens, Laytons, Blackstone and Buckhorn Creeks.

11-1-1754

GRIFFIN, James   Patent Book 42, Page 746

325 acres on Buffalo Creek, adjoining John
     Westmoreland, William Green, et als.
                                                   7-5-1774

GRIFFIN, William   Patent Book 32, Page 627

   500 acres on both sides of Buffalo Creek.
                                                   9-10-1755

GUNN, William   Patent Book 22, Page 80

   125 acres on south side of Roanoke River.
                                                   6-16-1744

GUNSTON, George   Patent Book 40, Page 847

   300 acres on Little Buffalo Creek, on south side of the
      Roanoke River, adjoining Newton, Hamlin, et als.
                                                   8-1-1772

HALL, Edmund   Patent Book 17, Page 383

   385 acres on both sides of Jeneto Creek.
                                                   8-15-1737

HARRIS, Benjamin   Patent Book 33, Page 562

   420 acres on a branch of Miles Creek.
                                                   5-7-1759

HARRIS, Samuel   Patent Book 26, Page 358

   353 acres on north side of Staunton River, adjoining
      land of Byrd and Munford.
                                                   4-5-1748

                                 Patent Book 34, Page 173

   2809 acres between Bluestone Creek and Roanoke River,
      adjoining Byrd.
                                                   2-7-1757

HARRIS, William   Patent Book 26, Page 362

   70 acres in Staunston River between Byrd's Island and
      Cargill's Island.
                                                   4-5-1748

                                 Patent Book 29, Page 29

   280 acres on both sides of Middle Bluestone Creek.
                                                   12-15-1749

HARRIS, William   Patent Book 31, Page 295

    940 acres on Bluestone and on Buffalo Creeks.

                                              Page 297

    1000 acres on Bluestone Creek.
                                              11-13-1752

                                   Patent Book 31, Page 559

    424 acres on Middle Bluestone Creek, adjoining his own land.
                                              9-10-1755

HARWELL, James   Patent Book 33, Page 1089

    1140 acres on both sides of the fork of Great Creek.
                                              8-7-1761

                                   Patent Book 34, Page 49

    373 acres adjoining Lankford' line.
                                              3-10-1756

HARWELL, Samuel   Patent Book 15, Page 190

    195 acres on north side of Roanoke River and on Allens Creek.
                                              3-23-1733

HATCHER, Frederick   Patent Book 33, Page 353

    485 acres on both sides of Laytons Creek, adjoining Huson's line.
                                              4-19-1757

HATSELL, William, Junr.   Patent Book 37, Page 85

    400 acres on a branch of Allens Creek, adjoining Akin.
                                              9-10-1767

HAWKINS, Thomas   Patent Book 32, Page 623

    420 acres on east, or lower side, of Butchers Creek, adjoining Blalock, Baker, et als.
                                              9-10-1755

                                   Patent Book 34, Page 189

    1950 acres on south side of Roanoke River, and on Buffalo and Grassy Creeks.
                                              12-15-1757

HAWKINS, William   Patent Book 32, Page 615

    304 acres on both sides of Meherrin River, adjoining Ravenscroft.
                                          8-22-1755

HAYNES, Anthony   Patent Book 28, Page 507

    424 acres on the ridge between Butchers Creek and Allens Creek, adjoining John Mitchell.
                                          1-10-1748

HAYWOOD, Francis   Patent Book 25, Page 591

    175 acres on south side of Roanoke River.
                                            1-12-1746

HERBERT, John   Patent Book 34, Page 109

    700 acres on south side of Roanoke River on Smith Creek
                                          8-10-1756

HESTER, Robert, Junr.   Patent Book 23, Page 949

    300 acres on a branch on south side of Butchers Creek.
                                          7-10-1745

HEWEY, Humphry   Patent Book 32, Page 346

    400 acres on head of Mill Branch of Parhams Creek.
                                          2-20-1754

HEWITT, John   Patent Book 42, Page 685

    85 acres on south side of Roanoke River, on Keiths Branch, adjoining Feild, Johnson, Burtchett, et als.
                                          7-5-1774

HIGHT, John and   Patent Book 33, Page 792
    John Beal

    770 acres on branches of Buckhorn and Laytons Creek, adjoining Weatherford.
                                          5-29-1760

HIGHTOWER, John   Patent Book 34, Page 111

    284 acres on a branch of Mountain Creek, adjoining James Arnold.
                                          8-10-1756

HILL, William   Patent Book 20, Page 88

    721 acres on a branch of Mitchells Creek.
                                            1-30-1741

                                   Patent Book 25, Page 202

    362 acres on west side of Butchers Creek.
                                            8-28-1746

                                   Patent Book 27, Page 273

    400 acres between Butchers and Allens Creeks.
                                            7-25-1749

                                   Patent Book 33, Page 795

    224 acres on a fork of Mitchells Creek.
                                            5-29-1760

HILL, Major William   Patent Book 39, Page 254

    260 acres on a branch of Eastland Creek, adjoining his own line and land of Eastland.
                                            2-16-1771

HILL, William   Patent Book 33, Page 694

    1380 acres on a branch of Bluestone Creek.
                                            3-3-1760

                                   Patent Book 38, Page 671

    386 acres on a branch of Bluestone Creek, adjoining Franklin, Parker, et als.
                                            7-14-1769

HIX, George   Patent Book 13, Page 60

    265 acres on north side of Roanoke River.
                                            10-31-1726

HIX, James   Patent Book 14, Page 70

    390 acres on Jeneto Creek and on south side of the Meherrin River.
                                            9-28-1728

HIX, Robert   Patent Book 14, Page 80

    580 acres on north side of Roanoke River.
                                            9-28-1728

HIX, Robert, Junr.   Patent Book 13, Page 60
    195 acres on north side of Roanoke River.
                                                                      10-31-1726

HOGWOOD, William   Patent Book 28, Page 53
    404 acres on east side of Stiths Creek.
                                                                      1-12-1746

HOLLOWAY, George   Patent Book 34, Page 108
    1063 acres in fork of Church Branch, adjoining Hubbard
        Ferrell.
                                                                      8-10-1756

HOLMES, Samuel   Patent Book 19, Page 1054
    400 acres on both sides of Miles Creek.
                                                                      7-6-1741

                                          Patent Book 22, Page 35
    101 acres on both sides of Allens Creek.
                                                                      3-1-1743

                                          Patent Book 27, Page 167
    348 acres on south side of Allens Creek on Byrd
        Lanier's line.
                                                                      5-20-1749

                                          Patent Book 31, Page 550
    175 acres on upper side of Miles Creek, adjoining line
        of Lark.
                                                                    9-10-1755

HOPPER, Michael   Patent Book 34, Page 100
    400 acres on south fork of Allens Creek.
                                                                      8-10-1756

HOUSE, Lawrence   Patent Book 21, Page 469
    195 acres on east side of Miles Creek.
                                                                      8-7-1743

HOWARD, Christopher   Patent Book 14, Page 91
    447 acres on south side of Jeneto Creek.
                                                                     9-28-1728

HOWARD, Francis					Patent Book 34, Page 220

    217 acres on south side of Roanoke River and on both sides of Cotton Creek.

                                                        5-22-1759

HOWARD, Henry					Patent Book 32, Page 659

    2800 acres on north side of Roanoke River, beginning at the mouth of Allens Creek.

                                                       12-15-1755

HOWARD, William					Patent Book 34, Page 241

    224 acres on south side of Roanoke River, adjoining Russell, Parham, et als.

                                                        5-12-1759

HUBBARD, Matthew					Patent Book 39, Page 382

    412 acres on middle fork of Little Bluestone Creek.

                                                        3-10-1771

HUDSON, John					Patent Book 32, Page 37

    314 acres on north side of Allens Creek, adjoining Humphry, Lanier, et als.

                                                        2-5-1753

HUDSON, Robert					Patent Book 34, Page 436

    200 acres on north side of Miles Creek, adjoining Booth

                                                        8-10-1759

HUGHES, Edward					Patent Book 23, Page 1123

    347 acres on both sides of Allens Creek.

                                                        8-20-1745

HUMPHREYS, William and			Patent Book 28, Page 141
    John, Thomas and Charles Humphreys

    366 acres on both sides of Allens Creek.

                                                        8-20-1747

HUNT, Memucan and				Patent Book 34, Page 188
    Samuel Harris

    3750 acres on a branch of Bluestone Creek, adjoining Evans, et als.

                                                       11-10-1757

HUTCHINS, Robert   Patent Book 39, Page 14

    370 acres on south side of Roanoke River, adjoining Stith, Pinson, et als.
                5-12-1770

HYDE, John   Patent Book 32, Page 84

    195 acres beginning at a run at Hyde's old line.
                5-9-1753

INGRAM, John   Patent Book 34, Page 456

    350 acres on both sides of Taylors Creek, adjoining Hix
                8-10-1759

JACKSON, Henry   Patent Book 34, Page 715

    775 acres on both sides of south fork of Allens Creek, adjoining Whittemore.
                9-10-1760

JEFFERSON, Feild   Patent Book 34, Page 604

    2200 acres on north side of Roanoke River, adjoining Howard, et als.
                7-15-1760

JOHNSON, Christopher   Patent Book 33, Page 51

    294 acres on south side of Meherrin River, beginning at the mouth of Buckhorn Creek.
                8-16-1756

JOHNSON, John   Patent Book 34, Page 583

    404 acres on Nutbush Creek, adjoining John Robinson.
                7-15-1760

JOHNSON, Philip   Patent Book 37, Page 111

    1097 acres on both sides of Russell's Creek.
                9-10-1767

JOHNSTON, Michael   Patent Book 33, Page 719

    262 acre on west side of the Canoe Gut, a branch of the Roanoke River.
                3-3-1760

JOHNSTON, Peter   Patent Book 32, Page 348

JONES, Frederick					Patent Book 28, Page 587

    425 acres on south side of Meherrin River.
                                                    6-20-1749

					Patent Book 33, Page 580

    1815 acres on west side of Cox Creek and on head branches of Miles Creek.
                                                    7-4-1759

JONES, John					Patent Book 23, Page 1133

    342 acres on a branch of Poplar Creek.
                                                    8-20-1745

					Patent Book 39, Page 386

    335 acres on south side of Roanoke River, adjoining Seat, Burwell, Griffin, et als.
                                                    3-10-1771

					Patent Book 41, Page 116

    406 acres on a branch of Aarons Creek, adjoining Joseph Gill and William Gill.
                                                    3-1-1773

JONES, Robert					Patent Book 33, Page 831

    220 acres on south side of Roanoke River, adjoining Scott.
                                                    7-15-1760

JONES, Robert, Junr.				Patent Book 32, Page 519

    345 acres on both sides of Grassy Creek.
                                                    Page 520

    82 acres on north side of Grassy Creek.
                                                    4-23-1755

JONES, Samuel					Patent Book 29, Page 247

    400 acres on Parhams Creek, adjoining Lewis Tanner.
                                                    7-12-1750

JONES, Stephen					Patent Book 34, Page 27

    200 acres on upper side of Great Creek, adjoining Rottenberry.
                                                    3-10-1756

JONES, William   Patent Book 26, Page 547

    665 acres on west side of Butchers Creek, adjoining the lands of Burwell and Ravenscroft.
                                                    8-20-1748

                                       Patent Book 34, Page 368

    425 acres on Allens Creek, adjoining Scott and Phifer.
                                                    8-10-1759

KEETON, Joseph   Patent Book 36, Page 953

    1204 acres on both sides of Buckhorn Creek and on the Long Branch of Laytons Creek, adjoining Turner, Thompson and Weatherfoed.
                                                    7-10-1766

KENNON, Robert   Patent Book 33, Page 797

    575 acres on north side of Miles Creek, adjoining Evans, Morgan, et als.
                                                  5-29-1760

KIDD, James   Patent Book 39, Page 105

    400 acres on Keiths Branch, adjoining his own land.
                                                  8-27-1770

KIMBALL, Charles   Patent Book 13, Page 182

    550 acres on south side of Roanoke River.
                                                  10-13-1727

KING, George   Patent Book 15, Page 114

    100 acres on south side of Roanoke River.
                                                  8-17-1733

KING, John   Patent Book 14, Page 74

    300 acres on south side of Roanoke River.
                                                  9-28-1728

                                       Patent Book 26, Page 655

    238 acres on both sides of Grassy Creek.
                                                  8-20-1748

                                       Patent Book 33, Page 560

    623 acres on Grassy Creek, adjoining Wilson.
                                                  4-3-1759

KING, Peter   Patent Book 23, Page 1112

    100 acres on both sides of Buffalo Creek.
                                                 8-20-1745

KING, William   Patent Book 30, Page 143

    400 acres on south side of Smith Creek, adjoining John
        Davis.
                                                 6-1-1750

KRUG, Andrew   Patent Book 34, Page 57

    200 acres on Allens Creek.
                                                 3-10-1756

LADD, William, Junr.   Patent Book 33, Page 472

    650 acres on south side of Taylors Creek.
                                                 8-19-1758

LAMBERT, William   Patent Book 38, Page 770

    132 acres adjoining his own land, and adjoining Fox.
                                                 7-14-1769

LANGLEY, Robert   Patent Book 32, Page 617

    1150 acres on a branch of Flatt Creek, adjoining Duke
        and Tanner.
                                                 9-10-1755

LANIER, Benjamin   Patent Book 26, Page 389

    368 acres on both sides of Allens Creek.
                                                 4-5-1748

LANIER, Byrd Thomas   Patent Book 28, Page 328

    374 acres on south side of Allens Creek.
                                                 1-12-1747

LANIER, Nicholas   Patent Book 28, Page 235

    415 acres on upper side of Mitchells Creek.
                                                 10-1-1747

                                        Patent Book 28, Page 669

    420 acres on south side of Meherrin River.
                                                 9-5-1749

LANIER, Thomas   Patent Book 26, Page 155

    380 acres on both sides of Mitchells Creek, adjoining his own line.
                                              1-12-1747

                                Patent Book 29, Page 475

    318 acres on lower side of Butchers Creek, adjoining William Hill, John Mitchell, et als.
                                              8-5-1751

                                Patent Book 33, Page 20

    415 acres on north side of Mitchells Creek.
                                              6-16-1756

                                Patent Book 33, Page 730

    400 acres on a branch of Allens Creek
                                              3-3-1760

                                Patent Book 37, Page 390

    838 acres on both sides of Mitchells Creek, adjoining William Hill and Thomas Eastland.
                                            9-20-1768

LANKFORD, John   Patent Book 34, Page 112

    200 acres on both sides of Great Creek, adjoining Rottenberry.
                                              8-16-1756

LARK, Dennis   Patent Book 30, Page 141

    284 acres on north side of Miles Creek, adjoining Johnson's line.
                                              6-1-1750

                                Patent Book 33, Page 53

    210 acres on south side of Dockery Creek, adjoining Baird.
                                              8-16-1756

                                Patent Book 33, Page 586

    32 acres on east side of Flatt Creek.
                                              7-4-1759

LETT, Francis   Patent Book 33, Page 59

325 acres on a branch of Miles Creek, adjoining Holmes.
8-16-1756

LETT, James Patent Book 33, Page 51

190 acres on a branch of Mountain Creek, adjoining Lett, Tabb and Clack.
8-16-1756

LETT, John Patent Book 28, Page 230

232 acres on north side of Miles Creek.
10-1-1747

LEWIS, James Patent Book 33, Page 537

376 acres on south side of Roanoke River, adjoining Gilliam.
3-3-1759

LIDDERDALE, William Patent Book 28, Page 513

288 acres on both sides of Little Bluestone Creek, adjoining Byrd.
1-10-1748

 Patent Book 33, Page 791

365 acres on both sides of the Middle Fork of Bluestone Creek.
5-29-1760

LIGHTFOOT, John Patent Book 28, Page 708

2050 acres on both sides of Buckhorn Creek.
3-12-1749

LOYD, Thomas, Junr. Patent Book 22, Page 327

424 acres on both sides of Butchers Creek.
8-1-1745

LUCAS, Charles Patent Book 14, Page 87

348 acres on south side of Great Creek.
9-28-1728

LUCAS, Samuel Patent Book 29, Page 489

297 acres on Dockery Creek, adjoining Lett and Gordon.
8-5-1751

LUCAS, Samuel   Patent Book 32, Page 707

    245 acres on Dockery Creek, adjoining William Lucas.

                                                                         3-10-1756

LUCAS, William   Patent Book 18, Page 41

    173 acres on south side of Miles Creek.

                                                                         7-20-1738

                                      Patent Book 19, Page 766

    200 acres on north side of Miles Creek.

                                                                         9-16-1740

                                      Patent Book 21, Page 478

    275 acres on his own line, and adjoining the line of
        John Day.

                                                                         8-30-1743

LYNCH, John   Patent Book 40, Page 523

    330 acres in fork of Bluestone Creek, adjoining Betts,
        Hudson, et als.

                                                                          8-3-1771

McCARTHY, Edmond   Patent Book 14, Page 29

    960 acres on both sides of North Fork of Jeneto Creek.

                                                                        9-28-1728

McDANIEL, James   Patent Book 19, Page 1033

    253 acres on both sides of Little Creek.

                                                                         7-6-1741

McDANIEL, James and   Patent Book 34, Page 401
        Edward McDaniel

    510 acres on south side of Meherrin River, adjoining
        Andrews.

                                                                      8-10-1759

McDANIEL, John   Patent Book 28, Page 130

    400 acres on both sides of a fork of Mountain Creek.

                                                                       8-20-1747

                                    Patent Book 36, Page 943

    400 acres on south side of Meherrin River below the
        mountain   7-10-1766

McHARG, Ebenezer   Patent Book 42, Page 650

    332 acres on north side of Roanoke River, and on both sides of Taylor's Ferry Road, adjoining Durham, Robertson et als.

                                                                               7-5-1774

McKINNEY, James   Patent Book 33, Page 1001

    220 acres on both sides of Miles Creek, adjoining Pennington, et als.

                                                                            2-14-1761

McKOY, John   Patent Book 34, Page 98

    373 acres on a branch of Flatt Creek, adjoining Gordon

                                                                             8-10-1756

McNEIL, Malcolm   Patent Book 28, Page 492

    167 acres on upper side of Grassy Creek, adjoining Munford.

                                                                             1-10-1748

MABRY, Joshua   Patent Book 33, Page 579

    350 acres on south side of Parhams Creek, adjoining Hewey and Timms.

                                                                             7-4-1759

                                    Patent Book 34, Page 609

    145 acres on Great and Parhams Creeks, adjoining **Timms**, et als.

                                                                             7-15-1760

                                    Patent Book 40, Page 536

    400 acres on a branch of Great Creek, adjoining Wright, Jones, et als.

                                                                             8-3-1771

MACLIN, John   Patent Book 24, Page 394

    995 acres on south side of Mitchells Creek.

                                                                             8-28-1746

                                    Patent Book 34, Page 112

    400 acres on Cox Creek, adjoining Farrar, Delony, et als.

                                                                             11-26-1756

MACLIN, John   Patent Book 34, Page 164

    484 acres on a fork of Cox Creek, adjoining Delony and
       McDaniel.
                                                  11-26-1756

MACLIN, William   Patent Book 23, Page 1127

    350 acres on north side of Miles Creek.
                                                  8-20-1745

                              Patent Book 29, Page 307

    400 acres on both sides of Miles Creek, adjoining his
       own line.
                                                  11-3-1750

MAJOR, Nicholas   Patent Book 19, Page 1069

    200 acres on north side of Butchers Creek.
                                                  7-25-1741

                              Patent Book 29, Page 25

    304 acres on Allens Creek, adjoining Benjamin Lanier.
                                                12-15-1749

MALONE, Drury and   Patent Book 29, Page 480
       Isham Malone

    970 acres on both sides of Jeneto Creek, adjoining
       William Nance.
                                                  8-5-1751

MALONE, Drury   Patent Book 34, Page 277

    300 acres on both sides of Jeneto Creek.
                                                  5-12-1759

                              Patent Book 34, Page 290

    390 acres on a branch of Jeneto Creek, adjoining
       Nathaniel Malone
                                                5-12-1759

MALONE, George   Patent Book 41, Page 378

    420 acres on a branch of Avents Creek and on Jeneto
       Creek, adjoining Pennington, et als.
                                                6-15-1773

MALONE, Thomas   Patent Book 34, Page 26

    194 acres on south fork of Great Creek, adjoining his father's line.

        3-10-1756

        Patent Book 34, Page 321

    705 acres on Jeneto Creek, adjoining Drury Malòne.

        5-12-1759

MALONE, William   Patent Book 18, Page 254

    247 acres on Taylors Creek.

        3-26-1739

        Patent Book 22, Page 125

    180 acres on south side of Meherrin River.

        6-16-1744

        Patent Book 24, Page 94

    234 acres on south side of Taylors Creek.

        9-20-1745

MANNING, Samuel   Patent Book 33, Page 440

    350 acres on Flatt Creek, adjoining his own line.

        6-2-1758

MARABLE, Matthew   Patent Book 32, Page 522

    490 acres on lower side of Laytons Creek.

        Page 523

    380 acres on both sides of King's Road.

        Page 524

    400 acres on both sides of the long fork of Laytons Creek, adjoining his own line.

        Page 525

    430 acres on both sides of the long fork of Laytons Creek.

        Page 525

    335 acres on Laytons Creek, adjoining Weatherford, Freeman, et als.

        4-23-1755

MARABLE, William   Patent Book 28, Page 84

    425 acres on the ridge between Bluestone Creek and the

Meherrin River.   6-25-1747

                                                            Page 85

   425 acres on branches of Bluestone and Finneywood
      Creeks.
                                                           6-25-1747

                                              Patent Book 33, Page 555

   100 acres on north side of Roanoke River.
                                                            3-3-1759

                                              Patent Book 41, Page 16

   71 acres at the head of Thomason's Branch.
                                                            8-1-1772

MARSHALL, Samuel   Patent Book 38, Page 587

   366 acres on Avents Creek, adjoining Despanes, Ezell,
      Pennington, et als.
                                                            4-6-1769

MARTIN, John   Patent Book 37, Page 96

   340 acres on a branch of Great Creek and on Parhams
      Creek, adjoining Ward, Epps, Harvell and Tanner.

                                                           9-10-1767

MATTHEWS, John, Junr.   Patent Book 34, Page 182

   180 acres on Finneywood Creek, adjoining Cox and
      Marable.
                                                           8-29-1757

MATHIS, James (Matthews)   Patent Book 14, Page 34

   850 acres on south side of Roanoke River.
                                                           9-28-1728

MILLER, Jacob   Patent Book 39, Page 13

   200 acres on a branch of Allens Creek, adjoining Hill.

                                                           5-12-1770

MILLER, Joseph   Patent Book 34, Page 712

   400 acres on a branch of Flatt Creek, adjoining Russell
                                                           9-10-1760

MITCHELL, James   Patent Book 17, Page 264

 330 acres on south side of Roanoke River.

 450 acres on Flatt Creek.   3-17-1736

          Patent Book 29, Page 454

 395 acres on south side of Roanoke River.

               7-5-1751

         Patent Book 29, Page 499

 1527 acres on south side of Roanoke River.

               8-5-1751

         Patent Book 33, Page 490

 404 acres on Mill Creek, adjoining Nathaniel and John Robinson.

              9-20-1758

         Patent Book 33, Page 491

 425 acres on Mill Creek, adjoining Robinson, Busby, et als.

              9-20-1758

MITCHELL, John   Patent Book 14, Page 507

 93 acres on north side of Roanoke River.

              9-28-1732

         Patent Book 17, Page 385

 400 acres on north side of Roanoke River.

              8-15-1737

MITCHELL, Robert   Patent Book 19, Page 795

 490 acres on south side of Roanoke River.

              9-16-1740

         Patent Book 28, Page 490

 40 acres on south side of Roanoke River, adjoining his own land.

              1-10-1748

         Patent Book 28, Page 520

 286 acres on south side of Roanoke River.

              1-10-1748

MITCHELL, Robert   Patent Book 28, Page 526

 135 acres on both sides of Island Creek and on the county line.
              1-10-1748

MITCHELL, Thomas   Patent Book 14, Page 34

 612 acres on north side of Raonoke River.
              9-28-1728

MITCHELL, William   Patent Book 34, Page 874

 204 acres on both sides of Mitchells Creek.
              7-14-1761

MOORE, John   Patent Book 24, Page 369

 170 acres on both sides of Long Branch.
              8-28-1746

MOORE, Seth   Patent Book 33, Page 581

 3600 acres on east side of Allens Creek, adjoining Ruffin and Baker.
              7-4-1759

MOORE, Thomas   Patent Book 38, Page 780

 411 acres on Butchers Creek, adjoining Maclin, Bracey, Brown, et als.
              7-14-1769

MORGAN, Philip   Patent Book 18, Page 17

 1000 acres on north side of Roanoke River.
              6-16-1738

         Patent Book 23, Page 922

 120 acres on both sides of Stiths Creek.
              7-10-1745

MORRIS, William   Patent Book 34, Page 268

 386 acres on a branch of Grassy Creek, adjoining Stith.
              5-12-1759

MUNFORD, James   Patent Book 14, Page 421

 808 acres on north side of Roanoke River.
              4-11-1732

MUNFORD, Robert   Patent Book 17, Page 69

    100 acres on south side of Roanoke River.
                                                    6-5-1736

                                          Patent Book 33, Page 794

    1150 acres on a branch of Finneywood Creek, adjoining
        John Ravenscroft.
                                                    5-29-1760

MUNFORD, Robert and   Patent Book 11, Page 88
    John Anderson

    2811 acres in the fork of Cox Creek.
                                                    5-15-1722

MUNFORD, Robert and   Patent Book 13, Page 115
    Richard Jones

    465 acres on north side of Roanoke River.
                                                    6-16-1727

MUNFORD, Robert   Patent Book 13, Page 427

    1000 acres on north side of Roanoke River.
                                                    9-28-1728

MUNFORD, William   Patent Book 14, Page 130

    390 acres on upper side of Cox Creek.
                                                    9-28-1728

                                          Patent Book 37, Page 306

    850 acres on lower side of Great Creek and upper side
        of Miles Creek, adjoining Jeremiah Ellis.
                                                    7-20-1768

MURRAY, James   Patent Book 28, Page 508

    395 acres on a branch of Allens Creek, adjoining Peter
        Jones.
                                                    1-10-1748

                                          Patent Book 36, Page 904

    2019 acres on Middle Fork of Bluestone Creek, adjoining
        Burwell, Evans, et als.
                                                    9-16-1765

MURPHY, Drury   Patent Book 40, Page 531

265 acres adjoining Lambert, Cole, Hayes, Davis, et als.
8-3-1771

MYRICK, Owen   Patent Book 26, Page 627

470 acres between Flatt Creek and Parhams Creek.
8-20-1748

NANCE, William   Patent Book 33, Page 63

390 acres on head branches of Great Creek, adjoining Malone, Harwell, et als.
8-16-1756

Patent Book 33, Page 223

400 acres on Roanoke River, adjoining Fox, et als.
8-16-1756

NANCE, William   Patent Book 25, Page 239

318 acres on south side of Jeneto Creek.
1-12-1746

NAPIER, John   Patent Book 13, Page 177

300 acres on north side of Roanoke River.
10-13-1727

NICHOLSON, Joshua   Patent Book 14, Page 304

106 acres on south side of Meherrin River.
8-25-1731

NOBLES, Robert   Patent Book 29, Page 224

400 acres on Roanoke River and Nutbush Creek, adjoining John Robinson.
6-1-1750

NORRILL, Hugh   Patent Book 34, Page 179

333 acres on both sides of Allens Creek.
2-7-1757

NORTHINGTON, Jabez   Patent Book E, Page 14

224 acres adjoining land of John Brown, Junr., Fowler, Nance, et als.
5-1-1775

OLIVER, James Patent Book 34, Page 596

    1900 acres on Allens Creek, adjoining Murray, et als.

    7-15-1760

PARHAM, Ephraim Patent Book 15, Page 411

    130 acres on south side of Roanoke River.

    1-27-1734

PARHAM, Lewis Patent Book 28, Page 218

    388 acres on both sides of middle fork of Bluestone Creek.

    10-1-1747

PARKER, John Patent Book 24, Page 259

    327 acres on north side of Dry Creek, adjoining Stephen Evans.

    6-5-1746

    Patent Book 25, Page 578

    278 acres on both sides of Little Creek.

    1-12-1746

PARRISH, James Patent Book 26, Page 46

    385 acres on west side of Butchers Creek.

    6-25-1747

PENNINGTON, James Patent Book 41, Page 400

    135 acres on Avents Creek adjoining his own land, and adjoining William Pennington.

    6-15-1773

PENNINGTON, Sack (Isaac) Patent Book 41, Page 399

    405 acres on Jeneto and Avents Creeks, adjoining Pennington, Malone, et als.

    6-15-1773

PENNINGTON, William Patent Book 19, Page 917

    274 acres on south side of Meherrin River, adjoining Malone and his own line.

    3-24-1740

    Patent Book 33, Page 66

367 acres on both sides of Stiths Creek, adjoining William Hagood.
8-16-1756

Patent Book 34, Page 1002

400 acres on both sides of Miles Creek, adjoining Hudson, et als.
3-25-1762

Patent Book 41, Page 401

410 acres on Avents Creek, adjoining his own land and adjoining John Brown, Junr., et als.
6-15-1773

PHIFER, Martin   Patent Book 32, Page 413

795 acres on head branch of south fork of Allens Creek.
11-1-1754

PINSON, Aaron   Patent Book 29, Page 495

404 acres on south side of Roanoke River.
8-5-1751

POINDEXTER, Philip   Patent Book 31, Page 645

1250 acres on south side of Meherrin River.
9-10-1755

POOL, Adam   Patent Book 34, Page 829

304 acres on west side of Flatt Creek, adjoining Taylor Duke.
2-14-1761

POOL, William   Patent Book 29, Page 228

330 acres on both sides of Flatt Creek, adjoining James Mitchell.
6-1-1750

Patent Book 29, Page 428

178 acres on upper side of Flatt Creek.
4-10-1751

Patent Book 30, Page 406

87 acres on lower side of Flatt Creek, adjoining Amos Timms.
11-3-1750

POOL, William   Patent Book 33, Page 442

     400 acres on Flatt Creek.

                                                  6-2-1758

                                 Patent Book 37, Page 104

     400 acres on both sides of Mill Branch of Flatt Creek, adjoining Robertson and Manning.

                                             9-10-1767

PULLIAM, Patterson   Patent Book 39, Page 274

     400 acres on branches of Little Bluestone Creek, adjoining Enroughty, White, et als.

                                           2-16-1771

PULLIAM, William   Patent Book 39, Page 398

     400 acres on Little Bluestone Creek, adjoining White, Hubbard, Parrish, et als.

                                           3-10-1771

PURYEAR, Peter   Patent Book 34, Page 670

     270 acres on east side of Butchers Creek, adjoining Bracey, et als.

                                           8-20-1760

RABOURN, John (Raiborne)   Patent Book 14, Page 73

     340 acres on south side of Roanoke River.

                                           9-28-1728

RAGSDALE, Peter   Patent Book 41, Page 34

     87 acres on Bluestone Creek, adjoining Hubbard, Abbitt, (Abbott) et als.

                                           8-1-1772

RAINEY, Francis   Patent Book 38, Page 622

     400 acres on Great Creek, adjoining Malone, Lankford, et als.

                                           4-6-1769

RANDLE, Josias   Patent Book 28, Page 455

     504 acres on Butchers Creek, adjoining John Mitchell.

                                           9-20-1748

RAVENSCROFT, Capt. John   Patent Book 20, Page 514

     450 acres on Jeneto Creek and on south side of the

Meherrin River.

6-30-1743

RAVENSCROFT, Robert   Patent Book 19, Page 802

    1000 acres on south side of Finneywood Creek.

9-16-1740

Patent Book 32, Page 203

    1000 acres on south side of Finneywood Creek, adjoining John Ravenscroft.

7-20-1753

RAVENSCROFT, Thomas   Patent Book 24, Page 334

    1050 acres on both sides of Butchers Creek.

7-25-1746

RICHARDSON, Richard   Patent Book 41, Page 402

    400 acres on Buffalo Creek, adjoining John Vaughan.

6-15-1773

RIDLEY, George   Patent Book 42, Page 529

    400 acres on a branch of Buckhorn Creek, adjoining Green and Hutchins.

7-5-1774

ROBERTS, John   Patent Book 33, Page 71

    575 acres on south side of Meherrin River, adjoining Bagwell, Walker, et als.

8-16-1756

ROBERTS, Philip   Patent Book 19, Page 792

    150 acres on south side of Roanoke River.

9-14-1740

ROBERTS, Thomas   Patent Book 33, Page 796

    366 acres on Flatt Creek.

5-29-1760

ROBERTSON, Henry   Patent Book 39, Page 161

    400 acres on Bluestone Creek, adjoining Clay, Rowland, et als.

8-27-1770

ROBERTSON, Isaac   Patent Book 14, Page 83

    670 acres on south side of Roanoke River.
                                                  9-28-1728

ROBERTSON, John   Patent Book 17, Page 123

    150 acres on south side of Roanoke River.
                                                  7-20-1736

ROBERTSON, John, Junr.   Patent Book 26, Page 322

    190 acres on north side of Roanoke River.
                                                  4-5-1748

                                  Patent Book 34, Page 278

    190 acres on north side of Roanoke River, adjoining
        Matthew Robertson.
                                                5-12-1759

ROBERTSON, Matthew   Patent Book 31, Page 151

    154 acres on north side of Roanoke River.
                                                7-15-1752

ROBERTSON, Nicholas   Patent Book 34, Page 591

    312 acres on west side of the Canoe Gut, adjoining
        Thomas Eastland.
                                                7-15-1760

ROBERTSON, William   Patent Book 31, Page 309

    300 acres on south side of Allens Creek.
                                                1-12-1753

                                Patent Book 38, Page 681

    344 acres on both sides of Island Creek, adjoining
        William Munford and William Wright.
                                                7-14-1769

ROBINSON, Abraham   Patent Book 33, Page 1008

    285 acres on south side of Roanoke River, adjoining
        Nathaniel Robinson
                                                2-14-1761

ROBINSON, John   Patent Book 29, Page 238

    400 acres on Nutbush Creek and on the county line.
                                                7-12-1750

ROBINSON, Nathaniel   Patent Book 33, Page 996

374 acres on both sides of Mitchells Mill Creek, adjoining the county line.

2-14-1761

ROFFE, William   Patent Book 42, Page 683

25 acres adjoining his own land, and adjoining the land of Phillips.

7-5-1774

ROTTENBERRY, Henry   Patent Book 33, Page 73

400 acres on both sides of lower fork of Great Creek.

8-16-1756

ROYAL, Joseph   Patent Book 26, Page 650

365 acres on both sides of Butchers Creek.

8-20-1748

ROYSTER, William   Patent Book 33, Page 825

1339 acres on south side of Roanoke River.

6-30-1760

RUFFIN, John   Patent Book 33, Page 535

870 acres on a branch of Allens Creek.

12-15-1758

                                   Patent Book 42, Page 775

978 acres adjoining land on which he now lives on Long Branch, and adjoining land of Moore, Parker, et als

7-5-1774

RUFFIN, Col. John and   Patent Book 32, Page 559
        Col. John Baker

13912 acres on east side of Allens Creek beginning at Humphries' line.

6-10-1755

RUFFIN, Robert   Patent Book 38, Page 678

3571 acres on Miles and Dockery Creeks.

7-14-1769

SANDEFER, William   Patent Book 29, Page 361

400 acres on upper side of Allens Creek.

11-30-1750

SATTERWHITE, Thomas   Patent Book 32, Page 208

    153 acres on both sides of Butchers Creek.
                                              7-20-1753

SCOTT, George   Patent Book 39, Page 305

    347 acres adjoining line of Henry King, formerly
        Granted to James Scott 11-3-1750.
                                              2-16-1771

SCOTT, James   Patent Book 28, Page 63

    404 acres on both sides of Allens Creek.
                                              1-12-1746

                                        Patent Book 32, Page 367

    400 acres on both sides of Allens Creek.
                                              5-11-1754

SCOTT, Robert   Patent Book 28, Page 82

    400 acres on both sides of Meherrin River.
                                              6-25-1747

SEAT, John   Patent Book 29, Page 236

    180 acres on south side of Roanoke River, and on lower
        side of Buffalo Creek.
                                              7-17-1750

SEAT, Josiah   Patent Book 29, Page 237

    383 acres on south side of Roanoke River and on upper
        side of Buffalo Creek, adjoining Byrd.
                                              7-12-1750

                                        Patent Book 39, Page 201

    360 acres on south side of Roanoke River, adjoining his
        own land.
                                              8-27-1770

SEAT, Robert   Patent Book 36, Page 655

    400 acres on Little Buffalo Creek.
                                              8-15-1764

SHELLEY, Amos Timms   Patent Book 24, Page 368

    326 acres on north side of Flatt Creek.
                                              8-28-1746

SHELLEY, Amos Timms   Patent Book 28, Page 484

    400 acres on lower side of Flatt Creek, adjoining his own line and Humphry Huey's (Hewey) line.
                                                                          1-10-1748

SHOTWELL, John   Patent Book 42, Page 740

    410 acres on a branch of Aarons Creek, adjoining Hutchins, Parrish, et als.
                                                                            7-5-1774

SMITH, Charles   Patent Book 14, Page 91

    180 acres on north side of Roanoke River.
                                                                             7-8-1728

SMITH, James   Patent Book 34, Page 672

    304 acres on both sides of the long branch of Allens Creek, adjoining Baker, Ruffin, et als.
                                                          8-20-1760

SMITH, John   Patent Book 29, Page 432

    265 acres on Butchers Creek, adjoining Nicholas Major.
                                                                    7-5-1751

                                             Patent Book 14, Page 77

    333 acres on north side of Jeneto Creek.
                                                                   9-28-1728

SMITH, Timothy   Patent Book 34, Page 645

    220 acres on the Old Mill Creek of Roanoke River, adjoining Bracey and Mitchell.
                                                          7-15-1760

SMITH, William   Patent Book 13, Page 182

    790 acres on south side of Roanoke River.
                                                             10-13-1727

SPARROW, James   Patent Book 42, Page 821

    400 acres on both sides of Little Mine Creek, adjoining Clark, Lanier, et als.
                                                          12-7-1774

SPEED, John   Patent Book 33, Page 67

    237 acres on east side of Cox Creek, adjoining

   Hubbard Ferrell, et als.

                  8-16-1756

STARKE, William   Patent Book 31, Page 324

  1050 acres on both sides of Butchers Creek.

                  4-26-1753

STEWART, Charles   Patent Book 24, Page 257

  300 acres on both sides of Allens Creek.

                  Page 271

  323 acres on south side of Allens Creek.

                  6-5-1746

STEWART, John   Patent Book 28, Page 514

  318 acres on both sides of Buffalo Creek.

                  1-10-1748

STITH, Buckner   Patent Book 39, Page 289

  727 acres on both sides of Cotton Creek, adjoining land
    of King.

                  2-16-1771

STITH, Drury   Patent Book 23, Page 687

  354 acres on north side of Mitchells Creek.

                  6-16-1744

            Patent Book 13, Page 414

  556 acres on north side of Roanoke River.

                  9-27-1729

            Patent Book 15, Page 205

  96 acres on north side of Roanoke River.

                  4-26-1734

            Patent Book 33, Page 124

  519 acres on a branch of Allens Creek, adjoining
    William Hill, et als.

                  8-16-1756

STITH, Drury and   Patent Book 28, Page 230
  Henry Morris and Michael Cadet Young

  412 acres on Little Bluestone and Middle Fork of
    Bluestone Creek.   10-1-1747

STITH, Drury and   Patent Book 28, Page 232
    Henry Morris and Michael Cadet Young

    637 acres on both sides of Bluestone Creek.
                                                            10-1-1747

                                   Patent Book 31, Page 346

    3070 acres on south side of Roanoke River and on both sides of Grassy Creek.
                                                            8-5-1753

STROUD, William   Patent Book 28, Page 498

    204 acres on a great branch of Allens Creek.
                                                            1-10-1748

TALLEY, Henry   Patent Book 34, Page 671

    650 acres on a branch of Laytons Creek, adjoining Hall and Marable.
                                                            8-20-1760

TANNER, Lewis   Patent Book 29, Page 188

    354 acres on Parhams Creek, adjoining Adam Tapley.
                                                             6-1-1750

                                   Patent Book 33, Page 914

    400 acres on Parhams Creek, adjoining Samuel Jones.
                                                             9-26-1760

TANNER, Thomas   Patent Book 32, Page 680

    220 acres on both sides of north fork of Allens Creek.
                                                            3-10-1756

TATE, Jesse   Patent Book 41, Page 235

    333 acres on a branch of Butchers Creek, adjoining Easter, Lewis, Wilkins, et als.
                                                             3-1-1773

TAYLOR, Edmund   Patent Book E, Page 28

    400 acres on both sides of Mitchell's fork of Bluestone Creek, adjoining Miller.
                                                             5-1-1775

TAYLOR, Edmund   Patent Book E, Page 30

   400 acres on branches of Bluestone Creek, adjoining
      Stith.
                                                     5-1-1775

TAYLOR, Thomas   Patent Book 33, Book 368

   370 acres on a branch of Wolfpit Fork of Flatt Creek,
      adjoining Duke's line.
                                                     6-8-1757

THOMERSON, William (Thomason)   Patent Book 28, Page 65

   314 acres on both sides of Butchers Creek.
                                                     1-12-1746

THOMPSON, John   Patent Book 34, Page 705

   400 acres on a branch of Buckhorn Creek.
                                                     9-10-1760

                                                Patent Book 37, Page 220

   400 acres on a branch of Buckhorn Creek, adjoining
      Keeton.
                                                     9-10-1767

THOMPSON, Wells   Patent Book 36, Page 759

   605 acres adjoining William Wright and George
      Pennington.   6-5-1765

THOMPSON, William   Patent Book 34, Page 15

   170 acres on Flatt Creek.
                                                     3-10-1756

TIBBS, William   Patent Book 33, Page 63

   400 acres on a branch of Bluestone Creek, adjoining
      Harris.
                                                     8-16-1756

TIMMS, Amos   Patent Book 13, Page 177

   200 acres on south side of Meherrin River.
                                                     10-13-1727

TOMSON, John (Thompson)   Patent Book 34, Page 305

   400 acres on Buckhorn Creek, adjoining Weatherford.
                                                     5-12-1759

TUCKER, James   Patent Book 33, Page 517

    324 acres on a branch of Allens Creek, adjoining
       Thomas Loyd.
                                            12-15-1758

                                                      Page 518

    940 acres on a ridge between Butchers and Allens
       Creeks.
                                            12-15-1758

                             Patent Book 42, Page 469

    800 acres on a branch of Allens Creek, adjoining
       Hutson, Bevill, Ruffin, Baker, et als.
                                           6-15-1773

TUNE, James (Toone)   Patent Book 42, Page 733

    45 acres adjoining his own land on north side of the
       Roanoke River.
                                            7-5-1774

TWITTY, John   Patent Book 32, Page 632

    435 acres on Allens Creek, adjoining Murray.
                                            9-10-1755

VAUGHAN, Stephen and   Patent Book 34, Page 411
       Reuben Vaughan

    795 acres at the head of Pine Creek.
                                            8-10-1759

VAUGHAN, William   Patent Book 33, Page 55

    400 acres on Buffalo Creek, adjoining Henry Green's
       line.
                                            8-16-1756

WALKER, David   Patent Book 17, Page 121

    250 acres on south side of Roanoke River.
                                            7-20-1736

                           Patent Book 20, Page 145

    400 acres on south side of Roanoke River.
                                            1-30-1741

                           Patent Book 29, Page 486

400 acres on Taylors Creek, adjoining Bates.
8-5-1751

Patent Book 14, Page 76

751 acres on south side of Roanoke River.
9-28-1728

WALTON, George   Patent Book 32, Page 41

850 acres on a branch of Mountain Creek, adjoining
Arnold, et als.   2-5-1753

Patent Book 12, Page 512

150 acres on south side of Meherrin River.
7-7-1726

WARD, Wade   Patent Book 34, Page 552

472 acres on Flatt Creek, adjoining Taylor Duke.
6-10-1760

WARREN, John   Patent Book 34, Page 553

192 acres on Flatt Creek.
6-10-1760

WATSON, John   Patent Book 17, Page 326

100 acres on Flatt Creek.   6-10-1737

Patent Book 19, Page 858

200 acres on south side of Meherrin River and on the
upper side of Mountain Creek.
12-1-1740

Patent Book 23, Page 610

300 acres on both sides of middle fork of Miles Creek.
11-25-1743

WEATHERFORD, Richard   Patent Book 33, Page 935

400 acres on Buckhorn Creek, adjoining Green.
9-26-1760

Patent Book 34, Page 263

800 acres on south fork of Meherrin River, adjoining
Lightfoot.   5-12-1759

WESTBROOK, William   Patent Book 17, Page 285

    428 acres on north side of north fork of Roanoke River.
                                                                      3-17-1736

WESTMORELAND, John   Patent Book 42, Page 610

    380 acres on Buffalo Creek, adjoining Taylor, Wall,
       Griffin, et als.
                                                           7-5-1774

WHEELER, Samuel   Patent Book 34, Page 262

    254 acres on south side of Roanoke River, adjoining
       Mitchell.
                                                      5-12-1759

WHISELL, Matthew   Patent Book 22, Page 60

    295 acres on south side of south fork of Allens Creek.

                                                   6-16-1744

WHITEHEAD, Benjamin   Patent Book 37, Page 228

    416 acres on a branch of Bluestone Creek, adjoining
       Parrish, Lidderdale and Miller.
                                                   9-10-1767

WHITLOW, Henry   Patent Book 41, Page 188

    150 acres on a branch of Bluestone Creek, adjoining
       Clay, Rowland, et als.
                                                      3-1-1773

WHITTEMORE, John   Patent Book 32, Page 625

    220 acres on a branch of the south fork of Allens
       Creek, adjoining Coleman.
                                                   9-10-1755

WILBOURN, John   Patent Book 33, Page 360

    400 acres on both sides of south fork of Bluestone
       Creek, adjoining Miller.
                                                   4-19-1757

WILES, Luke   Patent Book 30, Page 179

    204 acres on south side of Roanoke River.
                                                     7-12-1750

WILKINS, John   Patent Book 33, Page 45

    400 acres on a branch of Butchers Creek, adjoining Tabor.
                                                        8-16-1756

WILLIAMS, Benjamin   Patent Book 19, Page 787

    130 acres on both sides of Avents Creek.
                                                        6-1-1741

WILLIAMS, David   Patent Book 28, Page 161

    340 acres on the south side of Roanoke River.
                                                        8-20-1747

WILLIAMS, James   Patent Book 29, Page 429

    804 acres on south side of Meherrin River on Stiths Creek.
                                                        4-10-1751

WILLIAMS, Thomas   Patent Book 24, Page 256

    154 acres on north side of Butchers Creek.
                                                        6-5-1746

                                   Patent Book 27, Page 267

    425 acres on both sides of Bluestone Creek.
                                                       5-20-1749

                                   Patent Book 29, Page 409

    510 acres on lower side of Butchers Creek, adjoining John Maclin.
                                                     4-10-1751

                                   Patent Book 32, Page 16

    997 acres on branches of Finneywood and Otter Creeks, adjoining Munford, Howard, et als.
                                                   2-5-1753

WILSON, Nathaniel   Patent Book 14, Page 62

    650 acres on north side of Roanoke River.
                                                     9-28-1728

WINFIELD, Joshua (Wingfield)   Patent Book 42, Page 756

    705 acres adjoining the land of Jones, Douglas, Harwell Brothers, et als.
                                                   7-5-1774

WITTON, Richard   Patent Book 28, Page 90

  374 acres on west side of Blackstone Creek.
                   7-25-1747

              Patent Book 34, Page 89

  217 acres on a branch of Allens Creek, adjoining James Scott.
                   8-10-1756

             Patent Book 34, Page 878

  2750 acres on a branch of Allens Creek and on the Meherrin River.
                   8-7-1761

             Patent Book 36, Page 701

  549 acres on lower side of Blackstone Creek.
                   9-26-1764

             Patent Book 36, Page 859

  875 acres on head branch of Allens Creek.
                   9-16-1765

WOMACK, William   Patent Book 27, Page 450

  80 acres in the fork of Allens Creek.
                   9-5-1749

WOOD, John   Patent Book 34, Page 554

  400 acres on Dockery Creek, adjoining Clack.
                   6-10-1760

WOOD, Richard   Patent Book 24, Page 276

  347 acres on both sides of Allens Creek.
                   6-5-1746

WRAY, Francis   Patent Book 14, Page 63

  208 acres on east side of Jeneto Creek.
                   9-28-1728

WRIGHT, John   Patent Book 28, Page 462

  224 acres on Flatt Creek, adjoining Thomas Roberts.
                   1-10-1748

WRIGHT, John   Patent Book 28, Page 463

    386 acres on Flatt Creek, adjoining his own line and line of Thomas Roberts.

                                                       1-10-1748

YORK, Richard   Patent Book 23, Page 929

    204 acres on both sides of Butchers Creek.

                                                       7-10-1745

Note: Because of incomplete, or indefinite, description some patents have not been included in the foregoing list of Colonial patents.

MECKLENBURG COUNTY

CREEKS

1	Finneywood	19	Allens
2	Blackstone	20	Coleman
3	Buckhorn	21	Eastland
4	Pine	22	Butchers
5	Mountain	23	Little Bluestone
6	Stith	24	Middle Bluestone
7	Taylors	25	Bluestone
8	Jeneto	26	Aarons
9	Poplar	27	Buffalo
10	Grove	28	Little Buffalo
11	Great	29	Beaver Pond
12	Parhams	30	Grassy
13	Flatt	31	Island
14	Dockery	32	Mill
15	Miles	33	Nutbush
16	Cox	34	Cotton
17	Long Branch (of Laytons Creek)	35	Smiths
18	Laytons		

This list of the principal creeks in Mecklenburg County is appended as a key to the map on the next page. It was not feasible to designate every creek on a small map. Many names have changed. Mitchells Creek is now known as Eastland. The names of some of the streams referred to in patents and in deeds is now unknown, and evidently designated branches of the creeks listed above. Avents Creek, now known as Evans Creek, is not shown on the map, but is between Taylors and Jeneto Creeks. Persimmontree and Woodpecker (Peckerwood) Creeks are branches of the Blueston Creeks. The many branches of Butchers Creek are not usually named on extant maps, and are not shown on the map.

MECKLENBURG COUNTY

CREEKS

EARLY BRUNSWICK COUNTY DEEDS

Deeds, Wills, Etc. Book No. 1

BUTCHER, John   Book 1, Page 8

John Butcher to Gabriel Harrison ... on the river ....
south side of Butchers Creek on Roanoke River ....
(mutilated ... acreage not now legible) ... date not
legible.
                                      See Order Book 1, Page 10

HICKS, George   Book 1, Page 12

George Hicks and Sarah his wife of Surry County to
Daniel Carrell (Carroll) of Prince George County ......
265 acres ... adjoining Daniel Hicks ... on Poplar
Creek ... (mutilated).
Dated 4 Oct. 1732   Recorded 5 Oct. 1732

Witnesses: /s/ George Hicks
    Not legible   /s/ Sarah (X) Hicks

TUCKER, William   Book 1, Page 17

William Tucker of Brunswick County and Elizabeth his
wife to John Nipper of Brunswick County ... 150 acres
in St. Andrew's Parish ... on Cox's Creek ... being a
part of 400 acres granted to William Tucker (mutilated)
Witnesses: /s/ William (X) Tucker
    Mutilated   /s/ Elizabeth (X) Tucker
Dated 4 April 1732   Recorded 5 Oct. 1732

WALKER, David   Book 1, Page 51

David Walker of Bristol Parish, Prince George County,
to William Bird (Byrd), Esq. of Westover Parish, in
Charles City County ... 751 acres in St. Andrew's
Parish ... adjoining Robert Munford ... (mutilated)
Witnesses: /s/ David Walker
    Mutilated
Dated 2 May 1733   Recorded 7 June 1733

RAYLEY, Miles (Miles Reiley)   Book 1, Page 63

Miles Rayley of Brunswick County to David Allen of said
County ... 100 acres ... on Miles Creek ... on north
side of Roanoke River ... (mutilated).
Witnesses: /s/ Mutilated
    Mutilated
Dated 7 Jan. 1732/33   Recorded ( ) July 1733

MITCHELL, Robert   Book 1, Page 75

    Robert Mitchell of Surry County to James Anderson of
    Surry County ... 800 acres on River ... to a creek and
    to the river.
    Witnesses: /s/ Robert Mitchel
      None recorded
    Dated 4 May 1733   Recorded 6 Sept. 1733

MATTHEWS, James   Book 1, Page 76

    James Matthews and Anne his wife of Brunswick County to
    William Fletcher of same county ... 200 acres ... on
    south side of Roanoke River adjoining William Smith ...
    to line of Robert Mitchell ... granted to James
    Matthews by patent. (See Patent Book 14, Page 34)
    Witnesses:
      William Moore   /s/ James Mathis
      Charles Kimball   /s/ Anne Mathis
    Dated 26 Sept. 1733   Recorded 4 Oct. 1733

HICKS, Robert, Senr.   Book 1, Page 125

    Robert Hicks, Senr. of Brunswick County to Cornelius
    Keith ... 100 acres ... being the lowermost hundred
    acres .. on Col. Munford's line ... running up the
    river ... consideration ... for seating and cultivating
    part of a certain tract of land belonging to me in
    Brunswick County.
    Witnesses:
      W. Battersby   /s/ Robert Hix
      Byrd Thomas Lanier
    Dated 2 May 1734   Recorded 2 May 1734

KING, George   Book 1, Page 139

    George King of Brunswick County to William Stroud, Senr
    of same county ... 100 acres on south side of Roanoke
    River ... adjoining Lewis Parham ... thence up river.
    Witnesses:
      Michael C. Young   /s/ George King
      James Parish
      John Thomason
    Dated 31 July 1734   Recorded 5 Dec. 1734

DAVIS John   Book 1, Page 155

    John Davis of Brunswick County to William Toms ... 554
    acres on north side of Roanoke River ... adjoining line
    of Phillip Morgan.
    Witnesses: None recorded   /s/ John Davis
    Dated 4 Feb. 1735   Recorded 6 Feb. 1735

SUMERFORD, Jeffery   Book 1, Page 164

   Jeffery Sumerford, Planter, of Brunswick County to John
   Davis of same county ... consideration 8 pounds ... 69
   acres ... on south side of Roanoke River ... adjoining
   land that was taken up by John and Richard Brown by
   patent 13 Oct. 1727.
   Witnesses:
      John Hall   /s/ Jeffery Sumerford
      Lewis Delony
   Dated 2 April 1735   Recorded 3 April 1735

HIX, Robert, Senr.   Book 1, Page 165

   Robert Hix, Senr. of St. Andrew's Parish, Brunswick
   County to Samuel Clark, Junr. of Brunswick County ..for
   true love and natural affection ... 580 acres on north
   side of Roanoke River ... on line of Richard Jones ....
   except 100 acres where Cornelius Keith now lives.
   Witnesses:
      Moses Dunkley   /s/ Robert Hix Senr.
      Theophilus Feild
      Josias Randle
   Dated 7 July 1734   Recorded 3 April 1735

TOMS, William   Book 1, Page 178

   William Toms of St Andrew's Parish, Brunswick County to
   John Cleménts of same county ... 277 acres ... on north
   side of Roanoke River ... adjoining Gabriel Harrison
   and Phillip Morgan.
   Witnesses:
      Michael Cadet Young   /s/ William Toms
      Nicholas Edmunds
   Dated 4 June 1735   Recorded 5 June 1735

DICKSON, Henry   Book 1, Page 181

   Henry Dickson of Prince George County to James Jones of
   Surry County ... 262 acres ... on south side of Great
   Creek.
   Witnesses: /s/ Henry Dickson
      None recorded
   Dated 6 May 1735   Recorded 5 June 1735

CARGILL Cornelius   Book 1, Page 196

   Cornelius Cargill of Brunswick County, near Roanoke
   River, to Philip O'Reyly (O'Reily) ... 100 acres ...
   being half of a tract of land on north fork of Roanoke
   River ... on north side .. called Copper Hill ... also
   part of a tract called Cedar Hill ... being part of a
   survey made by Col. Thomas Cock(e) ... the patent

dated 9 June 1735 ... containing 50 acres.
Witnesses:
   Henry Beddingfield   /s/ Cornelius Cargill
   Richard Washington
   Edward Hood
Deed dated 2 July 1735
Acknowledged by Cornelius Cargill and Elizabeth, his wife - 3 July 1735

O'REILY, Phillip   Book 1, Page 200

Phillip O'Reily of Brunswick County to Edward Hood of North Carolina ... 1/10 part of 100 acres ... on north fork of Roanoke River ... known by name of Copper Hill ... part of a patent to Cornelius Cargill.
Witnesses:
   Henry Beddingfield   /s/ Philip O'Reily
   Richard Washington
   Redmond Caden
Dated 3 July 1735   Recorded 3 July 1735

O'REILY, Philip   Book 1, Page 203

Philip O'Reily of Brunswick County, near the Roanoke River, to Redman Caden ... 1/10 part of 100 acres .. on north side of Roanoke River ... part of a survey named Copper Hill ... surveyed for Cornelius Cargill.
Witnesses:
   Edward Hood   /s/ Philip O'Reily
   Henry Beddingfield
Dated 3 July 1735   Recorded 3 July 1735

O'REILY, Philip   Book 1, Page 206

Philip O'Reily of Brunswick County, near Roanoke River, to Richard Washington of North Carolina ... 1/10 part of 100 acres ... on north side of north fork of Roanoke River ... part of a survey named Copper Hill.
Witnesses:
   Edward Hood   /s/ Philip O'Reily
   Henry Beddingfield
Dated 3 July 1735   Recorded 3 July 1735

MITCHELL, Thomas   Book 1, Page 212

Thomas Michel (Mitchell) of Surry County to James Michel (Mitchell) of Brunswick County ... 250 acres on north side of Roanoke River ... lower part of a patent to said Thomas Mitchell 1 May 1728. At the river side marked by Robert Mitchell and James Mitchell for a dividing line between them with the consent of Thomas Mitchell the proprietor.
Witnesses:
   John Duke   /s/ Thomas Michel

Witnesses - Cont'd
   Charles King
   James Matthews
Dated 3 July 1735   Recorded 3 July 1735

MITCHELL, Thomas   Book 1, Page 213

Thomas Mitchell of Surry County to Robert Mitchell of same county ... 362 acres ... on north side of Roanoke River ... part of 612 acres granted to Thomas Mitchell 1 May 1728.
Witnesses:
   John Duke   /s/ Thomas Michel
   Charles King
   James Matthews
Dated 3 July 1735   Recorded 3 July 1735

AVENT, Thomas   Book 1, Page 220

Thomas Avent of Surry County to William Meriott (William Marriott) of Surry County ... 630 acres ... on south side of Meherrin River ...crost Avents Creek ... patented by William Avent of Surry County 30 Oct. 1727.
Witnesses:
   John Harris   /s/ Thomas Avent
   Edward Halin
   Robert Hicks
   George Walton
Dated 3 May 1735   Recorded 7 Aug. 1735

HICKS, Robert, Junr.   Book 1, Page 227

Robert Hicks, Junr. of Brunswick County to John Steed of same county ... 195 acres ... on north side of the Roanoke River ...on Poplar Creek .. adjoining line of George Hicks.
Witnesses:
   Clem Read   /s/ Robert Hicks
   W. Battersby
Dated 26 Aug. 1735   Recorded 4 Sept. 1735

BROWN, John   Book 1, Page 236

John Brown and Jane his wife, Richard Brown, son of the said John Brown, and Frances his wife, sell to John Davis ... all of Brunswick County ... 230 acres on side of the Roanoke River.
Witnesses: John Duke   /s/ John Brown
        Baxter Davis   Richard Brown
        John Scogin   Jane Brown
                                 Frans. Brown
Dated 4 Nov. 1735   Recorded 6 Nov. 1735

MORGAN, Phillip   Book 1, Page 241

    Phillip Morgan of Brunswick County to Patrick Dorum of
    same county ... 1000 acres at mouth of Island Creek ..
    beginning at Robert Munford's line on Roanoke River.
    Witnesses:
        James Mize   /s/ Philip Morgan
        Thomas Jarrod
        James Parran (Parham ?)
    Dated 3 April 1735   Recorded 6 Nov. 1735

EVANS, John   Book 1, Page 259

    John Evans of Brusswick County to William Browne, Junr
    of Surry County ... 376 acres on north side of Great
    Creek ... part of a patent to John Evans 20 June 1733.
    Witnesses:
        W. Poole,
        Hosea Tapley   /s/ John Evans
        Edward Clanton
    John Evans and Elizabeth his wife acknowledged deed.
    Dated 2 March 1736   Recorded 4 March 1736

TOMS, William   Book 1, Page 269

    William Toms and Margaret his wife, of St. Andrew's
    Parish, Brunswick County, sell to Thomas Robertson of
    same county ... 150 acres ... on south side of Roanoke
    River .... adjoining line of John Clements ... part of
    a tract granted to John Davis and sold by said Davis
    to William Toms.
    Witnesses:
        Cornelius Keith   /s/William (X) Toms
        Samuel Buckstone
        William Jinkines (Jenkins)
    Dated 4 Feb. 1735/36   Recorded 3 June 1736

CARGILL, Cornelius   Book 1, Page 283

    Cornelius Cargill of Brunswick County to Robert
    Munford of Prince George County ... 450 acres on north
    side of Roanoke River ... adjoining James Munford.
    Witnesses:
        None recorded   /s/ Cornelius Cargill
    Dated 6 April 1737   Recorded 7 April 1737

FLETCHER, William   Book 1, Page 291

    William Fletcher and Elizabeth his wife, of Brunswick
    County to John Smith of same county ... 100 acres on
    south side of Roanoke River ... adjoining line of
    Robert Mitchell.

Witnesses:
  None recorded   /s/ William (W) Fletcher
Dated - - 1735   Recorded 7 Oct. 1736

KIMBALL, Charles   Book 1, Page 296

Charles Kimball of St. Andrew's Parish, Brunswick County to Richard Fox of same parish and county ...550 acres ... on south side of Roanoke River.
Witnesses:
  Wm. Maclin
  William Wynne   /s/ Charles Kimball
  Richard Burch
Dated 1 Sept. 1736   Recorded 4 Nov. 1736

TOMS, William   Book 1, Page 306

William Toms of Brunswick County to Michael Cadet Young of the same county ... 125 acres ... on north side of Roanoke River ... adjoining Thomas Robertson and Philip Morgan ... part of a patent for 554 acres granted to John Davis.
Witnesses:
  John Parker
  Henry (X) Crackendale   /s/ William (X) Toms
  James (J) Riggby
Dated 3 March 1736   Recorded 3 March 1736

PARHAM, Ephraim   Book 1, Page 339

Ephraim Parham of Surry County to William Abbett (Abbott) of Brunswick County ... 130 acres on south side of Roanoke River ... granted to Ephraim Parham 27 Jan. 1734 by patent.
Witnesses:
  None recorded   /s/ Ephraim Parham
Dated 5 Aug. 1736   Recorded 2 June 1737

CARGILL, Cornelius   Book 1, Page 371

Cornelius Cargill and Elizabeth his wife, late Elizabeth Daniel, of Brunswick County to John Johnson (Johnston) of Goochland County ... 466 acres ... on south side of Jeneto Creek ... granted to Elizabeth Daniel while she was sole by patent 25 Aug. 1736.
Witnesses:
  Clem Read   /s/ Cornelius Cargill
  Drury Stith   /s/ Elizabeth (E) Cargill
  Moses Dunkley
Dated 2 March 1737   Recorded 2 March 1737

HALL, Edmund   Book 1, Page 396

Edmund Hall of Brunswick County to Drury Malone of
Surry County ... 200 acres ... on both sides of Jeneto
Creek.
Witnesses:
    Humphrey (X) Evans   /s/ Edmund (X) Hall
    Thomas Malone
Dated 1 March 1737   Recorded 2 March 1737

PARRISH, James   Book 1, Page 412

James Parrish of Brunswick County to John Parrish,
Senr, of Charles City County ... 150 acres on north
side of Great Creek ... part of 550 acres granted to
James Parrish 28 Aug. 1731.
Witnesses:
    None recorded   /s/ James Parrish
Dated 1 Nov. 1738   Recorded 1 Feb. 1738/39

WATSON, John   Book 1, Page 430

John Watson of Brunswick County to William Poole,
joyner, of the same county ... 100 acres ... at the
mouth of a branch (of Flatt Creek) (See patents).
Witnesses:
    Lewis Parham   /s/ John Watson
    Michael Wall
    John Ballard
Dated 2 March 1737   Recorded 2 June 1738

JOHNSTON, John   Book 1, Page 494

John Johnston, late of Brunswick County, pedlar, to
John Coles of Hanover County, merchant ... 466 acres
... on south side of Jenet's Creek (Jeneto), granted
to Elizabeth Daniel 25 Aug 1731, and conveyed to said
Johnston by Elizabeth and her husband Cornelius
Cargill.
Witnesses: /s/ J. Scott
    W. Battersby
    Joseph Scott
    Richard Booker
Dated 20 May 1740   Recorded 5 June 1740

Note: Land conveyed by John Scott under Power of Atty
      dated 16 May 1740 and recorded at page 494.

MORGAN, Philip   Book 1, Page 499

Philip Morgan of St. Andrew's Parish, Brunswick County
to John Wilkins of St. Martin's Parish, Hanover County
... 1000 acres ... on north side of Roanoke River, on
lower line of Robert Munford ... at mouth of Island

Creek. (Note: Appears to be same land conveyed to
    Patrick Dorum)
Witnesses:
    John Harris, Junr.   /s/ Philip Morgan
    Hugh Oneall (O'Neal ?)
Dated 2 Aug. 1739   Recorded 3 Jan. 1739/40

RUSSELL, John   Deed Book 2, Page 41

John Russell of Brunswick County to Andrew Moreman of
of Goochland County ... cons. 80 pounds ... 137 acres
on Staunton River.
Witnesses:
    John Twitty   /s/ John Russell
    Cornelius Cargill
    George King
Dated 6 Nov. 1740   Recorded 6 Nov. 1740

BUTCHER, John   Deed Book 2, Page 48

John Butcher of Brunswick County, Planter, to William
Baker of Hanover County, Planter ... 332 acres ... on
north side of Roanoke River ... cons. 45 pounds ...
part of 632 acres granted to John Butcher by patent. .
on upper, or south side, of Butchers Creek adjoining
Gabriel Harrison.
Witnesses:
    Samuel Baker
    William McDavid   /s/ John Butcher
    Richard Blalock
Dated 4 Feb. 1740   Recorded 5 March 1740

DUKE, John   Deed Book 2, Page 56

John Duke and Rejoyce, his wife, to Abraham Burton ...
cons. 25 pounds ... 200 acres .
Witnesses:
    Thomas Sisson   /s/ John Duke
    William Sisson   /s/ Rejoyce Duke
    Jehu Peebles
Dated 11 Feb. 1740   Recorded 2 April 1740

SMITH, William   Deed Book 2, Page 57

William Smith, Planter, St. Andrews Parish, Brunswick
County, to David Walker, Gent., Bristol Parish, Prince
George County ... cons. 20 pounds ... 500 acres ... on
south side of Roanoke River ... adjoining Charles Kimbell and John Davis ... part of 790 acres granted by
patent.
    No witnesses   /s/ William Smith
Dated 2 April 1741   Recorded 2 April 1741

SMITH, William   Deed Book 2, Page 59

    William Smith, Planter, St. Andrews Parish, to John
Davis, St. Andrews Parish ... cons. 40 pounds ... 300
acres ... part of patent.
Witnesses: /s/ William Smith
    None recorded
Dated 2 April 1741   Recorded 2 April 1741

CLARK, Joshua   Deed Book 2, Page 70

    Joshua Clarke of Brunswick County to Hewit Drew of Isle
of Wight County ... cons. 13 pounds ... 125 acres .. on
south side of Meherrin River ... surveyed for John
Mason.
Witnesses:
    Burrell Brown   /s/ Joshua Clark
    Nathaniel Hicks
    Mary Brown
Dated 7 May 1741   Recorded 7 May 1741

MATHIS, James   Deed Book 2, Page 73

    James Mathis of Colony of Virginia to Charles Kimball
of Province of North Carolina ... cons. 10 pounds ....
450 acres ... on south side of Roanoke River ... part
of patent for 850 acres to James Mathis dated 9-28-
1728.
Witnesses: /s/ James Mathis
    None recorded
Dated 4 June 1741   Recorded 4 June 1741

    Anne, wife of James Mathis, released dower right.

HARRISON, Gabriel   Deed Book 2, Page 94

    Gabriel Harrison of Prince George County to Abraham
Cook of Hanover County ... cons. 25 pounds ... 300
acres ... on north side of Roanoke River and on south
side of Butchers Creek.
Witnesses:
    John Dodd   /s/ Gabriel Harrison
    William Baker
Dated 6 Aug. 1741   Recorded 6 Aug. 1741

YOUNG, Michael Cadet   Deed Book 2, Page 100

    Michael Cadet Young of St. Andrews Parish, Brunswick
County, to Richard Blalock of St. Martin's Parish,
Hanover County ... cons. 25 pounds ... 125 acres on
north side of Roanoke River, part of a larger tract of

land granted to John Davis by patent.
Witnesses:
   John Ward
   Millington Blalock   /s/ Michael Cadet Young
   John Dodd
Dated 1 Sept. 1741   Recorded 3 Sept. 1741

CARGILL, Cornelius   Deed Book 2, Page 102

Cornelius (formerly) of Bristol Parish to William Pennington of Brunswick County ... 20 pounds ... 365 acres ... adjoining Munford and John Nipper.
Witnesses:
   None recorded   /s/ Cornelius Cargill
Dated 1 Aug. 1741   Recorded 1 Oct. 1741

KING, George   Deed Book 2, Page 106

George King to Andrew Hampton ... cons. 35 pounds .... 150 acres ... on south side of Roanoke River on line of Ephraim Parham.
Witnesses: /s/ George King
   None recorded
Dated 29 Sept. 1741   Recorded 1 Oct. 1741

Susanna, wife of George King, released dower right.

WATSON, John   Deed Book 2, Page 113

John Watson of Brunswick County to James Vaughan of the same county ... cons. 22 pounds ... 200 acres on south side of Meherrin River ... on upper side of Mountain Creek ... granted by patent to John Watson 12-1-1740.
Witnesses:
   None recorded   /s/ John Watson
Dated 29 Sept. 1741   Recorded 1 Oct. 1741

Rebecca, wife of John Watson, released dower right.

ROBERTS, Philip   Deed Book 2, Page 131

Philip Roberts of St. Andrew's Parish, Brunswick County to Samuel Hudson of same Parish and County ... cons. 14 pounds ... 150 acres on south side of Roanoke River at mouth of Grassy Creek ... Granted by patent to Philip Roberts.
Witnesses:
   William Poole   /s/ Philip Roberts
   John Ballard
Dated 6 Oct. 1740   Recorded 4 Feb. 1741

MITCHELL, John   Deed Book 2, Page 229

John Mitchell of Brunswick County to Thomas Eastland of same county ... cons. 70 pounds ... 400 acres ... on north side of Roanoke River ... granted to John Mitchell by patent 15 Aug. 1737.
Witnesses: /s/ John Mitchell
   None recorded
Dated 3 March 1742   Recorded 3 March 1742

Judith, wife of John Mitchell, released dower right.

KEITH, Cornelius   Deed Book 2, Page 236

Cornelius Keith to Thomas Twitty ... cons. 25 pounds .. 100 acres ... land conveyed to Cornelius Keith by deed of gift from Robert Hix, Senr. dated 2 May 1734 .... part of a patent to Robert Hix.
Witnesses:
   Clement Read   /s/ Cornelius Keith
   Michael C. Young
   Thomas Lanier
Dated 28 Feb. 1742   Recorded 3 March 1742

Elizabeth, wife of Cornelius Keith, released dower.

MITCHELL, James   Deed Book 2, Page 251

James Mitchell to John Taylor Duke ... cons. 30 pounds .. 450 acres on Flatt Creek.
Witnesses:
   Walter Campbell   /s/ James Mitchell
   Ralph Dunkley
   Adam Tapley
Dated 7 April 1743   Recorded 7 April 1743

Amy, wife of James Mitchell, released dower right.

HARWELL, Samuel   Deed Book 2, Page 276

Samuel Harwell of Prince George County to Mark Harwell of Brunswick County ... cons. 5 pounds ... 195 acres .. granted by patent to Samuel Harwell 23 March 1733.
Witnesses:
   Thomas Lanier
   Daniel Carrell   /s/ Samuel Harwell
   James Coleman
Dated 3 May 1743   Recorded 5 May 1743

DUKE, John Taylor   Deed Book 2, Page 277

John Taylor Duke of Brunswick County to John Duke, Gent of same county ... cons. 40 pounds ... 504 acres ... adjoining Taylor, Poole and Smith.

Witnesses:
  Nicholas Edmunds   /s/ John Taylor Duke
  Francis Bressie
  Thomas Twitty
Dated 5 May 1743   Recorded 5 May 1743

Jane, wife of John Taylor Duke, released dower.

WILLIAMS, Benjamin   Deed Book 2, Page 342

Benjamin Williams and Susanna, his wife, to William
Davidson ... cons. 12 pounds, 10 shillings ... 130
acres ... on both sides of Avents Creek.
Witnesses:
  James Parrish   /s/ Benjamin Williams
  Thomas Person   /s/ Susanna Williams
  Josias Randle
Dated 4 Aug. 1743   Recorded 4 Aug. 1743

HAYWARD, William   Deed Book 2, Page 360

William Hayward to Francis Hayward ... cons. 58 pounds
... 445 acres ... being one-fourth of land William
Hayward lately purchased of Col. John Allen.
Witnesses:
  William Poole   /s/ William Hayward
  George King
  Adam Tapley
Dated 6 Oct. 1743   Recorded 6 Oct. 1743

COLEMAN, James   Deed Book 2, Page 437

James Coleman to Andrew Moreman ... cons. 70 pounds ...
300 acres on Roanoke River.
Witnesses:
  G. Marr   /s/ James Coleman
  John Speed
  Edward Hulen
Dated 3 May 1744   Recorded 3 May 1744

Clary, wife of James Coleman, released dower right.

CLARK, Samuel   Deed Book 2, Page 449

Samuel Clark to Joshua Clark ... cons. 40 pounds ...
190 acres on south side of Meherrin River ... adjoining
Robert and Joshua Clark.
Witnesses:
  John Peebles   /s/ Samuel Clark
  Jeremiah Brown   /s/ Sarah (SC) Clark
  Robert Clark
Dated 5 June 1744   Recorded 7 June 1744

Sarah, wife of Samuel Clark, released her dower.

CLARK, Samuel   Deed Book 2, Page 451

    Samuel Clark of Brunswick County to John Peebles of
    Surry County ... cons. 50 pounds ... 200 acres.
    Witnesses:
      Jeremiah Brown
      Robert Clark   /s/ Samuel Clark
      Joshua Clark
    Dated 5 June 1744   Recorded 7 June 1744

    Sarah, wife of Samuel Clark, released her dower.

MUNFORD, James, Gent.   Deed Book 2, Page 454

    James Munford, Gent. of Prince George County, William
    Stark, and Theoderick Bland, Gent., "impowered by the
    court" as commissioners to dispose of and sell the
    estate of James Munford sell to William Byrd of Charles
    City County ... cons. 50 pounds ... 808 acres of land
    on north side of Roanoke River near the fork.
    Witnesses:
      John Wall   Walter Campbell   /s/ James Munford
      Samuel Gordon   Thomas Jones   /s/ Wm. Stark
      Robert Jones, Jr. John Scott   /s/ Theo'd Bland
      Theophilus Feild John Jones
    Dated 13 March 1743   Recorded 7 June 1744

ANDREWS, John   Deed Book 2, Page 478

    John Andrews of Surry County to Benjamin Harrison of
    Brunswick County ... 274 acres on the south side of the
    Great Creek.
    Witnesses: /s/ John Andrews
      None recorded
    Dated 2 Aug. 1744   Recorded 2 Aug. 1744

KILLCREASE, Robert   Deed Book 2, Page 482

    Robert Killcrease of Edgecomb County, N. C. to Patrick
    Boyd ... cons. 20 shillings ... 150 acres on south side
    of Dan River.
    Witnesses:
      Moses Dunkley   /s/ Robert Killcrease
      Byrd Thomas Lanier
      Thomas Durham
    Dated 2 Aug. 1744   Recorded 2 Aug. 1744

HUDSON, Samuel   Deed Book 2, Page 494

    Samuel Hudson, late of Virginia but now of Craven
    County, South Carolina to George Bearfoot ... cons. 100
    pounds ... 150 acres on south side of Roanoke River at
    mouth of Grassy Creek.

    Witnesses:
      Thomas Loyd
      Richard Hide (Hyde)   /s/ Samuel Hudson
      John Spencer
    Dated 22 June 1744   Recorded 6 Sept. 1744

TAYLOR, Ethread   Deed Book 2, Page 500

    Ethread Taylor of Isle of Wight County to Henry Taylor of Charles City County ... cons. 40 pounds ... 315 acres on south side of Meherrin River.
    Witnesses:
      J. Scett
      Lewis Parham   /s/ Ethread Taylor
      Robert Jones, Junr.
    Dated 3 Jan. 1744   Recorded 3 Jan. 1744

    Patience, wife of Ethread Taylor, released her dower.

DOUGLAS, William   Deed Book 2, Page 510

    William Douglas to Burrell Brown ... cons. 25 pounds .. 150 acres on south side of Meherrin River.
    Witnesses:
      Nathaniel Perry
      Thomas Rives   /s/ William Douglas
      James Turner
    Dated 30 Oct. 1744   Recorded 1 Nov. 1744

TILMAN, George   Deed Book 2, Page 517

    George Tilman to John Avery ... cons. 45 pounds 19 shillings ... 300 acres ... part of a larger tract of 504 acres.
    Witnesses:
      William Brewer   /s/ George Tilman
      William Tilman
      John King
    Dated 3 Jan. 1744   Recorded 30 Oct. 1744

WRAY, John   Page Book 2, Page 515

    John Wray to William Randle ... cons. 23 pounds 10 shillings ...250 acres on south side of Meherrin River, adjoining Francis Wray's line.
    Witnesses:
      John Randle   /s/ John Wray
      John Yarbrough
    Dated 3 Jan. 1744   Recorded 3 Jan. 1744

SMITH, Cuthbert   Deed Book 3, Page 48

    Cuthbert Smith to John Langley ... cons. 20 pounds ...

180 acres on north side of Roanoke River ... adjoining John Mitchell.
Witnesses:
   John Burch   /s/ Cuthbert Smith
   Charles King
Dated 1 Aug. 1745   Recorded 1 Aug. 1745

Elizabeth, wife of C. Smith, released her dower.

LETT, Francis   Deed Book 3, Page 51

Francis Lett to John Daniel ... cons. 20 shillings ... 180 acres on a branch.
Witnesses:
   Charles King   /s/ Francis Lett
   Wm. McKnight
Dated 6 Feb. 1744   Recorded 1 Aug. 1745

Amy, wife of Francis Lett, released her dower.

ALLING, Runall   Deed Book 3, Page 56

Runall Alling of Brunswick County to Andrew Presley of Amelia County ... cons. 25 pounds ... 100 acres on north side of Roanoke River ... adjoining Drury Stith and Philip Morgan.
Witnesses:
   George Curry   /s/ Runall Alling
   John Taylor   /s/ Mary (X) Alling
   Thomas (X) Duggins
Dated 1 Aug. 1745   Recorded 1 Aug. 1745

Mary, wife of Runall Alling, released her dower.

COOK, Abraham   Deed Book 3, Page 76

Abraham Cook and Sarah, his wife, to James Hester .... cons. 20 pounds ... 289 acres ... part of two tracts adjoining Davis.
Witnesses:
   Christopher Hudson   /s/ Abraham Cook
   Joseph Perrin
   Robert Hester
Dated 3 Oct. 1745   Recorded 3 Oct. 1745

WILKINS, John   Deed Book 3, Page 82

John Wilkins to William Tabor ... cons. 30 pounds ... 200 acres on Roanoke River ... adjoining Robert Munford.
Witnesses: /s/ John Wilkins
   Abraham Cook

Robert Hester
Christopher Hudson
Dated 1 Oct. 1745   Recorded 3 Oct. 1745

Mary, wife of John Wilkins, released her dower right.

ROBERTSON, Thomas   Deed Book 3, Page 84

Thomas Robertson and Mary, his wife, of Edgecomb County
N. C. to Christopher Hudson ... cons. 45 pounds ...
150 acres on north side of Roanoke River, adjoining
line of John Clements, deceased. Part of a tract John
Davis sold to William Toms, who sold to Robertson.
Witnesses:
   John Wilkins   /s/ Thomas Robertson
   Mary (X) Wilkins   /s/ Mary Robertson
   William Tabor
Dated 13 June 1745   Recorded 3 Oct. 1745

DAVIDSON, William   Deed Book 3, Page 98

William Davidson to William McKnight ... cons. 15
pounds ... 130 acres on both sides of Avents Creek.
Witnesses:
   None recorded   /s/ William Davidson
Dated 7 Nov. 1745   Recorded 7 Nov. 1745

IRVINE, Christopher   Deed Book 3, Page 104

Christopher Irvine to Rice Price ... cons. 16 pounds...
223 acres on both sides of Flatt Creek.
Witnesses:
   John Price   /s/ Christopher Irvine
   John Phelps   /s/ Mary Irvine
   Mark Hayes
   Joseph Miller
Dated 6 May 1745   Recorded 5 Dec. 1745

CARROLL, Benjamin   Deed Book 3, Page 139

Benjamin Carroll to Millington Blalock ... cons. 20
pounds ... 163 acres ... plantation where Benjamin
Carroll now lives.
Witnesses:
   George Sims   /s/ Benj. Carroll
   Charles Sims
   John Carroll
Dated 6 Feb. 1745   Recorded 21 Nov. 1745

YORK, Richard   Deed Book 3, Page 153

Richard York and Mary, his wife to Francis Bressie of Prince George County ... cons. 35 pounds ... 204 acres on both sides of Butchers Creek with grist mill.

Witnesses:
    Thomas Stevens   /s/ Richard York
Dated 4 March 1745   Recorded 4 March 1745

Mary, wife of Richard York, released her dower right.

MITCHELL, James   Deed Book 3, Page 156

James Mitchell to Jacob Mitchell ... cons. 20 pounds .. 130 acres on north side of Roanoke River ... part of a larger tract.

Witnesses: /s/ James Mitchell
    None recorded
Dated 6 March 1745   Recorded 6 March 1745

MITCHELL, James   Deed Book 3, Page 157

James Mitchell to Isaac Mitchell ... cons. 20 pounds .. 120 acres on north side of Roanoke River ... part of a larger tract.

Witnesses: /s/ James Mitchell
    None recorded
Dated 6 March 1745   Recorded 6 March 1745

KIMBALL, Charles   Deed Book 3, Page 159

Charles Kimball of Edgecomb County, N. C. to Walter Campbell ... cons. 5 pounds ... 450 acres on south side of Roanoke River ... part of a tract of 850 acres.

Witnesses:
James Mitchell   /s/ Charles Kimball
John Gilliam
Josiah Mitchell
Dated 6 March 1745   Recorded 19 Aug. 1745

LOYD, Thomas   Deed Book 3, Page 166

Thomas Loyd, the younger, to Drury Stith, Gent. .... cons. 20 pounds ... 424 acres on both sides of Butchers Creek. Granted to Thomas Loyd, Junr. by patent.

Witnesses:
    None recorded   /s/ Thomas Loyd, Jr.
Dated 3 April 1746   Recorded 3 April 1746

TUCKER, William   Deed Book 3, Page 168

William Tucker of Bath Parish, Prince George County to George Booth, Junr. of same parish and county ... cons. 55 pounds ... 211 acres on north side of Roanoke River and on Cox Creek.

Witnesses:
  Henry Jones   /s/ William Tucker
  Robert Tucker
  William McKinney
Dated 1 March 1746   Recorded 3 April 1746

CANNON, William   Deed Book 3, Page 172

William Cannon, Carpenter, of Goochland County to
Richard Ward of Goochland County .. cons. 55 pounds ...
492 acres. Land patented by John Martin.
Witnesses:
  John Cox
  Frederick Cox   /s/ William Cannon
  John Jones
Dated 29 March 1746   Recorded 3 April 1746

LUCAS, David   Deed Book 3, Page 179

David Lucas to Dennis Lark ... cons. 10 pounds ... 200
acres.
Witnesses:
  William Poole
  John Ezell   /s/ David Lucas
  David Dodd
Dated 29 April 1746   Recorded 1 May 1746

TITHE LIST - 1748

A list of the tithables taken in 1748 by Lewis Delony and names from the lists of Cornelius Cargill and Matthew Talbot who resided in that part of Lunenburg County which became Mecklenburg County in 1765.

Name	Count	Name	Count
ABBOTT, Samuel	1	CHAMLY, Nathaniel	1
" William	1	CHANDLER, Joseph	
ALLEN, Charles	1	William Chandler	2
" David	1	CLANCH, Jeremiah	1
" Robert	1	CLARKE, Edward	1
ANDREWS, Ephraim	1	" John	1
" Richard	1	COCKE, Richard	
" William	1	Wingfield Cobbs	2
ARNOLD, James	2	COLE, John	1
		COLEMAN, James	
BAIRD, Benjamin (List)	4	Timothy Carter	4
BALLARD, John	2	COLSON, Daniel	1
BATES, Henry	1	COOK, Benj. (Widow of)	3
" John	1	" Nathaniel	1
BERRINGER, Michael	1	COOPER, John McDonald	1
BIASSEE, John	1	COX, John	1
BILBO, John Peter		CULBREATH, John	1
James Bilbo	2	" Peter	1
BLACKWELDER, Caleb	1	" William	1
" John	1		
BLANKS, Thomas	1	DAVIS, Baxter	
" William	1	John King	3
BOLTON, Matthew	1	DAVIS, Edward	1
BOWEN, Robert	1	DAVIS, John	
BOWEN, William		William Halpin	10
David Bowen	2	DAVIS, William	1
BOWEN, William, Jr.	1	DECKER, Henry	1
BOWERS, Francis	1	DELONY, Henry	
BRACEY, Francis	4	John Challis	
BROADNAX, Mrs. Edward	4	James Vincent	3
BROOKS, William	1	DELONY, Lewis	
BROWN, Israel	1	John Freeman	8
BURNETT, Thomas	1	DELONY, Lewis, Jr.	
BURWELL, Armistead	7	Dennis Larke	6
BURWELL, Lewis		DISHMAN, William	1
Julius Nichols	9	DORTCH, David	2
BUTLER, William	1	DOUGLAS, William	1
BYRD, Col. William	10	DUKE, John	3
		" John Taylor	2
CALLIHAM, Nicholas			
David Calliham		EARLE, John	
John Calliham	3	John Carroll	2
CARGILL, Cornelius	4	EASTLAND, Thomas	
CELY, William	1	Joseph Eastland	2

EDLOE, John	8
ELLIDGE, Francis	3
ELLIS, Jeremiah	1
EVANS, Charles	1
EVANS, Thomas	
Solomon Harris	2
EZELL, George	
Michael Ezell	2
FINNEY, Thomas	1
FIRTH, Daniel	1
FLETCHER, John	1
FLOYD, Richard	1
FORREST, John	1
FOX, Richard	
George Floyd	2
FRANKLIN, Thomas	1
GARRETT, Humphry	1
GILL, William	1
GILLIAM, John	
Barnaby Bird	3
GLADDIN, Richard	
William Gladdin	2
GOING, John (Gowen)	2
GORDON, Gilbert	1
" John	1
GREEN, Henry	1
" John	1
" Lewis	1
GRIFFIN, Francis	1
" John	1
" Richard, Sr.	1
" William	1
GRISSELL, John	1
HAGOOD, Benjamin	1
HAGOOD, William	
William Hagood, Jr.	2
HARGROVE, Howell	1
HARRIS, Samuel	1
HARRIS, William	
Leonard Ashworth	2
HARRISON, Benjamin	2
HATCHELL, William	
Henry Hatchell	2
HATCHELL, William, Jr.	1
HAWKINS, Thomas	
William Lawrence	6
HEARN, John	1
HENRY, Edward	1

HEWEY, Humphry	1
HILL, William	1
HILTON, Thomas	1
HIX, James	1
" Joseph	1
HOGAN, William	1
HOLLOWAY, George	3
HOLMES, Samuel	
Isaac Holmes	
Samuel Holmes, Jr.	3
HOWARD, Francis	5
HOWARD, William	
Henry Howard	
Pinkethman Hawkins	
Andrew Pyle	
John Robinson	5
HUDSON, Christopher	1
HUMPHRYS, Charles	1
" John	1
" Thomas	1
" William	1
HYDE, John	2
JARRETT, Thomas	1
JEFFERSON, Feild	
THOMAS JEFFERSON	
Joseph Akin	
David Dodd	
William Edwards	
George Farrar	16
JONES, Robert, Jr.	1
" Thomas	1
" William	1
JONES, Capt. William	
John Gileness	2
KING, William	1
LANGFORD, John	1
LANGLEY, John	1
LANIER, Bird Thomas	
Zachariah Baker	3
LANIER, Thomas	1
LARK, Joseph	1
" Robert	1
LIDDERDAL, William	1
LUCAS, John	
John Thompson	2
LUNDY, Richard	1
McDANIEL, Michael	1

McDONALD, John	1	PARKER, William	1
McNEIL, Daniel	1	PARNELL, John	
" Malcolm	1	(Overseer for Thomas	
" Michael	1	Clarke of Isle of	
		Wight County)	3
MAJOR, Nicholas	1	PENNINGTON, John George	1
MALONE, Drury	3	PETTYPOOL, John	
" Thomas	2	John Sandford	2
MANNING, Henry	1	PETTYPOOL, Seth	
Samuel	1	Peter Pettypool	
MARABLE, William		Seth Pettypool, Jr.	4
Matthew Marable		PHIFER, Martin	1
Samuel Taylor	3	PINSON, Aaron	
MITCHELL, Daniel	1	Aaron Pinson, Jr.	2
" Henry	2	PODLE, William	
" Isaac	1	Robert Poole	2
" Jacob	1	POTTER, Daniel	
MITCHELL, James		Thomas Wells	2
James Mitchell, Jr.			
John Hannah	7	RAY, Francis (Wray)	
MITCHELL, Joab	1	Ralph Griffin	2
" John	1	REYNOLDS, Sherwood	1
MIZE, James	1	RIVERS, William	1
" James, Jr.	1	ROBERTS, James	1
MIZE, Jeremiah		" Thomas	1
John Mize	2	ROBINSON, Abraham	1
MIZE, Stephen	1	ROBINSON, John	
" William	1	Edward Robinson	
MOORE, Hugh	1	Mark Robinson	4
MOREMAN, Andrew		ROBINSON, John, Jr.	1
Andrew Moreman, Jr.		ROBINSON, Matthew	
Benjamin Moreman		William Hamblin	2
Charles Moreman	4	ROBINSON, Nathaniel	1
MORGAN, Philip	1	ROSE, Thomas	
" Reuben	1	William Rose	2
MULLEN, Valentine	1	ROTTENBURY, Henry	1
MURPHY, William	1	" John	1
MYRECK, Owen		ROYAL, Joseph	1
John Patrick	2	RUSSELL, Jeffrey	1
NIPPER, Alexander	1	SAGE, Henry	1
" James	1	SANDIFER, William	
NOTT, James (Knott)	1	John Young	2
		SATTERWHITE, Thomas	1
OSBORNE, Reps	1	SIZEMORE, Edward	1
OVERBY, Nicholas	1	" Ephraim	1
OVERBY, Peter, Sr.		" Henry	1
Peter Overby, Jr.	2	" James	1
OWEN, Edward	1	" William	1
" Joseph	1	SMITH, Charles	1
		" Luke, Jr.	1
PALMER, Richard	1	SPARROW, John	1

SPEED, John (Constable)	1
STEPHENS, Charles	1
" James	1
STEPHENS, Thomas	
Thomas Addiman	2
STEWART, James	1
SULLIVANT, John	1
" Owen	1
TABOR, William	1
TALLEY, Henry	
William Traylor	4
TANNER, Lewis	
Lucias Tanner	
Thomas Tanner	3
TATE, William (Constable)	
Nathaniel Tate	1
THOMASON, James	1
TIMMS, Amos, Sr.	
Amos Timms, Jr.	2
TUCKER, William	1
UPTON, Henry	1
VAUGHAN, George	1
VAUGHAN, James	
John Thompson	3
WADE, John	1
WALLER, John	1
WATSON, John	1
WATTS, Thomas	1
WEATHERFORD, Charles	1
WEATHERFORD, William	
Francis Tucker	2
WEEKES, Michael	1
" Thomas	1
WELLS, John	
John Wells, Jr.	2
WHITT, Edward	1
WILBORN, John	1
WILES, Luke	
Robert Wiles	
Thomas Wiles	3
WILKINS, Thomas	1
" William	1
WILLIAMS, James	1
" John	1
" William	1
WILSON, William	2
WOOD, William	1
WRIGHT, John	4
" Solomon	1
YORK, William	1
YOUNG, Lemuel	1

TITHE LIST - 1752

A list of the tithables taken in 1752 by Feild Jefferson and names from the lists of Richard Witton and Cornelius Cargill who resided in that part of Lunenburg County which became Mecklenburg County in 1765.

ABBOTT, Watt
   George Abbott
   William Abbott
ADAMS, Thomas
AKIN, John
   Daniel Akin
AKIN, Joseph
ALLEN, Charles
ANDREWS, Ephraim
  " , John
  " , Richard
  " , William
ARNOLD, James
AVERY, John
AVERY, Thomas
   Thomas Avery, Jr.

BAILEY, Henry
   William Bailey
BAKER, Zachariah
   James Avery
BALLARD, John
   William Ballard
BATES, Henry
BAZWELL, Samuel (Bizwell)
   Barzilia Bazwell
   Robert Bazwell
BEALE, William
BELL, William
BEVILL, William
BILBO, James
   John Bilbo
BLACK, John
BLACKWELL, John
BLANKS, Amy
   Isaac Blanks
   Harry Blanks
BLANKS, Hannah
   William Blanks
   Richard Blanks
   David Craddock
BOWEN, Robert
    , William
BRACEY, Thomas
BRESSIE, Francis

BROOKS, Robert, Jr.
BROOKS, Richard
BROWN, Valentine
  " , John, Jr.
BRYANT, David
BUGG, Edmond
BUGG, Sherwood
   John Bugg
BURGEMY, William
BURKE, Charles
   James Burns
BURNETT, Richard
   (Taxed to Edward
   Davis of
   Dinwiddie Co.)
BURNETT, Thomas
BURTCHETT, Joseph
BURTON, Hutchins
   Bartholomew Stovall
   Charles Smith
BURTON, James
BURWELL, Armistead
BUSBY, John
BUTLER, George
BYRD, William
   Thomas Pool
   Jacob Royster
   William Royster
   Thomas Anderson
   (Overseers)

CALLIHAM, David
   John Thomas
CARGILL, Cornelius, Sr.
   John Cargill
   Cornelius Cargill, Jr,
CARLETON, Thomas
CARTER, Timothy
   Matthew Orchard
CHAMBLISS, Nathaniel
CHANDLER, Joel
  " , Joel, Jr.
  " , John
CHANDLER, Joseph
   James Chandler

CHANDLER, William, Sr. *
    William Chandler, Jr.
    * (Carpenter)
CHAVIS, George
    Robert Hudson
    Robert Hudson, Jr.
CHISWELL, James
CLAUNCH, Jeremiah
    George Mack
CLAUNCH, John
COATES, Henry
COCKERHAM, Philip
    ", Henry
COLEMAN, James
CONNELL, Robert
COOK, Benjamin
    ", James
COOK, Nathaniel
    John Lett
COOK, Reuben
COX, John
CRENSHAW, Joseph
    Joseph Crenshaw, Jr.
    James Downing
CRENSHAW, Gideon
CRUMP, Stephen
    William Brooks
CULBREATH, John
CUNNINGHAM, James

DAVIES, Joseph
DAVIS, Baxter
DAVIS, Baxter
    John King
DAVIS, John
    William Davis
    Stephen Houseman
DAVIS, William
DECKER, Henry
DELONY, Henry
DORTCH, David
    Elisha McCoy
DUKE, John Taylor
DUNCAN, John
DUNMAN, William
    ", James
    ", Joseph

EARL, John
EAST, Isham
    Joseph East
EASTLAND, Joseph
    ", Thomas

EDLOE, William
    Philemon Russell
ELLIDGE, Francis
    (Estate)
ELLIS, Abraham
    ", Jeremiah
EPPS, Edward
    Peter Epps
    Isaac Epps
EVANS, Charles
    Thomas Evans
    Major Evans
EVANS, Gilbert
    ", Stephen
EVANS, Thomas
    John Evans

FARRAR, George
    Feild Farrar
FARRAR, Thomas
    Thomas Akin
FLINN, James
    George Flinn
FLOYD, Richard
FLOWERS, Samuel
FOWLER, John
FOX, Richard
    John Spradley

GAFFORD, Thomas
GARRETT, Thomas
GEE, James
    William Gee
    Nevil Gee
GENTRY, David
GILL, Henry
    ", Joseph
    ", William
GILLIAM, John
    Robert Gilliam
GISH, Benjamin
GLASS, John
GOIN, Joseph (Gowen)
GOODE, Edward
GORDON, Gilbert
    ", John
GORRE, Daniel
    ", John
GOWEN, John (Goin)
GREER, Joseph
    John Maxey
    John Currie
    Richard Wilkins

GRIFFIN, John

HAGOOD, William, Jr.
HALPIN, William
HARDEN, Gabriel
" , William
HARRIS, Samuel
    Stephen Wade
    Charles Harris
    David York
HARRIS, William
HARRISON, Benjamin
    Thomas Harrison
HATCHELL, John
HATCHELL, William
    Stephen Hatchell
HATCHER, Jeremiah
" , Robert
HAWKINS, Pinkethman
" , Thomas
HEARN, John
HENRY, Edward
HIGHTOWER, Thomas
HILL, Nicholas
    (Taxed to Benjamin
      Baird, Surry Co.)
HILL, William
    John McAdum
HICKS, John
HIX, James
HOBSON, Nicholas
    John Hobson
HOGWOOD, William
    John Hogwood
HOLLOWAY, George
HOLMES, Samuel
    Samuel Holmes, Jr.
    William Holmes
HOOPER, Obadiah
HOPSON, John
    Richard Hopson
HOWARD, Henry
HOWELL, John
    William Scott
HUDSON, James
    Richard Hudson
HUDSON, Peter
    Daniel Hudson
HUEY, Humphry
HUMPHREYS, John

JEFFERSON, Feild
    John Fain

JOHNSON, Christopher
" , John
" , Michael
" , William
JONES, James
JONES, Robert, Jr.
    David Dodd

KILLINGSWORTH, Edward
KING, William
KIRKS, Samuel

LANGFORD, John
    Henry Langford
LANIER, Thomas
LARKE, Dennis
" , Robert
LAX, William
LETT, Francis
LETT, James
    John Dean
LEWIS, Edward
LIDDERDALE, William
LUNDY, Richard
    Henry Jackson

MACLIN, Thomas (McLin)
    Edward Peters
    Benjamin Scott
McDANIEL, John
    James McDaniel
McDONALD, James
    James McDonald, Jr.
McKAY, John Noble
McQUIE, Michael
MABRY, Ephraim
MAJOR, Nicholas
    Abraham Coleson
    Jacob Coleson
MALLETT, Stephen, Sr.
    William Mallett
MALLETT, Stephen, Jr.
MALONE, Drury
MALONE, Thomas
    James McKenney
MANNING, Henry
MANNING, Samuel
    William Manning
    John Manning
    Samuel Manning, Jr.
MARABLE, William
MARTIN, John
MAYES, John

MAYES, Matthew
MINOR, James
" , Joseph
MITCHELL, Isaac
" , Jacob, Sr.
" , Jacob, Jr.
MITCHELL, James
    James Mitchell, Jr.
    John Mitchell
    David Mitchell
MIZE, Jeremiah
    John Mize
    Henry Mize
MIZE, James
" , Stephen
" , William
MOORE, Robert
MORGAN, John
" , Philip
" , Reuben
MORROW, John
MULLINS, Valentine
MURPHEY, Benjamin
MURPHY, William
MYRECK, Owen

NEWSOM, Amos
    (Taxed to Col. John
    Ruffin, Surry Co.)
NICHOLS, Julius
NICHOLS, William
    Nicholas Cook
NORRILL, Hugh
    Thomas Norrill
NORTON, Stephen

ORGAIN, Matthew
OVERBY, Nicholas
    Overby, Peter, Jr.
OVERBY, Peter, Sr.

PALMER, Richard
PARKER, John
    William Parker
PARKER, Samuel
PARRISH, Peter
PENNINGTON, John George
PERINGER, Michael
PINSON, Aaron
POINDEXTER, Philip
POOLE, William
    Robert Poole
    William Poole, Jr.
    Adam Poole

PRICE, John

RAGSDALE, John, Sr.
REILY, Charles
    Charles Reily, Jr.
RICHARDS, Jonathon
RICHARDSON, William
ROBERTS, Thomas
" , William
ROBERTSON, David
" , Henry
ROBERTSON, John
    Edward Robertson
    Robert Robertson
ROBERTSON, John
ROBERTSON, Abraham
" , John, Jr.
" , Mark
" , Nathaniel
" , Nicholas
ROBERTSON, William
    (Taxed to Mary Ferrell
    Brunswick County)
ROGERS, Richard W.
ROTTENBERRY, Henry
    , John
RUSSELL, Jeffrey
" , Philip

SAFFOLD, William
    Lewis Scarborough
SAGE, Henry
SANDIFER, William
    Samuel Young
    William Calvin
SANTHORPE, Thomas
SATTERWHITE, Thomas
    Michael Satterwhite
    John Satterwhite
SAUNDERS, Thomas
SEARCY, Reuben
SMITH, James
" , John
SMITH, James
SPEARS, Augustine
SPEED, John
    William Taylor
    Terrence McMullan
STAGNER, John
STEVENS, Thomas
STONE, William
SWEPSON, Richard

TABOR, John

TALLEY, John
    David Talley
    Joseph Talley
TANNER, Lewis
" , Lucias
" , Matthew
" , Thomas
TATE, Thomas
THOMASON, James
THOMPSON, John
" , John
" , Richard
TUCKER, James
    Warner Tucker
TUCKER, William
    William Whittemore
TUREMAN, George

VAUGHAN, Reuben

WADE, Robert
    Charles Wade
WALLACE, William
    John Wallace
WARD, Wade
WARREN, Thomas
WATSON, John
    William Watson
    John Watson, Jr.
WEATHERFORD, Charles
WEATHERFORD, John
    John Boone
WEATHERFORD, William
WESTCOTT, Thomas

WELLS, John
    John Wells, Jr.
WELLS, Thomas
    James Bryant
WHEELER, Samuel
WHITE, William
WHITT, Richard
    John Whitt
WILBOURN, John
WILES, Robert
" , Stephen
" , Thomas
WILKINS, James
    John Wilkins
WILKINS, Thomas
WILLIAMS, Matthew
" , William
WILLIS, Edward
WILSON, Edward
    Robert Wilson
WILSON, Henry
" , Samuel
" , William
WINDERS, Adam
WITTON, Richard
    Andrew Graham
    Daniel McGowan
WOODING, Robert
WRIGHT, John
    John Shepherd
WRIGHT, John
" , Solomon
" , Thomas
YOUNG, Lemuel

Note: The number of tithables charged to each of those listed above has been omitted as not being pertinent to these records.

    The tithables indented were chargeable to the preceding name.

EARLY LUNENBURG COUNTY DEEDS

HOWARD, William   Deed Book 1, Page 14

    William Howard and Sarah, his wife, of Lunenburg County to Feild Jefferson of Henrico County ... 580 acres in Lunenburg County.
    Witnesses:
        Francis Howard   /s/ William Howard
        William Seeley
        Thomas Hawkins
    Deed dated 1 May 1746   Recorded 19 June 1746

    Sarah, wife of William Howard, released dower 6-28-46.

WILKINS, John   Deed Book 1, Page 28

    John Wilkins of Lunenburg County to Thomas Satterwhite of same county ... cons. 100 pounds ... 400 acres on north side of Roanoke River ... adjoining Tabor, John Cox, William Lidderdale and Richard Blalock.
    Witnesses:
        William Tabor
        Thomas Wilkins   /s/ John Wilkins
        Valentine Mullins
    Dated 27 June 1746   Recorded 7 July 1746

    Mary, wife of John Wilkins, released dower right.

HUDSON, Christopher   Deed Book 1, Page 30

    Christopher Hudson and Cary, his wife, of Cumberland Parish, Lunenburg County, to Richard Palmer of Fredericksville Parish, Louisa County ... cons. 80 pounds ... 150 acres on north side of Roanoke River ... adjoining John Clemens (Clements), Thomas Robertson (one of the former proprietors of this land now conveyed) and William Toms.
    Witnesses: /s/ Christopher Hudson
        Anthony Pouncey   /s/ Cary Hudson
        Julius Nichols
    Dated 7 July 1746   Recorded 7 July 1746

    Cary, wife of Christopher Hudson, released dower.

TWITTY, John   Deed Book 1, Page 50

    John Twitty of Lunenburg County to John Hall of Amelia County ... cons. 10 pounds ... 150 acres at mouth of Blackston's (Blackstone) Creek ... part of a larger tract granted by patent.
    No witnesses recorded   /s/ John Twitty
    Dated 18 July 1746   Recorded 4 Aug. 1746

HOWARD, Francis   Deed Book 1, Page 91

    Francis Howard of Cumberland Parish, Lunenburg County
to Feild Jefferson of Dale Parish, Henrico County, Gent.
... cons. 240 pounds ... 445 acres on Roanoke River ...
adjoining Andrew Moreman and Jefferson's own line.
Witnesses:
  William Howard
  L. Delony   /s/ Francis Howard
  John Speed
  Henry Delony
Dated 7 May 1746   Recorded 16 Oct. 1746

    Diana, wife of Francis Howard, released dower.

CLARK, Samuel   Deed Book 1, Page 99

    Samuel Clark of Brunswick County to Thomas Twitty of
Brunswick County ... cons. 15 pounds ... 480 acres on
Roanoke River ... devised to Clark by deed of gift from
Robert Hicks ... part of a tract conveyed to Cornelius
Keith by Hix which has been conveyed to Twitty by Keith
Witnesses:
  Clément Read
  William Hill   /s/ Samuel Clark
  Thomas Lanier
Dated Feb. 5, 1746   Recorded 1 Dec. 1746

BRESLAR, Andrew   Deed Book 1, Page 106

    Andrew Breslar and Anne, his wife, of Lunenburg County*
to Robert Jones, Junr., attorney-at-law, of Surry
County ... cons. 32 pounds 10 shillings ... 100 acres
on north side of Roanoke River ... at mouth of Miles
Creek ... adjoining Philip Morgan.
Witnesses:
  L. Delony
  John (X) Freeman   /s/ Andrew Breslar
  Anne Delony
  Anne Delony, Junr.
Dated 3 Feb. 1746   ? Recorded 2 March 1746

    Anne, wife of Andrew Breslar, released dower right.

  * The county of Lunenburg was created by an Act of the
    House of Burgesses on 26 March 1745, and to be effec-
    tive 1 May 1746. Some of the dates above appear to
    have been recorded in error.

SHEARMAN, John   Deed Book 1, Page 113

    John Shearman and Katherine, his wife, of Cumberland
Parish, Lunenburg County, to William Wood of same
Parish and County ... cons. 30 pounds ... 100 acres on

          south side of Roanoke River.
       Witnesses: /s/ John Shearman
          Thomas Hawkins
          William Seeley
       Dated 2 March 1746   Recorded 1 Nov. 1746

       Katherine, wife of John Shearman, released dower.

HILL, William   Deed Book 1, Page 227

       William Hill and Catherine, his wife, of Cumberland
       Parish, Lunenburg County, to Francis Bressie of same
       Parish and County ... cons. 45 pounds ... 362 acres on
       west side of Butchers Creek ... patented by William
       Hill.
       Witnesses: /s/ William Hill
          Walter Campbell   /s/ Catherine Hill
          John Speed
          David Dodd
       Dated 7 Sept. 1747   Recorded 7 Sept. 1747

COLEMAN, James   Deed Book 1, Page 239

       James Coleman to William Willie of Surry County, Clerk,
       cons. 35 pounds 7 shillings 6 pence ... 100 acres on
       north side of Roanoke River ... being the plantation
       and land where John Roper formerly lived ... adjoining
       Andrew Mooreman and land that Robert Jones, Junr.,
       purchased of Andrew Breslar.
       Witnesses: /s/ James Coleman
          Clement Read   L. Claiborne, Sr.
          Buckner Stith Robert Jones, Jr.
       Dated 5 Oct. 1747   Recorded 5 Oct. 1747

HOUSE, Lawrence   Deed Book 1, Page 264

       Lawrence House of Brunswick County to Benjamin Baird of
       Surry County .... cons. 10 pounds ... 195 acres on east
       side of Miles Creek.
       Witnesses: /s/ Lawrence House
          John Holloway   John Lett
          Robert (X) Hobbs James Lett
          Job (X) Hobbs   Isaac Holmes
       Dated 18 Sept. 1747   Recorded 2 Nov. 1747

LETT, John   Deed Book 1, Page 266

       John Lett of Lunenburg County to Benjamin Baird of
       Surry County ... cons. 10 pounds ... 116 acres on Miles
       Creek, adjoining Dennis Lark.
       Witnesses:
          L. Claiborne, Sr.   /s/ John Lett

John Given
Charles Talbott
Dated 3 Nov. 1747   Recorded 3 Nov. 1747

WALKER, David   Deed Book 1, Page 280

David Walker of Prince George County to Robert Brooks
of Brunswick County ... cons. 16 pounds ... 100 acres
... part of a tract patented by William Munford.
Witnesses:
   J. Scott   /s/ David Walker
   L. Claiborne, Sr.
   John Cox
Dated 7 Jan. 1747   Recorded 1 Feb. 1747

SMITH, Luke, Senr.   Deed Book 1, Page 283

Luke Smith, Senr. for love and affection gives to son
Luke Smith, Junr. and Martha, his wife, ... 250 acres
on south side of Dan River and on Tewayhomony (Aarons)
Creek.
Witnesses:
   Richard Griffin   /s/ Luke Smith, Sr.
   Aaron Pinson, Jr.
   Aaron Pinson
Dated 30 Jan. 1747   Recorded 1 Feb. 1747

PARKER, John   Deed Book 1, Page 295

John Parker of Brunswick County to Joseph Minor of
Lunenburg County ... tract of land on Dry Creek ... 327
acres ... granted by patent to said Parker 5 June 1746.
Witnesses:
   John Twitty   /s/ John Parker
   George Walton
   William Hagood
Dated 19 Feb. 1747   Recorded 7 March 1747

DUKE, John Taylor   Deed Book 1, Page 312

John Taylor Duke to Edward Goodrich of Brunswick
County ... cons. 30 pounds ... 100 acres on east side
of Flatt Creek ... part of a tract of land patented by
James Mitchell 17 March 1736.
Witnesses:
   John Duke   /s/ John T. Duke
   Rireyel Duke
Dated 18 March 1747   Recorded 4 April 1747

Jane, wife of John Taylor Duke, released dower.

WILKINS, John   Deed Book 1, Page 318

John Wilkins for love and affection for his son Thomas
Wilkins ... 100 acres ... land where he now lives ....
joining my line.
Witnesses:
   Thomas Satterwhite
   John Long   /s/ John Wilkins
   Jesse Flower
Dated 10 Oct. 1747   Recorded 4 April 1748

BROOKS, Robert   Deed Book 1, Page 329

Robert Brooks to Nicholas Gentry ... cons. 12 pounds .
... 108 acres ... on both sides of Meherrin River ....
land patented by Robert Brooks.
Witnesses: /s/ Robert Brooks
   None recorded
Dated 4 June 1747   Recorded 6 June 1748

WATSON, John   Deed Book 1, Page 348

John Watson to John MacDonald, cooper,... cons. 5
pounds Sterling ... 50 acres on south side of middle
fork of Miles Creek ... part of patent granted to John
Watson.
Witnesses:
   James Williams   /s/ John Watson
   Francis Ellidge
   John Twitty
Dated 25 Sept. 1748   Recorded 8 Oct. 1748

Rebecca, wife of John Watson, released dower right.

WATSON, John   Deed Book 1, Page 351

John Watson to Francis Lett of Brunswick County ...
cons. 20 pounds ... 100 acres on north side of middle
fork of Miles Creek. Granted Watson by patent.
Witnesses:
   John High
   Thos. Hardaway, Sr.   /s/ John Watson
   Susanna Simmons
Dated 12 Sept. 1748   Recorded 3 Oct. 1748

Rebecca, wife of John Watson, released dower right.

HUMPHREYS, William   Deed Book 1, Page 356

William Humphreys to Christopher Hudson, Planter ...
cons. 40 pounds ... 90 acres on upper side of Allens
Creek ... part of land granted to William, John,
Thomas and Charles Humphreys.
Witnesses:

```
        John Speed
        James Williams              /s/ William Humphreys
        Julius Nichols
        Dated 3 Oct. 1748                Recorded 3 Oct. 1748
```

Mary, wife of William Humphreys, released dower.

CLEMONS, Susanna (Clements)   Deed Book 1, Page 359

Susanna Clemons to Thomas Satterwhite ... cons. 5 pounds ... 50 acres on north side of Roanoke River ... land left her by will of her father.
Witnesses:
    John Twitty   /s/ Susanna Clements
    John Wilkins
    Richard Palmer
Dated 18 July 1748   Recorded 3 Oct. 1748

RAY, Francis (Wray)   Deed Book 1, Page 363

Francis Ray and Rachel, his wife, to James Mize ... 33 pounds consideration ... tract of land granted to Wray by patent.
Witnesses:
    Richard (X) Andrews   /s/ Francis Ray
    Ephraim (E) Andrews
    Ralph (T) Griffin
    John Howell
Dated 2 July 1748   Recorded 3 Oct. 1748

Rachel, wife of Francis Ray, released dower right.

WILKINS, John   Deed Book 1, Page 389

John Wilkins to his son William Wilkins ... natural love and affection for son ... 100 acres ... in the fork of Little Creek, adjoining line of Munford.
Witnesses:
    Thos. Satterwhite   /s/ John Wilkins
    Christopher Hudson
    John Lucas
Dated 1 April 1749   Recorded 5 June 1749

MAJOR, Nicholas   Deed Book 1, Page 391

Nicholas Major to Peter Piryere (Puryear) ... cons. 62 pounds ... 200 acres ... on north side of Butchers Creek.
Witnesses:
    Christopher Hudson   /s/ Nicholas Major
    John Wilkins
    John Lucas
Dated 5 Dec. 1748   Recorded 5 June 1749

Mary, wife of Nicholas Major, released her dower right.

ELLIDGE, Francis   Deed Book 1, Page 393

Francis Ellidge of Cumberland Parish, Lunenburg County, to Thomas Clarke of Isle of Wight County ... two tracts of land containing together 730 acres ... being contiguous ... patented by said Ellidge 20 August 1747.
Witnesses:
    Thos. Clifton
    Thomas (X) Pyland   /s/ Francis Ealidge
    Hannah Pyland
Dated 11 Oct. 1748   Recorded 5 June 1749

HOWARD, Francis   Deed Book 1, Page 405

Francis Howard to John Hyde ... cons. 20 pounds ... 150 acres on Roanoke River ... part of 175 acres lately patented by Francis Howard.
Witnesses:
    William Howard   /s/ Francis (X) Howard
    William Sandifer
    George (X) Holloway
Dated 2 Feb. 1749   Recorded 5 June 1749

Diannah, wife of Francis Howard, released her dower.

HOMES, Samuel (Holmes)   Deed Book 1, Page 407

Samuel Homes, Planter, to Julius Nichols ... cons. 40 pounds ... 101 acres ... bounded as by letters patent to Samuel Homes (Holmes) 1 March 1743.
Witnesses:
    Robert Wade
    Fran. Bressie   /s/ Samuel (Sam) Homes
    Christopher Hudson
Dated 5 June 1749   Recorded 5 June 1749

Anne, wife of Samuel Holmes, released dower right.

McCONNEL, John   Deed Book 1, Page 413

John McConnel to Joseph Minor ... cons. 80 pounds .... 178 acres on Flat Rock Creek.
Witnesses:
    Lyddall Bacon   /s/ John McConnel
    Hampton Wade
    James Williams
Dated 4 July 1749   Recorded 4 July 1749

MOARMAN, Andrew (Mooreman)   Deed Book 1, Page 420

Andrew Moarman to Hutchins Burton of Goochland County
cons. 235 pounds ... 300 acres on north side of Roanoke
River... adjoining lower line of Feild Jefferson.
Witnesses:
    Thos. Jefferson
    Andrew Moarman (Jr. ?)   /s/ Andrew (A) Moarman
    John Fain
Dated 10 Nov. 1748   Recorded 3 Oct. 1749

MALONE, Drury   Deed Book 1, Page 432

Drury Malone to Daniel Nance of Albemarle Parish, Surry
County ... cons. 10 pounds ... 50 acres on north side
of Jeneto Creek. Patented to Edward Hall (Edmund) 15
Aug. 1737.
Witnesses:
    James Hicks, Junr.   /s/ Drury Malone
    James McKenney
    Josias (Jo) Floyd
Dated 2 Oct. 1749   Recorded 3 Oct. 1749

NANCE, Daniel   Deed Book 1, Page 437

Daniel Nance and Elizabeth, his wife, of Surry County,
to Thomas Malone .... cons. 125 pounds... 230 acres on
north side of Jeneto Creek. Part of 385 acres patented
by Edmund Hall 15 Aug. 17 7.
Witnesses:
    James McKenney   /s/ Daniel Nance
    Josias (Jo) Floyd   /s/ Elizabeth Nance
    James Hicks, Jr.
Dated 3 Oct. 1749   Recorded 3 Oct. 1749

STEWART, Charles   Deed Book 1, Page 439

Charles Stewart and Anne, his wife, of Brunswick County
to Lewis Parham of same county ... 495 acres on both
sides of Allens Creek. (Part of patents to Stewart.)
Witnesses:
    Sterling Clack
    Drury Stith   /s/ Charles Stewart
    John Embry
Dated 26 July 1749   Recorded 3 Oct. 1749

STITH, Drury et als   Deed Book 1, Page 463

Drury Stith, Henry Morris and Michael Cadet Young of
St. Andrews Parish, Brunswick County, to John Thompson
of Cumberland Parish, Lunenburg County ... cons. 44
pounds ... 637 acres on both sides of Bluestone Creek.
Patented by Stith, Morris and Young 1 Oct. 1747. Adjoining land of William Byrd.

Witnesses:
  James Parrish
  John (O) Murphy
  John (X) Humphries
Dated 26 Sept. 1749

/s/ Drury Stith
/s/ Henry Morris
/s/ M. Cadet Young

Recorded 3 Oct. 1749

CARTER, James   Deed Book 1, Page 466

James Carter of Surry County to Julius Nichols of Lunenburg County ... cons. 12 pounds 10 shillings ... 83 acres on both sides of Allens Creek.
Witnesses:
  J. Scott
  L. Claiborne, Sr.   /s/ James Carter
  Robert Jones, Junr.
Dated 19 June 1749   Recorded 3 Oct. 1749

BURWELL, Armistead   Deed Book 1, Page 473

Armistead Burwell of Williamsburg, Gent. to John Cox, Planter ... cons. for sundry work, labor and services performed by Cox in improving a tract of land in Lunenburg County and 5 shillings ... 100 acres on south side of south fork of Meherrin River (bounded as by plat and survey made by George Walton) at mouth of Finneywood Creek.
Witnesses:
  Wm. Dobyns
  Sam'll Harris   /s/ Armist^d Burwell
  Matt'w Talbot, Junr.
Dated 23 Oct. 1749   Recorded 2 Jan. 1749/50

COOK, Nathaniel   Deed Book 2, Page 7

Nathaniel Cook to John Watson ... cons. 20 pounds ... 400 acres ... on both sides of a branch.
Witnesses:
  Sam'l Bizwell   /s/ Nathaniel (X) Cook
  William (O) Edwards
  Isaac (I) Holmes
Dated 12 Dec. 1749   Recorded 3 July 1750

NANCE, Daniel   Deed Book 2, Page 10

Daniel Nance of Surry County to Drury Malone ... cons. 5 shillings ... 152 acres on south side of Jeneto Creek ... Part of a patent of 385 acres to Edmund Hall.
Witnesses:
  Thomas Malone
  John (L) Langford   /s/ Daniel Nance
  James McKenney
Dated 7 April 1750   Recorded 3 July 1750

TWITTY, John   Deed Book 2, Page 17

    John Twitty to Joseph Chandler ... cons. 25 pounds ....
247 acres on both sides of south fork of Meherrin River
... part of a patent.
Witnesses: /s/ John Twitty
    None recorded
Dated 3 July 1750   Recorded 3 July 1750

HOLMES, Samuel   Deed Book 2, Page 18

    Samuel Holmes, Planter, to Julis Nichols ... cons. 40
pounds ... 348 acres ... bounded as shown by patent to
Holmes 20 May 1749.
Witnesses:
    Lydall Bacon   /s/ Samuel (Sa) Holmes
    Henry Delony
    Drury Allen
Dated 3 July 1750   Recorded 3 July 1750

MITCHELL, Robert   Deed Book 2, Page 23

    Robert Mitchell of the Province of North Carolina to
John Davis of Lunenburg County ... cons. 10 pounds ....
40 acres on north side of Roanoke River.
Witnesses: /s/ Robert Mitchell
    None recorded
Dated 3 April 1750   Recorded 3 July 1750

CARGILL, Cornelius   Deed Book 2, Page 29

    Cornelius Cargill, Planter, Lunenburg County to Hugh
Miller, Merchant, Prince George County ... sells slaves
to Miller ... cons. 118 pounds 11 shillings.
Witnesses: /s/ Cornelius Cargill
    None recorded
Dated 9 April 1750   Recorded 3 July 1750

COLEMAN, James   Deed Book 2, Page 36

    James Coleman to Martin Phifer ... cons. 5 shillings ..
20 acres ... part of land James Coleman now lives on.
Witnesses:
    None recorded   /s/ James Coleman
Dated 30 March 1750   Recorded 3 July 1750

    Clary (Clarissa), wife of James Coleman, released dower

HILL, William   Deed Book 2, Page 40

    William Hill to Richard Stith of Brunswick County ...
cons. 43 pounds ... 400 acres on a ridge between
Allens and Butchers Creeks ... adjoining Ravenscroft ..

```
              land patented by Hill 25 July 1749.
              Witnesses:
                 Thomas Lanier           /s/ William Hill
                 Martin Fifer
              Dated 20 Oct. 1749               Recorded 3 July 1750
```

Catherine, wife of William Hill, released dower right.

HUMPHREYS, John et als   Deed Book 2, Page 47

    William, John, Thomas and Charles Humphreys to Lewis Delony ... 48 pounds ... 91½ acres ... one fourth part of patent 20 Aug. 1747 to William, John, Thomas and Charles Humphreys ... on lower side of Allens Creek.
```
              Witnesses:
                 None recorded           /s/ John (I) Humphreys
              Dated 1 Jan. 1749                Recorded 3 July 1750
```

HARRIS, William   Deed Book 2, Page 57

    William Harris to Samuel Harris ... cons. 60 pounds ... 70 acres ... consisting of plantation and island in the Staunton River ... between Byrd's Island and Cargill's Island.
```
              Witnesses:
                 John Cargill            /s/ William Harris
                 William Hunt
              Dated 3 July 1750                Recorded 3 July 1750
```

Judith, wife of William Harris, released dower right.

BAIRD, Benjamin   Deed Book 2, Page 74

    Benjamin Baird to Robert Lark ... cons. 10 pounds sterling ... 195 acres on east side of Miles Creek and on Dockery Creek ... tract of land granted by letters patent to Lawrence House.
```
              Witnesses:
                 Dennis Lark
                 Thomas Wills            /s/ Benj. Baird
                 Michael Kirk
                 John (F) Wells
              Dated 1 March 1749               Recorded 3 July 1750
```

LETT, John   Deed Book 2, Page 85

    John Lett of Province of North Carolina to Nathaniel Cook ... cons. 20 pounds ... 116 acres on Miles Creek.. one moiety of 232 acres patented by John Lett and one part sold to Benjamin Baird of Surry County.
```
              Witnesses:
                 L. Delony
                 John Watson             /s/ John (E) Lett
                 William Williams
```

Dated 1 Dec. 1749   Recorded 3 July 1750

RANDLE, Josias   Deed Book 2, Page 94

Josias Randle to Richard Stith of Brunswick County ...
cons. 50 pounds ... 504 acres on east side of Butchers
Creek, adjoining John Mitchell.
Witnesses:
    Thos Nash
    Clemt Read   /s/ Josias Randle
    Thos Stith
Dated 20 June 1750   Recorded 3 July 1750

MORGAN, Philip   Deed Book 2, Page 110

Philip Morgan, Planter, to Robert Jones, Junr.,
Attorney-at-law, of Surry County. ... cons. 8 pounds 13
shillings 3 pence ... 120 acres on both sides of Miles
Creek. Patented by Philip Morgan.
Witnesses:
    William Howard   Henry Delony
    Francis Ellidge   John Speed   /s/ Philip (P) Morgan
    Thos Jefferson   L. Delony
Dated 4 April 1750   Recorded 4 July 1750

PARHAM, Lewis   Deed Book 2, Page 120

Lewis Parham to Hugh Miller of Bristol Parish, Prince
George County ... cons. 70 pounds ... 388 acres on both
sides of Middle Fork of Bluestone Creek. Patented by
Lewis Parham 1 Oct. 1747.
Witnesses: /s/ Lewis Parham
    None recorded
Dated 2 Oct. 1750   Recorded 2 Oct. 1750

WOMACK, William   Deed Book 2, Page 135

William Womack to Richard Lunday (Lundy) ... cons. 35
pounds ... 80 acres on a fork of Allens Creek.
Witnesses: /s/ William (X) Womack
    None recorded
Dated 2 Sept. 1750   Recorded 2 Oct. 1750

LANIER, Benjamin   Deed Book 2, Page 154

Benjamin Lanier to John Humphreys ... cons. 40 pounds .
.. 368 acres on both sides of Allens Creek.
Witnesses:
    Christopher Hudson
    John Mayse (Mayes)   /s/ Benjamin Lanier
    William White
Dated 2 Oct. 1750   Recorded 2 Oct. 1750

HUMPHREY, John et als   Deed Book 2, Page 169

    John, William, Thomas and Charles Humphreys to James
    Tucker .... cons. 96 pounds ... 183 acres ... on both
    sides of Allens Creek.
    Witnesses:
        Christopher Hudson   /s/ John (I) Humphrey
        John Mayse (Mayes)   /s/ William Humphrey
        William White   /s/ Thomas (X) Humphrey
                                /s/ Charles (C) Humphrey

    Dated 1 Jan. 1750   Recorded 2 Oct. 1750

PARRISH, James   Deed Book 2, Page 187

    James Parrish of St. Andrew's Parish, Brunswick County,
    to Thomas Hawkins of Cumberland Parish, Lunenburg
    County ... cons. 80 pounds ... 385 acres on Butchers
    Creek ... Adjoining the line of Thomas Baker ... land
    patented by Parrish 25 June 1747.
    Witnesses:
        None recorded   /s/ James Parrish

    Dated 7 April 1750   Recorded 2 April 1751

MOORE, Thomas   Deed Book 2, Page 191

    Thomas Moore to John Roberson (Robertson) ... cons. 30
    pounds ... 215 acres ... on a branch of Allens Creek.
    Witnesses:
        William Goode   Thomas Hawkins
        Thomas Farrar   Matthew Tanner   /s/ Thomas Moore
        William Roberts
    Dated 29 Dec. 1750   Recorded 2 April 1751

    Mary, wife of Thomas Moore, released her dower right.

HALL, John   Deed Book 2, Page 195

    John Hall of Amelia County to John Twitty ... cons. 10
    pounds ... 150 acres .. at mouth of Blackstone Branch
    ... part of a larger tract patented by Twitty. *
    * John Twitty sold this land to John Hall, who sold it
    back to Twitty.
    Witnesses:
        Wm. Dendy
        Eliza (EO) Dendy   /s/ John Hall
        Martha (MD) Dendy
    Dated 7 Jan. 1750   Recorded 2 April 1751

MAJOR, Nicholas   Deed Book 2, Page 202

    Nicholas Major to Pinkithman Hawkins ... cons. 25

pounds ... 200 acres ... part of a tract of land where
Nicholas Major now lives.
Witnesses: /s/ Nicholas Major
  None recorded
Dated 2 April 1751   Recorded 2 April 1751

Mary, wife of Nicholas Major, released dower right.

TWITTY, Thomas   Deed Book 2, Page 211

Thomas Twitty to Julius Nichols ... cons. 80 pounds ...
580 acres and also an island in the Roanoke River containing 21 acres.
Witnesses:
  Henry Seward   /s/ Thomas Twitty
  Richard Russell   /s/ Mary Twitty
  Th. Taylor
  John Taylor Duke
Dated 11 Dec. 1750   Recorded 2 April 1751

LARK, Joseph   Deed Book 2, Page 222

Joseph Lark to John Dortch of Southampton County ...
cons. 50 pounds ... 384 acres on Miles Creek ...
adjoining Dennis Lark.
Witnesses:
  Dennis Lark
  Thomas Wells   /s/ Joseph Larke
  David Dortch   /s/ Anne Larke
  John (I) Wells
Dated 3 Nov. 1750   Recorded 2 April 1751

SCOTT, James   Deed Book 2, Page 242

James Scott of Amelia County to William White of Cumberland Parish, Lunenburg County ... cons. 48 pounds ..
404 acres on both sides of Allens Creek.
Witnesses:
  James Hill, Senr.
  William Jones   /s/ Jas. Scott
  Edw. Booker, Junr.
Dated 9 March 1751   Recorded 3 April 1751

RAY, Francis (Wray)   Deed Book 2, Page 275

Francis Ray for love and affection for my son-in-law
William Allen ... 200 acres.
Witnesses:
  John Williams   /s/ Francis (1-1) Ray
  Richard Blanks   /s/ Rachel (X) Ray
  John Blackwell
Dated 1 Oct. 1751   Recorded 1 Oct. 1751

Rachel, wife of Francis Ray, released her dower right.

FLETCHER John   Deed Book 2, Page 279

    John Fletcher and Amy, his wife, to Charles Lewis of
    Amelia County ... cons. 25 pounds ... 53 acres on north
    side of Roanoke River.
    Witnesses: /s/ John (X) Fletcher
        None recorded
    Dated 3 Sept. 1751   Recorded 1 Oct. 1751

NANCE, John   Deed Book 2, Page 281

    John Nance to George Wells of Orange County ... cons.
    70 pounds ... 200 acres on south side of Meherrin River
    ... part of a patent.
    Witnesses:
        George Walton
        Barnaby (B) Wells   /s/ John Nance
        Francis Moor Petty
        Richd Tomson
    Dated 4 Sept. 1751   Recorded 1 Oct. 1751

DORTCH, John   Deed Book 2, Page 285

    John Dortch of Southampton County to Charles Burkes,
    Junr. of Amelia County ... cons. 60 pounds ... 384
    acres on a fork of Miles Creek ... adjoining Dennis
    Larke.
    Witnesses:
        John Speed   /s/ John Dortch
        John Ballard
        Robert Wooding
    Dated 29 Sept. 1751   Recorded 1 Oct. 1751

    Ruth, wife of John Dortch, released her dower right.

WILKINS, John   Deed Book 2, Page 297

    John Wilkins for love and affection for my son James
    Wilkins ... 100 acres of land ... where I now live
    after my death and the death of my wife.
    Witnesses:
        Thomas Satterwhite   /s/ John Wilkins
        Michael Satterwhite
        John Satterwhite
    Dated 8 Sept. 1751   Recorded 1 Oct. 1751

    Hannah, wife of John Wilkins, released dower right.

HUMPHREYS, John   Deed Book 2, Page 300

    John Humphreys to Warner Tucker of Prince George County
    ... cons. 25 pounds ... 168 acres on upper side of
    Allens Creek... part of land bought of Benjamin Lanier.

```
        Witnesses:                  /s/ John (I) Humphreys
           None recorded
        Dated 1 July 1751              Recorded 1 Oct. 1751
```

Marisucar (?), wife of John Humphreys, released dower.

TWITTY, John   Deed Book 2, Page 339

John Twitty to Thomas Pettus of Amelia County ... cons. 100 pounds ... 404 acres on Blackstone Creek ... land patented by John Cox and sold to Twitty.
```
        Witnesses:
           James Scott
           Thomas Claiborne           /s/ John Twitty
           Andrew Graham
        Dated 17 May 1751              Recorded 1 Oct. 1751
```

HAGOOD, William   Deed Book 2, Page 371

William Hagood to James Williams ... cons. 47 pounds 10 shillings ... 404 acres on east side of Stiths Creek.
```
        Witnesses:
           L. Delony                  /s/ Wm Hagood
        Dated 2 May 1748 *             Recorded 2 May 1748
```

* This deed and the three following deeds apparently were not recorded by the clerk, and were recorded in the deed book at the January Court 1752.

THOMASON, William Turner   Deed Book 2, Page 384

William Turner Thomason to Thomas Hawkins ... cons. 45 pounds ... 314 acres on Butchers Creek ... adjoining Francis Bressie.
```
        Witnesses:
           J. Scott                   /s/ William Turner Thomason
           John Twitty                /s/ Mary (N) Thomason
           John Cargill
        Dated 7 Dec. 1747              Recorded Dec. Court 1747
```

MITCHELL, Robert   Deed Book 2, Page 396

Robert Mitchell of Granville County, N. C. to John Davis ... cons. 135 pounds ... 417 acres on north side of Roanoke River ... adjoining Isaac Mitchell ... the plantation where Thomas King now lives.
```
        Witnesses:
           L. Delony                  /s/ Robert Mitchell
        Dated 7 Sept. 1747             Recorded 7 Sept. 1747
```

MITCHELL, James   Deed Book 2, Page 399

James Mitchell to John Roberson, Senr. (Robertson) ....

cons. 25 pounds ... 130 acres on south side of Roanoke River ... on Mitchell's line.
Witnesses:
   None recorded   /s/ James Mitchell
Dated 7 March 1747   Recorded 7 March 1747

GOODRICH, Edward   Deed Book 2, Page 402

Edward Goodrich of Brunswick County to Ephraim Mabry .. cons. (not stated) ... acreage not stated ... tract of land on east side of Flatt Creek.
Witnesses:
   Robert Jones, Junr.   /s/ Edward Goodrich
   Wm. Embry
   John Embry
Dated 2 Jan. 1751   Recorded 7 Jan. 1752

NICHOLS, Julius   Deed Book 2, Page 408

Julius Nichols to Stephen Mallett, Junr. ... cons. 70 pounds ... 83 acres on both sides of Allens Creek ... patented by James Carter and sold to Julius Nichols.
Witnesses:
   James Bilbo
   John Gorre'   /s/ Julius Nichols
   Stephan Mallett, Senr.
Dated 2 July 1751   Recorded 7 Jan. 1752

HAWKINS, Thomas   Deed Book 2, Page 412

Thomas Hawkins to Matthew Tanner ... cons. 35 pounds .. 198 acres ... adjoining Easter ... part of tract of land Thomas Hawkins purchased from James Parrish.
Witnesses:
   None recorded   /s/ Thomas Hawkins
Dated 11 March 1752   Recorded 7 April 1752

TUCKER, James, Senr.   Deed Book 2, Page 418

James Tucker, Senr. of Prince George County to William Bevill, Junr. ... cons. 41 pounds ... 200 acres on the lower side of Allens Creek ... part of a larger tract James Tucker bought from John Humphreys.
Witnesses: /s/ James (X) Tucker, Senr.
   Pat. Mullen   Christopher Hudson
   Edward Bevill   Joseph Bevill
   Joseph Ragsdale   Warner Tucker
   James (I) Tucker, Junr.
Dated 20 Jan. 1752   Recorded 7 April 1752

RUSSELL, Philip   Deed Book 2, Page 423

Philip Russell and Elizabeth, his wife, to Richard

Tomson (Thompson) ... cons. 5 pounds ... 200 acres on north side of Miles Creek ... adjoining Maclin and Jeffrey Russell.
Witnesses:
   John Tomson
   Jefery Russel
Dated 27 March 1752

/s/ Philip Russel
/s/ Elizabeth Russel

Recorded 7 April 1752

TUCKER, Warner   Deed Book 2, Page 432

Warner Tucker to Thomas Hawkins ... cons. 37 pounds 12 shillings 6 pence ... 168 acres on upper side of Allens Creek.
Witnesses:
   James (I) Tucker   /s/ Warner (X) Tucker
   Nicholas Major
   William Bevill
Dated 6 April 1752   Recorded 7 April 1752

ROYAL, Joseph   Deed Book 2, Page 455

Joseph Royal to John Roberson (Robertson) ... cons. 20 pounds ... 100 acres on both sides of Butchers Creek.
Witnesses:
   Thomas Hawkins
   Thomas Farrar   /s/ Joseph Royal
   William Farrar
   Thos Moore
Dated 10 March 1752   Recorded 7 April 1752

HOWARD, Henry   Deed Book 2, Page 459

Henry Howard to Hutchins Burton ... cons. 40 pounds ... 50 acres with a water mill on it ... on Miles Creek.
Witnesses:
   John Speed   /s/ Henry Howard
   Pinkithman Hawkins
   John Hyde
Dated 26 March 1752   Recorded 7 April 1752

COLEMAN, James   Deed Book 2, Page 461

James Coleman to Hutchins Burton ... 235 pounds cons. ... 400 acres on north side of Roanoke River ... adjoining David Allen.
Witnesses:
   Feild Jefferson
   Clary (C) Coleman   /s/ James Coleman
   Margret (W) Burch
Dated 21 Jan. 1752   Recorded 21 Jan. 1752

DELONY, Henry   Deed Book 2, Page 468

Henry Delony to Isham East ... cons. 30 pounds ... 300
acres on south east side of Cox Creek ... adjoining
Delony, Hayward and Harwell.
Witnesses:
    Feild Jefferson
    Julius Nichols   /s/ Henry Delony
    Charles Burkes
    Joseph East
Dated 18 Feb. 1752   Recorded 7 April 1752

Frances, wife of Henry Delony, released her dower.

MITCHELL, James   Deed Book 2, Page 470

James Mitchell to Feild Jefferson ... cons. 80 pounds .
.. 395 acres on south side of Roanoke River ... includ-
ing an island.
Witnesses:
    Robert Wade, Junr.   /s/ James Mitchell
    Robert Wooding
    William Chassels
Dated 7 April 1752   Recorded 7 April 1752

TOMSON, John   Deed Book 2, Page 480

John Tomson (Thompson) and wife Mary to John Flynn ....
cons. 20 pounds ... 181 acres on north side of
Bluestone Creek ... on William Byrd's line ... part of
a larger tract Thomson purchased of Drury Stith, Henry
Morris and Michael Young.
Witnesses: /s/ John (I) Thompson
    None recorded   /s/ Mary (X) Thomson
Dated 7 April 1752   Recorded 7 April 1752

Mary Thomson, wife of John Thomson, released dower.

RUSSELL, Philemon   Deed Book 2, Page 484

Philemon Russell and Elizabeth his wife to Peter
Parrish ... cons. 5 pounds ... 200 acres on south side
of Miles Creek.
Witnesses: /s/ Philip Russell
    John Tomson   /s/ Elizabeth Russell
    Jefery Russel
Dated 3 April 1752   Recorded 7 April 1752

PARHAM, Lewis   Deed Book 2, Page 490

Lewis Parham, Merchant, of Brunswick County to William
Hill ... cons 215 pounds ... 495 acres purchased by
Lewis Parham from Charles Stewart.
Witnesses: /s/ Lewis Parham
    None recorded
Dated 5 May 1752   Recorded 5 May 1752

Sarah Parham, wife of Lewis Parham, released her dower right 5 May 1752.

WRAY, Francis   Deed Book 2, Page 499

Francis Wray to David Allen ... for love and affection for my son-in-law ... 75 acres.
Witnesses: /s/ Francis (II) Wray
   None recorded
Dated 5 May 1752   Recorded 5 May 1752

HYDE, John   Deed Book 2, Page 508

John Hyde to Samuel Bugg of Henrico County ... cons. 170 pounds ... 150 acres of land on south side of the Roanoke River ... granted to Francis Howard and sold by him to John Hyde.
Witnesses:
   Henry Howard
   Penuel (X) Wood   /s/   John Hyde
   Edmund Bugg
   Sherwood Bugg
Dated 16 Jan. 1752   Recorded 6 May 1752

Martha, wife of John Hyde, released her dower right.

WOOD, William   Deed Book 3, Page 3

William Woode to Sherwood Bugg ... cons. 70 pounds ... 100 acres on south side of Roanoke River ... granted to John King who sold to William Wood.
Witnesses:
   George Walton   /s/ William (W) Wood
   Matt. Marable
   Jos. Williams
Dated 2 Jan. 1752   Recorded 2 June 1752

ROBERTSON, John   Deed Book 3, Page 5

John Robertson to Richard Robertson of Chesterfield County ... cons. 42 pounds 10 shillings ... 215 acres ... adjoining Thomas Moore, Thomas Hawkins and John Maclin. (Tract of land lately bought from Thomas Moore)
Witnesses:
   None recorded   /s/ John Robertson
Dated 2 June 1752   Recorded 2 June 1752

Mary, wife of John Robertson, released her dower.

POOL, William   Deed Book 3, Page 7

William Pool (Joyner) to William Bell, (Planter) .... cons. 15 pounds ... 87 acres ... on north side of Flatt

Creek adjoining Amos Timms, Philip Roberts and Adam
Tarpley.
Witnesses:
    Samuel Bizwell   /s/ Willm Poole
    Ephraim Mabry
    William (W) Poole, Junr.
Dated 1 June 1752   Recorded 2 June 1752

JONES, Robert, Junr.   Deed Book 3, Page 22

Robert Jones, Junr., of Surry County, to William Willie
of Surry County, Clerk ... cons. 60 pounds ... 100
acres on south bounded by Roanoke River, on west and
north by land of William Willie and on east by Miles
Creek. Land Robert Jones purchased of Andrew Breslar.
Witnesses:
    None recorded   /s/ Robert Jones Jun.
Dated 6 June 1750   Recorded 7 July 1752

WILLIE, William   Deed Book 3, Page 24

William Willie of Surry County to George Baskervill of
Cumberland County ...cons. 160 pounds ... 3 tracts of
land ... 267 acres in all ... bounded south on Roanoke
River, west and northwest by Hutchins Burton and east
on Miles Creek.
Witnesses: /s/ Wm Willie
    None recorded
Dated 7 July 1752   Recorded 7 July 1752

STITH, Richard   Deed Book 3, Page 30

Richard Stith of Brunswick County to John Hyde ... cons
45 pounds ... 504 acres lyinh between Butchers and
Allens Creeks, Adjoining John Mitchell.
Witnesses: /s/ Richard Stith
    None recorded
Dated 7 July 1752   Recorded 7 July 1752

POOL, William   Deed Book 3, Page 56

William Pool to John Mclain of Brunswick County ....
cons. 20 pounds ... 178 acres on upper side of Flatt
Creek.
Witnesses: /s/ Wm Poole
    Samuel Bizwell
    Thos (T) Roberts
    Robt (R) Poole
Dated 1 Sept. 1752   Recorded 1 Sept. 1752

HARWELL, Mark   Deed Book 3, Page 58

Mark Harwell of Prince George County to John Earl ....

cons. 30 pounds ... 195 acres on north side of Roanoke
River on Allens Creek.
Witnesses:
    James Coleman   /s/ Mark Harwell
    Martin Fifer (Phifer)
    Peter Farrar
Dated 9 March 1751   Recorded 1 Sept. 1752

TATE, Thomas   Deed Book 3, Page 65

Thomas Tate to Thomas Wilkins ... cons. 25 pounds ...
50 acres on south side of Little Creek ... adjoining
line of Tabor and James Wilkins.
Witnesses:
    Thomas Satterwhite
    Mich^1 Satterwhite   /s/ Thomas Tate
    John Satterwhite
Dated 2 Oct. 1752   Recorded 3 Oct. 1752

WILKINS, Thomas   Deed Book 3, Page 75

Thomas Wilkins to Thomas Tate ... cons. 50 pounds ...
50 acres ... adjoining Tabor and Thomas Wilkins.
Witnesses:
Thomas Satterwhite
John Satterwhite   /s/ Thomas (T) Wilkins
Mich^1 Satterwhite
Dated 2 Oct. 1752   Recorded 3 Oct. 1752

Hannah, wife of Thomas Wilkins, released her dower.

TANNER, Lewis   Deed Book 3, Page 85

Lewis Tanner to sons Lucius Tanner and Thomas Tanner ..
all that tract of land where Lewis Tanner now lives ...
354 acres ... to be divided equally between them ...
son Lucius to have his part now, and Thomas at death of
his father, or mother if she lives longest.
Witnesses:
    Amos Timms, Jr.
    Thomas Bracey   /s/ Lewis Tanner
    Ephraim Mabry
Dated 10 July 1752   Recorded 7 Nov. 1752

ROBERTSON, Matthew   Deed Book 3, Page 91

Mathew Roberson to John Davis ... cons. 40 pounds ...
154 acres on north side of Roanoke River ... adjoining
the upper corner of Rebecca Mitchell.
Witnesses:
    Henry Delony   /s/ Mathew Robertson
    Tho. Hawkins
    John Speed
Dated 7 Nov. 1752   Recorded 7 Nov. 1752

Sarah, wife of Matthew Robertson, released her dower.

HOWARD, Henry   Deed Book 3, Page 94

    Henry Howard to Samuel Bugg of Amelia County ... cons. 250 pounds ... 400 acres on north side of the Roanoke River ... on Allens Creek ... adjoining John Earl.
    Witnesses:
        Pink^n Hawkins   /s/ Henry Howard
        John Hyde
        Samuel Young
    Dated 22 May 1752   Recorded 7 Nov. 1752

HOWARD, Henry   Deed Book 3, Page 96

    Henry Howard to Jacob Bugg of Chesterfield County ... cons. 250 pounds ... 400 acres on north side of Roanoke River ... beginning at the mouth of Allens Creek .... adjoining John Earl.
    Witnesses:
        Samuel Young   /s/ Henry Howard
        John Hyde
        Pink^n Hawkins
    Dated 22 May 1752   Recorded 7 Nov. 1752

    Rebecca Hawkins, wife of Henry Hawkins, released her dower right in the foregoing tracts of land.

MOORE, Thomas   Deed Book 3, Page 108

    Thomas Moore to Richard Robertson of Chesterfield County ... cons. 8 pounds 12 shillings ... 30 acres ... on a branch adjoining Moore and Robertson.
    Witnesses:
        None recorded   /s/ Thos Moore
    Dated 6 Nov. 1752   Recorded 7 Nov. 1752

    Mary, wife of Thomas Moore, released her dower right.

MOORE, Thomas   Deed Book 3, Page 110

    Thomas Moore to Joseph Rudd of Chesterfield County .... cons. 120 pounds ... 185 acres ... part of a tract of land Thomas Moore bought from Thomas Hawkins.
    Witnesses:
        None recorded   /s/ Thos Moore
    Dated 6 Nov. 1752   Recorded 7 Nov. 1752

    Mary, wife of Thomas Moore, released dower right.

FARRAR, Feild   Deed Book 3, Page 113

    Feild Farrar to Henry Talley ... cons. 45 pounds .... 447 acres on both sides of Cox Creek.

    Witnesses:
      Robert Wooding   /s/ Feild Farrar
      Robert Stokes
      John Glass
    Dated 6 Nov. 1752   Recorded 7 Nov. 1752

    Martha, wife of Feild Farrar, released her dower right.

WALKER, David   Deed Book 3, Page 138

    David Walker of Dinwiddie County to Daniel McNeal
    (McNeil) ... cons. 14 pounds ... 400 acres on south
    side of Roanoke River ... on Grassy Creek ... to mouth
    of creek.
    Witnesses:
      L. Claiborne, Jr.   /s/ David Walker
      Henry Parrish
      Lewis Parham
    Dated 14 Nov. 1752   Recorded 5 Dec. 1752

HARRIS, William   Deed Book 3, Page 160

    William Harris to James Thomson Bardin ... cons. 40
    pounds ... 940 acres lying on branches of Bluestone
    Creek ... adjoining Barnes ... and on branches of
    Buffalo Creek. *
    Witnesses: /s/ William Harris
      None recorded
    Dated 6 Feb. 1753   Recorded 6 Feb. 1753

  * A part of this land appears to have been located in
    Charlotte County.

GOODE, William   Deed Book 3, Page 163

    William Goode to William Elam of Dinwiddie County ....
    cons. 60 pounds ... 400 acres on the west, or upper
    side of Bluestone Creek.
    Witnesses:
      George Walton   /s/ Wm Goode
      James (S) Stanley
      Reps (I) Osborn(e)
    Dated 8 Dec. 1752   Recorded 6 Feb. 1753

    Feeby Goode (Phoebe ?), wife of said Goode, released
    her dower right in land.

MUNFORD, Edward   Deed Book 3, Page 165

    Edward Munford and his wife, Mary Munford, of Dinwiddie
    County to Frederick Jones of Dinwiddie County ... cons.
    400 pounds ... 811 acres in the counties of Brunswick
    and Lunenburg ... beginning at Cocke's Creek *   ....

part of 2811 acres granted to Robert Munford and John
Anderson by patent dated 15 May 1722 ... devised to
Edward Munford by Robert Munford by his will dated 20
April 1734.
Witnesses: /s/ Edward Munford
  James Anderson Peter Jones /s/ Mary Munford
  James Hownam   John Thornton
  David Haliburton
  William Jones   Ant° Walke
Dated 25 Nov. 1752   Recorded 6 Feb. 1753

GOODE, William   Deed Book 3, Page 168

William Goode to Edward Elam ... cons. 30 pounds ...200
acres on west, or upper side, of Bluestone Creek. ....
part of a larger tract of land.
Witnesses:
  George Walton   /s/ Wm Goode
  James (S) Stanley
  Reps (I) Osborn(e)
Dated 8 Dec. 1752   Recorded 6 Feb. 1753

Feeby, wife of William Goode, released her dower right.

WILLIAMSON, Thomas   Deed Book 3, Page 186

Thomas Williamson and wife Martha Jones (Williamson) to
Branch Tanner of Amelia County ... cons. 200 pounds ...
997 acres on head branches of Finneywood and other
Creeks.
Witnesses: /s/ Thos Williamson
  Thom^s Claiborne /s/ Martha Jones (X) Williamson
  Robert Wooding
  William Robert
Dated 6 March 1753   Recorded 6 March 1753

Martha Jones, wife of Thomas Williamson, released her
dower right in land.

FARRELL, James (Ferrell)   Deed Book 3, Page 197

James Farrell of Brunswick County to Nathaniel Edwards
of Brunswick County ... cons. 30 pounds ... 223 acres
on south side of upper fork of Miles Creek.
Witnesses: /s/ James Farrell
  None recorded
Dated 6 March 1753   Recorded 6 March 1753

POOLE, William   Deed Book 3, Page 224

William Poole to Richard Evans, son of Morris Evans ...
for love and good will ... 50 acres ... on north side
of Flatt Creek.

Witnesses:
   Eph Mabry
   Adam Tupley (Tarpley)(Tapley)   /s/ Willm Poole
   Robert Poole
Dated 1 March 1753   Recorded 3 April 1753

MALLETT, Stephen, Senr.   Deed Book 3, Page 229

Stephen Mallett, Senr., to son William Mallett ... for love and affection ... 348 acres on south side of Allens Creek ... adjoining Byrd Lanier ... land that Stephen Mallett purchased from Julius Nichols.
Witnesses:
   Stephen Mallett, Junr.
   James Bilbo   /s/ Stephen Mallett, Senr.
   Martin Phifer
Dated 3 April 1753   Recorded 3 April 1753

MAJOR, Nicholas   Deed Book 3, Page 237

Nicholas Major to Abraham Coleson, alias Reignwater (Rainwater) ... cons. 5 pounds ... 100 acres on north side of Allens Creek ... adjoining Tucker.
Witnesses:
   Pink^n Hawkins   William Bevill
   Winney (X) Coleson   /s/ Nicholas Major
   Jacob (I) Coleson
   John (X) King
Dated 5 Feb. 1753   Recorded 1 May 1753

POOL, William   Deed Book 3, Page 241

William Pool to Robert Pool ... for love and affection ... 100 acres ... on south side of Flatt Creek.
Witnesses:
   Samuel Bizwell   /s/ Wm Poole
   Ephraim Mabry
   William Poole, Junr.
Dated 8 May 1752   Recorded 1 May 1753

Elizabeth Poole, wife of William Poole, released dower.

ROBINSON, John   Deed Book 3, Page 259

John Robinson and wife, Mary Robinson, to John Johnston ... cons. 39 pounds ... 180 acres on south side of the Roanoke River ... adjoining Matthews.
Witnesses:
   Reuben Searcy   /s/ John Robinson
   James Mitchell   /s/ Mary (X) Robinson
Dated 7 July 1752   Recorded 5 June 1753

Mary, wife of John Robinson, released her dower right.

BANISTER, John   Deed Book 3, Page 262

    John Banister of Dinwiddie County to Samuel Jones ....
cons. 150 pounds ... 250 acres on south side of the
Roanoke River ... adjoining John Alexander ... part of
a patent 13 October 1727 ... being all of the land that
falls within the dividing line between Virginia and
North Carolina.
Witnesses:
    Abraham Smith   /s/ John Banister
    Robert Stanfield
    John Hightower
Dated 27 July 1752   Recorded 5 June 1753

COX, Henry   Deed Book 3, Page 273

    Henry Cox of Elizabeth City County, Bricklayer, to
Joseph Akin ... cons. 5 shillings ... 400 acres on
Keith's Branch ... adjoining Richard Fox.
Witnesses:
    Abraham Martin   /s/ Henry (H) Cox
    Henry Delony
    John Maxcedan
Dated 15 June 1753   Recorded 3 July 1753

BLALOCK, Richard   Deed Book 3, Page 284

    Richard Blalock of Louisa County to Henry Ward of
Amelia County ... cons. 80 pounds ... 400 acres on east
side of Butchers Creek ... adjoining Hawkins.
Witnesses:
    Thos Nash
    Ben Harris   /s/ Richd Blalock
    James Claiborne
    Paul Carrington
Dated 29 June 1753   Recorded 3 July 1753

TABOR, John   Deed Book 3, Page 287

    John Tabor to Robert Wade of Halifax County ... cons.
180 pounds ... 200 acres on north side of Roanoke River
... adjoining Munford's line on Little Creek.
Witnesses:
    Memucan Hunt   /s/ John Tabor
    Mich^l Satterwhite
    Robert Wiles
Dated 3 July 1753   Recorded 3 July 1753

    Rachel Tabor, relict of William Tabor, deceased, relea-
sed her dower right in this land.

HYDE, John   Deed Book 3, Page 295

John Hyde to Samuel Bugg, Senr., ... cons. 20 pounds 195 acres on south side of the Roanoke River ..... adjoining Gunn and William Wood.
Witnesses: /s/ John Hyde
   None recorded
Dated 7 Aug. 1753 Recorded 7 Aug. 1753

HICKMAN, Joseph Deed Book 3, Page 304

Joseph Hickman of Brunswick County to William Riddle .. cons. 18 pounds ... 400 acres on north side of Roanoke River ... near the horseford.
Witnesses:
   C. Courtney
   Julius Nichols /s/ Jos. Hickman
   William Lindsey
   Henry Parrish
Dated 24 July 1753 Recorded 8 Aug. 1753

LANIER, Thomas Deed Book 3, Page 318

Thomas Lanier to John Hubbard of Cumberland County .... cons. 40 pounds ... (318 acres) land patented by Thomas Lanier 5 August 1751 ... on lower side of Butchers Creek ... adjoining Drury Stith and William Hill.
Witnesses:
   None recorded /s/ Thomas Lanier
Dated 7 Aug. 1753 Recorded 7 Aug. 1753

Elizabeth Lanier, wife of Thomas Lanier, being privately examined, released her dower right in land.

WEATHERFORD, William Deed Book 3, Page 335

William Weatherford to William Booker of Amelia County ... cons. 60 pounds ... 400 acres on a branch of Buckhorn Creek.
Witnesses: /s/ William Weatherford
   None recorded /s/ Sarah (X) Weatherford
Dated 6 November 1753 Recorded 6 Nov. 1753

Sarah, wife of William Weatherford, released dower.

SAFFOLD, William Deed Book 3, Page 338

William Saffold to Leonard Cheatham of Amelia County .. cons. 35 pounds ... 293 acres ... adjoining Edloe.
Witnesses:
   Philip Hobson /s/ Wm Saffold
   James Cheatham /s/ Temperance (I) Saffold
   William (X) Traylor
Dated 15 Oct. 1753 Recorded 6 Nov. 1753

Temperance Saffold, wife of William Saffold, released her dower right in this land.

MARABLE, William   Deed Book 3, Page 343

William Marable to Matthew Marable ... cons. 5 shillings ... 484 acres on a branch of Bluestone Creek ... part of William Marables Finneywood tract of land.
Witnesses:
    None recorded   /s/ William Marable
Dated 6 Feb. 1754   Recorded 6 Feb. 1754

MAJOR, Nicholas   Deed Book 3, Page 354

Nicholas Major to Jacob Coleson, alias Reignwater, ... cons. 5 pounds ... 100 acres on north side of Allens Creek ... adjoining lines of Thos. Clarke, deceased, Thomas Farrar and James Tucker.
Witnesses:
    Pink[n] Hawkins
    William Bevill   /s/ Nicholas Major
    John (X) King
    Winney (X) Coleson
Dated 5 Feb. 1753   Recorded 1 May 1753

BRESSIE, John   Deed Book 3, Page 336

John Bressie to David Bullock of St. Paul's Parish, Hanover County ... cons. 35 pounds ... 100 acres ..... adjoining Munford, Tabor and Thomas Wilkins.
Witnesses:
    Tho Satterwhite   /s/ John Bressie
    Edward Lewis
    John Satterwhite
Dated 24 July 1753   Recorded 4 Sept. 1753

Mary Bressie, wife of John Bressie, and Sarah Wilkins released dower right to this land.

HESTER, James   Deed Book 3, Page 364

James Hester of St. Martin's Parish, Louisa County to John Paisley of Fredericksville Parish, Louisa County ... cons. 57 pounds 16 shillings ... 289 acres .... adjoining William Davis.
Witnesses:
    Tho[s] Williamson   /s/ James Hester
    Gideon Crenshaw   /s/ Frances (X) Hester
    Henry Isbell
Dated 2 Oct. 1753   Recorded 2 Oct. 1753

Frances Hester, wife of James Hester, released her dower right in land.

BURKS, Charles   Deed Book 3, Page 373

    Charles Burks to Hutchins Burton and Henry Delony ...
cons. 65 pounds ... 400 acres on Miles and Dockery
Creeks ... adjoining John Cardwell, Dennis Larke, John
Patrick and David Dortch.
Witnesses:
    Feild Jefferson
    William Nichols   /s/ Charles Burks
    Mary Nichols
    James Coleman
    Wm Williams
Dated 23 March 1753   Recorded 2 Oct. 1753

AKIN, Joseph   Deed Book 3, Page 385

    Joseph Akin to James Cary, Junr., of Nansemond County
... cons. 12 pounds ... 400 acres on south side of the
Roanoke River ... land deeded by Henry Cox to Joseph
Akin.
Witnesses:
    Ben Harris   /s/ Joseph Akin
    Henry Delony
    Ch. Talbot
Dated 4 Sept. 1753   Recorded 6 Nov. 1753

SANDIFER, William   Deed Book 3, Page 388

    William Sandifer to Samuel Young ... cons. 100 pounds
... 323 acres on Allens Creek (land William Sandifer
lately bought from Charles Stewart).
Witnesses: /s/ William Sandifer
    None recorded
Dated 6 Nov. 1753   Recorded 6 Nov. 1753

    Elizabeth, wife of William Sandifer, released dower.

MITCHELL, Joab   Deed Book 3, Page 390

    Joab Mitchell to John Davis ... cons 107 pounds 10
shillings ... 240 acres on north side of Beaver Pond
Creek.
Witnesses:
    Tho. Hawkins   /s/ Joab (M) Mitchell
    Richd Palmer
    William Davis
    Matthew Tanner
Dated 1 Oct. 1753   Recorded 1 Oct. 1753

    Mary Mitchell, wife of Joab, released her dower right.

COLE, John   Deed Book 3, Page 403

John Cole to Lewis Wells, son of Thomas and Susannah
Wells ... for love and affection ... 56 acres ... where
Thomas Wells now lives.
Witnesses:
    Saml Bizwell   /s/ John (I) Cole
    Charles Burks
    John (I) Wells, Junr.
Dated 11 June 1753   Recorded 6 Nov. 1753

SMITH, Thomas   Deed Book 3, Page 406

Thomas Smith of Brunswick County to James Daniel of
Albemarle County ... cons. 30 pounds ... 100 acres on
south side of Roanoke River ... adjoining John Gilliam,
Thomas Stephens and John Maclin.
Witnesses:
    William Love   /s/ Thomas (S) Smith
    Andrew Throughten
    George Cane
Dated 21 July 1753   Recorded 1 Jan. 1754

LARK, Dennis   Deed Book 3, Page 428

Dennis Lark to Henry Delony ... cons. 130 pounds ....
200 acres on north side of Miles Creek.
Witnesses:
    John Speed
    George Baskervill   /s/ Dennis Lark
    Thos Moore
    Edward Carter
Dated 17 Nov. 1753   Recorded 5 Feb. 1754

MILLER, Hugh   Deed Book 3, Page 432

Hugh Miller of Prince George County to Benjamin
Ragsdale ... cons. 150 pounds ... 678 acres on both
sides of the middle fork of Bluestone Creek.
Witnesses:
    James Stark   Ben Harris   /s/ Hugh Miller
    John Baird   Jacob Royster
    William Royster
Dated 21 Dec. 1753   Recorded 5 Feb. 1754

MYRICK, Owen   Deed Book 3, Page 436

Owen Myrick of Southampton County to Dennis Lark ...
cons. 105 pounds ... 470 acres between Flatt Creek and
Parhams Creek.
Witnesses: /s/ Owen (O) Myrick
    Amos Timms Shelley
    Henry Delony   Joshua Mabry
    Thomas Wells   Thos (T) Roberts
Dated 12 Nov. 1753   Recorded 5 March 1754

WADE, Robert   Deed Book 3, Page 439

    Robert Wade of Halifax County to Peter Perear (Puryear)
    of Henrico County ... cons. 195 pounds ... 200 acres on
    north side of Roanoke River ... adjoining Munford.
    Witnesses:
        Robert Wade, Junr.
        Joseph Greer   /s/ Robert Wade
        Thos Moore
        Fran Bressie
    Dated 4 Dec. 1753   Recorded 5 March 1754

ROBERTSON, Richard   Deed Book 3, Page 446

    Richard Robertson to Henry Robertson ... cons. 20
    pounds ... 100 acres ... adjoining Joseph Rudd, Thomas
    Hawkins and John Maclin. Part of 215 acres that Rich-
    ard Robertson lately bought of John Robertson.
    Witnesses:
        John Twitty   /s/ Richard (X) Robertson
        Robert Wade, Junr.
        Tho. Hawkins
    Dated 2 April 1754   Recorded 2 April 1754

McNEIL, Daniel   Deed Book 3, Page 468

    Daniel McNeil to John Clark ... cons. 12 pounds 10
    shillings ... 100 acres on Grassy Creek ... land where
    John Clark now lives.
    Witnesses: /s/ Daniel McNeil
        None recorded
    Dated 8 Oct. 1753   Recorded 2 April 1754

STARK, William et als   Deed Book 3, Page 477

    William Stark, Gent., of Prince George County and
    Thomas Ravenscroft of Brunswick County to Frederick
    Jones of Dinwiddie County ... cons. 400 pounds ... for
    all interest due Stark & Ravenscroft in a tract of land
    patented by William Stark 26 April 1753 on both sides
    of Butchers Creek containing 1050 acres.
    Witnesses:
        John Eppes, Junr.
        James Hownam   /s/ Wm Stark
        Peter Jones
        Ed Powell
        Patrick Boyd   /s/ Thos Ravenscroft
        Tho. Eggleston
        John Jones
    Dated 21 Nov. 1753   Recorded 7 May 1754

GOODE, William   Deed Book 3, Page 487

William Goode to William Kay ... cons. 12 pounds ....
75 acres on a branch of Bluestone Creek ... adjoining
the Courthouse Road.
Witnesses:
    Robert Wade   /s/ Wm Goode
    Joseph Minor
    Ja^s Taylor
Dated 2 April 1754   Recorded 7 May 1754

Feeby, wife of William Goode, released her dower right.

TALLEY, Henry   Deed Book 3, Page 491

Henry Talley to Richard Newman of Dinwiddie County ...
cons. 110 pounds ... 450 acres on both sides of north
fork of Cox Creek.
Witnesses:
    T. Claiborne   /s/ Henry (H) Talley
    Francis (~~II~~) Ray
    Christopher Johnson
Dated 7 May 1754   Recorded 7 May 1754

Judith, wife of Henry Talley, released her dower right.

BURTON, Hutchins et als   Deed Book 3, Page 505

Hutchins Burton and Henry Delony to Charles Cousens of
Amelia County ... cons. 70 pounds ... 384 acres on
Miles Creek ... adjoining Dennis Lark.
Witnesses:
    Feild Jefferson   /s/ Hutchins Burton
    Reuben Searcy
    Samuel Bugg   /s/ Henry Delony
    Cornelius Cargill
Dated 4 June 1754   Recorded 4 June 1754

BARNES, John   Deed of Gift   Deed Book 3, Page 512

John Barnes of Cumberland County to James Barnes of
Cumberland County ... for love and affection for his
brother ... 704 acres on both sides of Williams fork of
the Horsepen Creek (a branch of Bluestone Creek).
Witnesses:
    Cornelius Cargill   /s/ John Barnes
    Luke Smith, Junr.
    Mich^l Satterwhite
Dated 4 June 1754   Recorded 4 June 1754

BARNES, John   Deed Book 3, Page 513

John Barnes of Cumberland County to Francis Barnes of
the same county ... cons. 5 shillings and love and
affection for his brother ... 2000 acres on Bluestone

Creek ... part of a patent.
Witnesses:
   Cornelius Cargill   /s/ John Barnes
   Luke Smith, Junr.
   Mich[l] Satterwhite
Dated 4 June 1754   Recorded 4 June 1754

TWITTY, John   Deed Book 3, Page 515

John Twitty to Joseph Boswell ... cons. 280 pounds ... 1493 acres on the south side of the Meherrin River and on both sides of Blackstones Creek ...adjoining Witton, Hatcher, Pettus and Poindexter.
Witnesses: /s/ John Twitty
   None recorded
Dated 2 July 1754   Recorded 2 July 1754

LARKE, Dennis   Deed Book 3, Page 524

Dennis Larke to James Hamner, Planter ... cons. 80 pounds 10 shillings ... 284 acres on Miles Creek .... adjoining Johnson.
Witnesses:
   Geo. Baskervill   /s/ Dennis Larke
   John Ballard
   W[m] Marsten Lightfoot
Dated 2 July 1754   Recorded 2 July 1754

MITCHELL, Robert   Deed Book 3, Page 527

Robert Mitchell to Francis Wagstaff of Henrico County ... cons. 350 pounds ... 490 acres on south side of the Roanoke River on Island Creek.
Witnesses:
   Reuben Searcy   /s/ Robert Mitchell
   Samuel Bugg, Senr.
   Samuel Bugg, Junr.
Dated 30 May 1754   Recorded 2 July 1754

Hannah, wife of Robert Mitchell, released her dower.

SCOTT, James   Deed Book 3, Page 532

James Scott of Amelia County to William White ... cons. 48 pounds ... 404 acres on both sides of Allens Creek.
Witnesses:
   David Halliburton   /s/ Ja[s] Scott
   Samuel Taylor   /s/ Grisel (R) Scott
   Henry Wade
Dated 9 June 1754   Recorded 2 July 1754

Grisel, wife of James Scott, released her dower right.

LIGHTFOOT, William Marston   Deed Book 3, Page 543

   William Marston Lightfoot to Henry Talley ... cons. 44
pounds ... 400 acres on Buckhorn Creek ... adjoining
Booker, Johnson and Cox.
Witnesses:
    John Weatherford   /s/ Wm Marston Lightfoot
    Charles Weatherford
    John (X) Morgan
Dated 12 Aug. 1754   Recorded 3 Sept. 1754

JONES Samuel   Deed Book 3, Page 547

   Samuel Jones to Joshua Mabry ... cons. 40 pounds ...
400 acres ... adjoining Lewis Tanner and Roberts. Land
patented by Samuel Jones 12 July 1750.
Witnesses:
    Feild Jefferson
    John Speed   /s/ Samuel Jones
    Richard W. Rogers
Dated 3 Sept. 1754   Recorded 3 Sept. 1754

LAND PROCESSIONING

The only extant early land processioning record for the area now Mecklenburg County, which had been made before the county was created in 1765, is that for the year 1759. This order for the processioning of land was entered at a meeting of the Vestry of Cumberland Parish on September 17, 1759.

This order divided the parish into twenty eight precincts of which nineteen were in the area now Mecklenburg County and nine in the present Lunenburg County. Only ten of the nineteen precessioning returns for Mecklenburg have been found.

The processioners for the nineteen precincts are listed in the following pages. The four precincts south of the Roanoke River in Mecklenburg County are easily identified. They were: East of Cotton Creek; from Cotton Creek to Nutbush Creek; Nutbush Creek to Grassy Creek; and from Grassy Creek to Aarons Creek now the Halifax County boundary line. The area comprised in some of the precincts is not now readily identified as reference is primarily to roads no longer in existence.

Cumberland Parish in 1759 was composed of the area now Lunenburg and Mecklenburg Counties. Antrim Parish in Halifax County had been formed in 1752, Russel Parish covering most of Bedford County in 1754 and Cornwall Parish in Charlotte County in 1757.

An "Act to divide Brunswick County" was passed on March 26, 1745. Cumberland Parish was created under this act and was co-extensive with Lunenburg County as established by the act.

Lunenburg County at the time comprised all of the territory now in the counties of Lunenburg, Mecklenburg, Charlotte, Halifax, Pittsylvania, Henry, Patrick and Franklin, the greater part of Bedford and Campbell, and a part of the present county of Appomattox.

Cumberland Parish was divided again in 1761. This division created St. James Parish which became Mecklenburg County in 1764. All of the early St. James Parish records have been lost. The Register for Cumberland Parish has been lost or destroyed also.

The Register as well as the Vestry Book, by law, were required to be kept by the Clerk of the Vestry, but in actual practice the minister kept the Register.

PROCESSIONING PRECINCTS - 1759

Precinct	Boundary of Precinct	Processioners Named
No. 1	Roanoke River-Brunswick Line-Fox's Road-Pennington's Old Road	Drury Malone Thomas Malone
No. 2	Brunswick Line-Meherrin River-Duke's Old Road to Mize's Ford-Pennington's Old Road	John Pennington George Vaughan John Ezell William Pennell
No. 3	Roanoke River-Miles Creek-Pennington's Old Road-Fox's Road	Dennis Larke Joshua Mabry Amos Timms, Junr.
No. 4	Mize's Ford Road-Duke's Old Road-Pennington's Old Road	David Dortch Howell Collier William Lucas Robert Larke
No. 5	Mize's Ford Road-Miles Creek-Mountain Creek Road	James Hamner William Holmes James Lett
No. 6	Miles Creek-Roanoke River-Cox Creek-Mountain Creek Road	Randolph Bracey John Speed Jacob Bugg George Baskervill John Ballard Henry Delony
No. 7	Cox Creek-Allens Creek-Mountain Creek Road	John Humphreys John Clark Thomas Farrar Hugh Norvell
No. 8	Allens Creek-Roanoke River-Taylor's Ferry Road	Samuel Bugg Samuel Young Isaac Mitchell Joseph Eastland James Coleman Stephan Mallett
No. 9	Roanoke River-County Line-Cotten Creek	Robert Alexander Richard Fox William Davis
No. 10	Cotten Creek-County Line Nutbush Creek-Roanoke River	George Farrar Peter Feild Jefferson

| No. 10 | Cont'd | Edmund Bugg |
| | | Anselm Bugg |

No. 11	Meherrin River-Mountain Creek Road-Buckhorn Creek	James Arnold
		Reuben Vaughan
		Ephraim Andrews

No. 12	Buckhorn Creek-Mountain Creek Road-Boswell's Road-Meherrin River	Joseph Gill
		John Thompson
		Edward Goode

No. 20	Butchers Creek-Mize's Ford Road-Allens Creek Witton's Road	Joseph Freeman
		Christopher Hudson
		John Hyde

No. 21	Meherrin River-Boswell's Road-Witton's Road-Court House-Marable's Road-Parish Line (Cornwall)	Guy Smith
		John Cox, Junr.
		Joseph Boswell

No. 22	Mouth of Butchers Creek-Bluestone Creek-Court House-Witton's Road-Allens Creek	Richard Palmer
		Thomas Anderson
		Thomas Carleton

No. 23	Bluestone Creek-Roanoke River-Parish Line	William Harris (F)
		Stephan Evans
		William Harris (P)

No. 24	Nutbush Creek-County Line-Grassy Creek-Roanoke River	John Bracey
		James Lewis
		Nathaniel Robertson

No. 25	Grassy Creek-County Line-Aarons Creek-Roanoke River	Richard Yancey
		William Culbreath
		William Royster
		Thomas Wiles
		Peter Overby
		Nicholas Overby

No. 28	Taylor's Ferry Road-Roanoke River-Butchers Creek-Mize's Ford Road	Tignal Jones
		Francis Jones
		Zachariah Baker

Note: William Harris (F) - Lived on Finneywood Creek

William Harris (P) - Lived on Peckerwood Creek

RETURNS OF LAND PROCESSIONING

Processioned under Vestry Order of September 17, 1759

Land Owner	Present at Processioning

Precinct 1 - Processioners: Drury Malone-Thomas Malone

BARTLETT, William	John Lankford
	John Boseman
BOSEMAN, John	John Lankford
	George Lankford
CLEATON, William	John Lankford
	John Cleaton
DIXON, Thomas	Robert Hudson
	Ephraim Hudson
EPPS, Edward	John Lankford
	William Cleaton
LANKFORD, George	Francis Rainey
	John Boseman
LANKFORD, John	George Lankford
MALONE, Drury	Isham Malone
MALONE, Isham	Joel Wingfield
	Thomas Nance
MALONE, Thomas	Joel Wingfield
	Thomas Nance
NANCE, Daniel	Joel Wingfield
	Thomas Malone
NANCE, William	William Nance
PARHAM, William	Robert Hudson
	Ephraim Hudson
RAINEY, Francis	John Lankford
	George Lankford

Precinct 3 - Processioners: Joshua Mabry-Dennis Larke
Amos Timm, Jr.

BELL, William	William Bell
BENNETT, Joseph	Joseph Bennett
BLANTON, William	William Blanton
	Humphrey Hewey
BUGG, Sherwood	Sherwood Bugg
	John Patrick
COURTNEY, Clack	Clack Courtney
	Thomas Taylor, Sr
DAVIS, Capt. William	William Rottenberry
	Humphrey Hewey
EVANS, Charles	Labon Wright

EVANS, Dick	Dick Evans
BROOKS, Robert	Samuel Rottenberry
	John Rottenberry
HENDRICK, John	William Davis
	Humphry Hewey
HEWEY, Humphry	John Rottenberry
	William Blanton
JONES, Robert, Junr.	Reuben Morgan
	William Head
LANGLEY, Robert	Dick Evans
MABRY, Joshua	William Blanton
MANNING, Samuel	John Manning
MORGAN, Reuben	Labon Wright
McLIN, John	William Pool
	John Watson
McLIN, Thomas	Thomas McLin
PATRICK, John	Sherwood Bugg
POOL, William, Senr.	Clack Courtney
	Adam Pool
ROBERTSON, John	John Sargent
	Adam Pool
TANNER, Lucias	Thomas Tanner
TANNER, Thomas	Lucias Tanner
TAYLOR, Thomas, Senr.	William Pool, Senr.
	John Watson
TAYLOR, Thomas, Junr.	Thomas Taylor, Senr.
	Clack Courtney
TIMMS, Amos	Amos Timms
WATSON, John	William Pool, Senr.
	Thomas Taylor
WRIGHT, Labon	Philip Morgan
	Thomas Roberts

Precinct 4   Processioners: David Dortch-Howell Collier
                             William Lucas-Robert Larke

CAMPBELL, Robert	Robert Campbell
COLLIER, Howell	Howell Collier
COLLIER, Nathaniel	Howell Collier

COZENS, Charles	Charles Cozens
DORTCH, David	David Dortch James Hamner
DUKE, Taylor	Taylor Duke
LARKE, Dennis	Dennis Larke
LARKE, Robert	Robert Larke
LUCAS, Samuel	Dennis Larke
LUCAS, William	William Lucas
WARD, Wade	Wade Ward

Precinct 5   Processioners: James Hamner-William Holmes
                              James Lett

BAIRD, Benjamin	Nathaniel Cook James Ferrell
BUTLER, Hannah	John Watson, Senr.
COOK, Nathaniel	Nathaniel Cook
DELONY, Henry	William Holmes Isaac Holmes
HAMNER, James	William Holmes Isaac Holmes
HARWELL, James, Senr.	James Harwell, Junr.
HOLMES, Samuel	Isaac Holmes
LETT, Francis	John Watson, Senr.
LETT, James, Senr.	Jacob Matthews Isham Lett
LETT, James, Junr.	John Lett
LETT, John	Francis Lett John Watson
WATSON, John, Senr.	John Watson, Senr.
WHITTEMORE, Abraham	John Whittemore
WHITTEMORE, William	Francis Lett

Precinct 6   Processioners: George Baskervill-John Speed
                              Henry Delony-John Ballard
                              Jacob Bugg

ADAMS, Thomas	Joseph Gray Bennett Holloway
BALLARD, John	William Williams

BASKERVILL, George	Bennett Holloway
	Hutchins Burton
BRACEY, Randolph	
BUGG, Jacob	John Earl
BURTON, Hutchins	John Jefferson
CORDELL, Bryant	Thomas Adams
	James Ferrell
COZENS, Robert	James Ferrell
	Joseph Gray
DELONY, Henry	James Ferrell
	Isaac Holmes
EARL, John	John Earl
EDMUNDSON, Thomas	
FERRELL, James	James Ferrell
	John Earl
HIGHTOWER, John	
HOLLOWAY, Bennett	George Jefferson
JEFFERSON, Feild	George Jefferson
LINDSEY, William	Thomas Adams
	Henry Talley
MORGAN, Reuben	Reuben Morgan
NEWMAN, Richard	Henry Talley
	Spettle Pully
PARRISH, Peter	Thomas Adams
	James Ferrell
RUFFIN, John	Joseph Gray
	Spettle Pully
RUFFIN, Robert	Thomas Adams
	Peter Parrish
SPEED, John	Bennett Holloway
	James Ferrell
WILLIAMS, William	Bennett Holloway

PRECINCT 10 - Processioners: George Farrar-Anselm Bugg
Edmund Bugg

BUGG, Anselm	Samuel Hopkins
BUGG, Edmund	Anselm Bugg
	Edmund Bugg
BIRTCHETT, Joseph	Joseph Birtchett
COCKE, James	Samuel Hopkins

CUNNINGHAM, James	Thomas Adams
HOPKINS, Samuel	Samuel Hopkins
HOWARD, Francis	Francis Howard
HOWARD, William	William Howard
JOHNSON, Daniel	Thomas Adams
STEPHENS, Mary	Thomas Adams

Precinct 12 - Processioners: Edward Goode-Joseph Gill
John Thompson

BOOKER, Richard	John Thompson
COLEMAN, Cluverius	Cluverius Coleman William McDowell
GILL, Joseph	Peter Gill
GOODE, Edward	Edward Goode
GREER, Joseph	Joseph Greer
HUMPHREYS, John	John Humphreys Abraham Colson
PLEASANT, John	John Childress
TALLEY, Henry	Abraham Talley
WEATHERFORD, John	William Weatherford
YOUNGHUSBAND, Isaac	Peter Gill

Precinct 20 - Precessioners: Christopher Hudson
Joseph Freeman-John Hyde

BEVILL, Edward	Edward Bevill John White
BOSWELL, Joseph	
BURWELL, Col. Lewis	Thomas Carleton, Overseer
BURWELL, Col. Lewis	John Jeffries, Overseer Richard Swepson
CROWDER, Abraham	Abraham Crowder
DRAPER, Solomon	Solomon Draper
EDWARDS, William	Joseph Freeman Christopher Hudson
FREEMAN, Joseph	Joseph Freeman

HUBBARD, John	John Hubbard
	Thomas Carleton
HUDSON, Christopher	James Tucker
HUGHES, Anthony	Anthony Hughes
HYDE, John	James Tucker
JONES, Capt. Peter	Hugh Franklin
JONES, William	
PALMER, Pirmenas	Pirmenas Palmer
ROYAL, Sarah	John Royal
STITH, Richard	
TUCKER, James	James Tucker
WHITE, John	John White
	Edward Bevill

<u>Precinct 22</u> - Processioners: Thomas Anderson-Richard Palmer-Thomas Carleton

ALIBURTON, David	John Jeffries
	Richard Swepson
AVERY, James	Matthew Tanner
r	Edward Hogan
AVERY, Ophans of Thomas	Matthew Tanner
	Edward Hogan
BRACEY, Francis	George Bruce
	Richard Long
BRUCE, George	William Donithon
BULLOCK, David	Edward Lewis
	James Wilkins
EASTER, Robert	Matthew Tanner
	Edward Hogan
EVANS, Stephen	John Jeffries
	Richard Swepson
DONITHON, William	William Donithon
FOLIO, Luke	Valentine Mullins
	Riah Tabor
HARRIS, William	Stephen Evans
	John Camp
HAWKINS, Orphans of Thomas	Benjamin Pulliam
	Richard Long
HILL, William	John Jeffries
	Richard Russell
LEWIS, Edward	Edward Lewis

MAYES, Orphans of John	Matthew Tanner
	Edward Hogan
LIDDERDAL, Orphans of Wm.	Edward Lewis
	James Wilkins
MULLINS, Valentine	Matthew Tanner
	Edward Hogan
MUNFORD, Robert	Valentine Mullins
	Riah Tabor
MURRAY, John	Stephen Evans
	John Camp
PALMER, Richard	James Wilkins
PURCER, John	Valentine Mullins
	Riah Tabor
PURCER, Peter	James Wilkins
SATTERWHITE, Thomas	James Wilkins
TABOR, Rachel	Valentine Mullins
	Riah Tabor
TABOR, Orphans of William	George Bruce
	Benjamin Pulliam
TANNER, Matthew	Matthew Tanner
	William Tate, Jr.
TATE, Orphans of William	Matthew Tanner
	William Tate, Jr.
WARD, Henry	Matthew Tanner
	Edward Hogan
WAGSTAFF, Basil	William Donithon
WILKINS, James	James Wilkins
	Edward Lewis
WILKINS, John	Valentine Mullins
WILKINS, Mary Ann	Valentine Mullins
	Riah Tabor

Note: There was no attendance at the processioning where no name is listed opposite the name of the landowner.

It is regretable that no other land processioning records have been preserved before 1765.

The list of tithables taken by Edmund Taylor in St. James Parish, Lunenburg County, for the year 1764.

Names:	Tithes	Land
ADAMS, David		
William Solomon	1	200 Acres
ADAMS, Thomas		
William Adams	3	400 "
AKIN, Joseph		
Thomas Craig		
Thomas Langley	4	280 "
AKIN, Peter		
Charles Piron	4	
ALEXANDER, Robert	10	450 "
ALLGOOD, Ishmael		
Edward Allgood	2	
ALLGOOD, John	1	
ANDERSON, Thomas		
Aaron George	12	1050 "
ARMISTEAD, John, Junr.		
Michael Thompson		
Samuel Traylor	4	1000 "
ARNOLD, James, Junr.	1	540 "
BAILEY, Robert		390 "
BAKER, Zachariah	3	300 "
BARLEY, William	1	400 "
BASKERVILL, George		
John Baskervill	9	520 "
BATES, John	2	168 "
BENNETT, Absolem	1	
BIDDEY, Edward	4	300 "
BLACK, William (Quarters)		
James Whitlock	7	250 "
BLACKWELDER, William	1	
BLAND, Marriott (Constable)		200 "
BLANTON, George	3	
" William	4	300 "
BIRTCHETT, Joseph	2	413 "
BOWEN, David	1	75 "
" Jesse	1	
" Jesse	1	
" Robert	1	125 "
BOZEMAN, John	2	290 "
BRAME, Richins (Quarters)		
James Brame	3	400 "
BREWER, Reese	1	
BROOKS, Elisha	4	200 "
BROOKS, George		
Thomas Brooks	2	
BROOKS, Robert	4	500 "
BROWN, Fadias	1	

BROWN, Henry		
Alexander Morson	2	150 Acres
BROWN, Henry, Junr.	1	150 "
" James	1	
" William	1	
BROWN, William, Senr.		
Charles Brown	2	
BROWN, William, Junr.	1	
BUCHANAN, Nevill	1	
BUGG, Anselm		
George Tureman	5	220 "
BUGG, Edmund	7	120 "
" John	1	
BUGG, Samuel		
Jesse Bugg	6	450 "
BUGG, Sherwood		
Robert Lark		
Thomas Russell	9	
BURNS, Equator	2	399 "
BURTON, Hutchins		
John Burton		
Thomas Brandon		
Robert Corn		
William Head	14	1100 "
BURTON, James	1	
" Josiah	1	
BUSBY, Henry	1	270 "
CAMP, John		
John Hudson (Overseer)	4	490 "
CARMICHAEL, Duncan	1	
CARROLL, Dennis	1	
" Elias	1	
CAVINESS, Henry		
Thomas Caviness		
William Caviness	3	230 "
CAIN, William	1	
CHAMBERLAIN, Thomas		
Elijah Hughes	4	424 "
CHAVOUS, Henry	1	
CHAVOUS, Jacob		
James Chavous	2	100 "
CHILDRESS, John	1	
CLARK, Archibald	1	200 "
" Francis	1	150 "
" James	2	350 "
" Jesse	2	400 "
" John	3	548 "
" John (Grassy Creek)	2	100 "
CLEATON, John	1	
CLEATON, William		
William Cleaton, Junr.	2	375 "

Name		Acres
COCKE, William	5	430 Acres
COLEMAN, Benedict		
Ben Coleman	2	
COLEMAN, Christopher	2	
COLEMAN, James		
William Coleman		
John Leach	6	650 "
COLEMAN, Robert		
Phil Coleman		
Abner Coleman	5	368 "
COLLIER, Howell		
William Ladd	5	1340 "
COOK, John Lett	1	400 "
" Nathaniel	1	116 "
COOK, Reuben		
Nathaniel	2	
COPE, Thomas	1	
CROWDER, Joshua	1	
" Robert	1	
CULBREATH, Edward	2	600 "
" John	1	500 "
CULBREATH, Mary		
Joseph Culbreath	1	200 "
CULBREATH, Peter	2	451 "
CULBREATH, William		
William Culbreath, Junr.	5	671 "
CUNNINGHAM, William	1	
DANIEL, Josiah	5	400 "
DAVIS, Baxter (Estate)		
John Fain	8	827 "
DAVIS, Baxter, Junr.		
William Talbert	7	240 "
DAVIS, Edward	1	
DAVIS, Edward (Estate)		
Edward Davis, Junr.		
Joel Fain	5	150 "
DAVIS, John		
Joseph Crews	7	600 "
DAVIS, Capt. William		
James Shuffly		
William Stroud	13	4374 "
DIXON, Judith		
Peter Thomas	5	300 "
DONALD, Alexander		
Nathaniel Adams	2	
DOUGLAS, John	1	
DOUGLAS, William		
George Douglas	3	290 "
DRAPER, Joshua		
Martin Hammond	2	213 "
DUKE, John Taylor	3	370

EARL, John		
George Holloway		
James Holloway	5	100 Acres
EASTER, John	3	100 "
EDMONDS, Thomas	1	
EDMUNDSON, Richard	1	150 "
ELLIS, Abraham	1	100 "
ELLIS, James		
John Robinson	2	170 "
EVANS, Dick	1	
" Thomas	1	
FANN, William		
Jesse Fann	3	290 "
FARRAR, Feild	2	
" William	1	450 "
FEAGIN, Edward		
Richard Green	2	157 "
FERRELL, James		
Ephraim Ferrell	4	370 "
FOWLER, John	2	
" Alexander, Junr.	1	
FLINN, James	1	400 "
FLOYD, Richard	1	
FOX, Richard		
Jacob Fox	12	
FOX, William	1	
FRAIL, John	1	
" Patrick		200 "
FRANKLIN, Owen		
Jesse Chandler	5	200 "
GILES, Edward		
Edward Epps	2	96 "
GILES, John		
Samuel Hughes		
Elias Scott		
Elias Wildman	4	
GILL, William		
Joseph Gill	3	508 "
GLADDIN, Richard		
John Glass	2	297 "
GLASSCOCK, John	1	180 "
GLEBE LAND (St. James Parish)		400 "
GOLD, Daniel	1	145 "
GOODE, John		
John Gaines	8	225 "
GRAVES, Mary		
Elijah Graves	10	174 "
GREEN, Frederick	1	157 "
GREEN, John		
Gardiner Green	2	157 "
GREEN, Stephen	1	157 "

GRIFFIN, James	1	Acres
" John	1	200 "
" William	1	300 "
GUNSTON, George	1	
HARGROVE, James	1	
HARRIS, Benjamin (Quarters)		
Isaac Bryant	7	1017 "
HARRIS, Solomom	1	
HARWOOD, Col. William (Quarters)		
Henry Street		
Richard Street	26	1989 "
HATSELL, Stephen	1	
" William (Hatchell)	1	400 "
HAWKS, Isaac	1	
HAYES, John		
John Hayes, Junr.	2	650 "
HAZLEWOOD, Daniel	5	440 "
HESTER, Abraham		
James Hester	12	816 "
HEWEY, James	1	
" John	2	
HILL, William (Quarters)	4	945 "
HIX, Amos		
James Hix	5	450 "
HOGAN, Edward (Quarters)		
Evan Owen	2	145 "
HOLLOWAY, William	1	340 "
HOLMES, Isaac		
William Butler	2	150 "
HOLMES, Samuel	2	100 "
" Samuel, Junr.	1	150 "
" William	1	175
HOMES, Charles	2	200 "
HOOD, Robert	1	
HOPKINS, Samuel	8	904 "
HOWARD, Henry	9	1315 "
HUDSON, Christopher		
Christopher Hudson, Junr.	5	550 "
HUDSON, Ephraim	1	
" Richard		50 "
HUDSON, Robert		
William Hudson	3	200 "
HUNTER, James		
Isaac Austin	2	
HUSKY, William	1	50 "
JACKSON, Henry	1	400 "
" John	1	
JEFFRIES, John		
Swepson Jeffries	6	626 "
JOHNSON, Daniel		
Jacob Lantor	4	200 "

JOHNSON, John	1	180	Acres
" Michael	1	400	"
JONES, Harwood (Quarters)			
Tignal Jones, Junr.	2	750	"
JONES, John	3	220	"
" Peter	2		
JONES, Peter (Quarters)			
Richard Russell	4	1050	"
JONES, Robert, Esquire			
John Anderson	10	2004	"
JONES, Stephen	1	420	"
" Tabitha	2	200	"
" Tignal, Senr.	5	565	"
" William	1	171	"
JONES, William			
Jeremiah Russell	4	665	"
Jones, Vinckler	1		
JUSTICE, John	1		
KENDRICK, John			
James Morrison	3	220	"
KIDD, Lewis	1		
KIRK, James	1	75	"
" Stephen	1		
KITCHEN, John	1		
LADD, John	1		
" Joseph	1	150	"
" Thomas	1	100	"
LAMBERT, James	1	200	"
" Jervis	1	100	"
" John	1		
" Joseph	1		
LAMBERT, Cleaton	1	100	"
" Hugh	1		
" Joseph	1		
" William	1		
LANIER, John	1		
LANKFORD, John	1	200	"
LANKFORD, Henry			
John Lankford	2		
LARK, Dennis			
John Lark	4	510	"
LEE, Walter (Leigh)	4		
LETT, James	1		
" John	1		
LEWIS, Howell (Quarters)			
Zachariah Baughan	5	210	"
LEWIS, James (Estate)			
James Holloway	15	1353	"
LONG, Richard			
George Long	2		

LUCAS, William		
Thomas Beddingfield	5	450 Acres
LYNCH, John		
Josiah Glass		
Thomas Glass		
William Glass		
William Rainey	5	
MABRY, Joshua		
Joshua Mabry, Junr.	9	750 "
MALLETT, Stephen	6	489 "
MALONE, Drury	9	1250 "
" Isham	1	410 "
" John	1	
" Phillip	1	
" Thomas	3	705 "
MANGUM, John	1	
MANNING, Samuel		
John Samuel	6	485 "
MARABLE, William	2	
MASON, Richard	1	164 "
MAYNARD, John	2	
MAYNARD, Nicholas		
Henry Mitchell	6	815 "
MEALER, Ann		
Matthew Mealer	2	400 "
MICHAUX, Jacob, Junr.		
Benjamin Pulliam		
Abraham Searcy	4	1069 "
MILLER, Brice		
Robin Newton	2	190 "
MITCHELL, Jacob	5	457 "
MOORE, George	2	100 "
" Thomas	4	300 "
MOORE, Thomas, Junr.		
Richard Johnson	6	
MORGAN, Reuben	4	520 "
MULLINS, Richard	1	
" Valentine	1	
MUNFORD, Robert, Esquire		
Drury Smith	34	2002 "
MURPHEY, William		
William Murphey, Junr.	2	460 "
MUSAMPE, George		
William Musampe	2	
McCARTY, John	1	
McDANIEL, Edward	2	110 "
McNEIL, Daniel	2	317 "
NEWTON, Henry	1	
" John, Senr.	1	
" John, Junr.	1	

NEWTON, William	1	158 Acres
NIPPER, John, Junr.	1	
NORMENT, William		
John Johns	4	220 "
NORRELL, Mary	1	
" Thomas	2	333 "
OVERBY, Nicholas	3	100 "
OVERBY, Peter (Constable)		
Obadiah Overby	1	182 "
PALMORE, Edward (Palmer)	3	400 "
PANKEY, John		
Stephen Pankey	2	225 "
PATRICK, John		300 "
PEASLEY, The Rev. William	1	
PENNINGTON, James	3	400 "
" John George	2	227 "
PERRY, William	1	200 "
PHILLIPS, Thomas	1	
PINSON, Aaron	1	478 "
" John	1	
PINSON, Thomas		
Moses Grigg	2	150 "
POOL, Adam		
William Taylor	2	50 "
POOL, William	2	100 "
" William, Junr.	1	200 "
POWELL, John		
Richard Powell	2	
PULLIAM, Benjamin		340 "
PURYEAR, John	7	570 "
PURYEAR, John, Junr.		
Thomas Akin	6	
RAINEY, Francis	4	100 "
RAGSDALE, William	3	300 "
RICHARDSON, William		
William Brown	2	
ROBERTS, James	1	
" Thomas	1	366 "
" Thomas (Junr.)	1	
ROBERTSON, Richard	2	
ROBINSON, Henry	1	
" John	1	400 "
" John	1	404 "
" Nathaniel (Constable)		
" William	2	318 "
ROCKETT, Richard (Lockett ?)	6	400 "
ROTTENBERRY, John		
Samuel Rottenberry	2	
ROYAL, John	1	

		Acres
ROYSTER, Jacob		
Robert Scott	4	
ROYSTER, William	4	370 "
RUDD, Joseph	5	182 "
RUFFIN, Robert (Quarters)		
James Watson	11	1914 "
RUSSELL, Richard (Quarters)	3	400 "
SALLE', Isaac	3	400 "
SANDIFER, Elizabeth		
Phillip Sandifer	3	
SANDIFER, James		
William Sandifer	3	200 "
SANDIFER, William		
William Sandifer, Junr.	3	200 "
SATTERWHITE, Thomas		
Bartlett Satterwhite	7	400 "
SAUNDERS, Meriwether	1	
SCOTT, Robert		120 "
SEATON, William	1	170 "
SERGEANT, John	1	300 "
SHOCKLEY, David	1	82 "
SIZEMORE, John	1	
" William	1	400 "
SMITH, Guy	4	380 "
SMITH, Obadiah (Quarters)		
William Martin	6	427 "
SPEED, John, Junr.	4	384 "
STEVENS, John	1	
" Mary		400 "
" Thomas	1	
SWEPSON, Richard		
James Toney	6	580 "
TANNER, Lewis	1	177 "
" Matthew	3	198 "
" Thomas	2	377 "
TATE, William	1	154 "
TAYLOR, Edmund	20	2400 "
" Goodwyn	2	
" James	1	
" John	1	
" Thomas	4	1120 "
" Thomas, Junr.	3	150 "
" William	1	
THOMASON, James		
John Thomason	2	290 "
THOMPSON, John Farley		
John Thompson	7	929 "
THOMPSON, Richard	1	600 "
TUCKER, James		
Gardiner Tucker	4	642 "

VAUGHAN, George		1	200 Acres
" James			200 "
VAUGHAN, Reuben			
James Vaughan			
William Cooper			
Samuel Oldham		7	400 "
VAUGHAN, William			
James Vaughan			
John Vaughan		5	400 "
WAGSTAFF, Bazell		5	150 "
WARD, Henry (Quarters)			
Edward Hogan		7	755 "
WATSON, Henry			
Burwell Watson			
George Watson		3	
WATSON, William		1	
WHITE, George			
Thomas Caviness			
George Duncan			
Samuel Hazelrig		5	374 "
WHITE, James		1	
WILES, Robert		1	353 "
" Thomas		1	102 "
WHITTEMORE, Abraham		2	240 "
John Whittemore		4	800 "
WILKINS, James		1	124 "
WILLIAMSON, John		2	150 "
WILLIS, Richard			300 "
WILLS, Matthew		2	
" Richard Wills		1	
WILSON, Elimileck		2	345 "
" Samuel		1	
" William		1	191 "
WOOD, Richard		1	
" Richard, Junr.			200 "
WOODWARD, William		3	270 "
WOOTEN, Samuel		3	460 "
WRIGHT, Laban			
YATES, William		1	100 "
YOUNG, Samuel		7	1323 "

The list of tithables taken by Edmund Taylor in St. James Parish, Lunenburg County, for year 1764 - List No. 2.

Names:	Tithes	Land
ABBOTT, George	2	Acres
ALEXANDER, Robert	12	
AVERY, James		
Henry Avery	2	100 "
BACON, Nathaniel		
John Potter		
John Robinson	18	2196 "
BILBO, James	1	560 "
BLANTON, James (Constable)	3	
BOWLES, Jeremiah		400 "
BOYD, Alexander		
James Speed	2	
BRESSIE, Elizabeth		
William Bressie	5	204 "
BUGG, Jesse		200 "
CHANDLER, James	1	497 "
CHANDLER, Joel		
Samuel Chandler	5	250 "
CROWDER, James	1	100 "
CROWDER, Stephen	1	
CUNNINGHAM, Jonathon	1	250 "
DODSON, Joseph	1	382 "
EASLEY, William		
William Renn	3	325 "
EASTLAND, Joseph		
William Eastland	2	
EASTLAND, Thomas	1	380 "
EVANS, Charles	1	60 "
" Major	1	
FARRAR, John		
George Farrar	5	125 "
FEAGIN, Henry	1	189 "
FEILD, Theophilus (Quarters)		
John Bagwell	4	4808 "
FOWLER, Alexander	5	
" William	1	
GLASS, Samuel	1	
GREGORY, Isaac	1	50 "
HARRISON, Benjamin	3	262 "
HOLMES, George	1	

Name		Acres
HUDGINS, Josiah	1	
JEFFERSON, George		
William Morgan		
William Howard	9	965 "
JEFFERSON, Feild		1224 "
" Peter Feild	6	
" John	10	194 "
JOHNSON, John	1	200 "
JONES, Vinkler	7	
KING, George		
William King	2	300 "
KING, Henry	1	400 "
" John	1	100 "
KING, William		
Overby King	2	116 "
LACKS, Henry (Lax)	1	
LEWIS, Edward	5	442 "
LOCKLAIN, Randolph	1	
MILES, George	1	200 "
MITCHELL, Daniel		
Matthew Avery	4	
MITCHELL, Isaac	4	463 "
MUNROE, John		
Richard Stevens	2	
PALMORE, John (Palmer)	1	300 "
POPE, John		
Peter Williams	2	50 "
PULLY, Spettle	2	200 "
ROWLAND, Robert	3	100 "
STRANGE, Mitchell	1	
TALLEY, David	1	
TARRY, Samuel		
Robert Crawley		
William Townsend	27	1000 "
TUCKER, Isham	1	
WHITE, John	1	
" William, Senr.	1	400 "
WILLIS, William	1	
YANCEY, Richard		
Charles Yancey	3	485 "

The list of tithables taken by Richard Witton, Gent., in
St. James Parish, Lunenburg County, for the year 1764.

Names:		Tithes	Land
ADAMS, John		1	100 Acres
AKIN, Lewis		1	100 "
ANDERSON, James		1	
ANDREWS, Eleazar		1	280 "
" Ephraim		1	280 "
" John		1	280 "
" William		1	413 "
ARNOLD, James, Senr.			
Joseph Arnold		7	770 "
BAIRD, John Batte		7	514 "
BALLARD, John			
Edmund Ballard			
William Ballard		7	403 "
BENNETT, Joseph		3	353 "
BEVILL, Edward		3	550 "
" Luke		1	
BOND, Richard		1	33 "
BOOKER, Richard		6	492 "
BOSWELL, Joseph			
William Edens		13	1280 "
BOSWELL, Samuel		1	
BROOKS, Richard		1	400 "
" Thomas		1	200 "
BROWN, Abram		2	200 "
" George (Constable)		1	
" Thomas		3	260 "
" Thomas		3	
BUGG, Jacob			
Philip Morgan			
John Ramsey		9	700 "
BULLOCK, David		1	700 "
BURTON, AAbram			
William Palmer, Junr.		3	350 "
BURTON, Robert			
John Griggs		3	
BURWELL, Armistead (Estate)			
John Oliver (Overseer)	10		
George Tureman (Overseer)	9		
John Westbrook (Overseer)	15	34	3003 "
BURWELL, Col. Lewis			
Thomas Carleton (Overseer)	8		
Hugh Franklin (Overseer)	18		
John Jeffries, Jr. (Overseer)	17	43	10866 "
BUSH, John			
Thomas Draper		4	200 "
CAMPBELL, James		1	

CARDIN, John	1	250 Acres
CARLETON, Thomas		
Anthony Kitchen	6	412 "
CHAMBERLAIN, Thomas	1	200 "
CHANDLER, William	1	375 "
CHRISTOPHER, David		
John Stembridge	5	595 "
CHRISTOPHER, Robert	1	600 "
CONNELL, Robert	2	340 "
CORDELL, Bryant		100 "
COX, Frederick	3	338 "
" John, Senr.	7	640 "
" John, Junr.	4	752 "
COLLEY, Edward	1	567 "
COX, John, Senr.		
Bolling Cox		
Thomas Cox	3	235 "
COX, John, Junr.	1	
" William	1	
CROWDER, Jeremiah		
Batt. Crowder	4	397 "
DARDEN, David	1	190 "
DELONY, Henry		
Henry King		
John Thompson	12	1350 "
DOWSING, William	3	496 "
DORTCH, David		
Noah Dortch		
Henry Speed	6	
DUKE, Henry	1	
DUNMAN, Joseph		100 "
EASTER, James	2	
EDWARDS, Nathaniel		
John Edwards	2	
ELAM, Joel	6	70 "
ERSKINE, Thomas		
John McCutcheon		
Alexander McNabb		
Thomas Robertson	7	831 "
ESTES, Benjamin	2	
EVANS, Morris	1	
" Robert	1	425 "
EVANS, Stephen, Senr.		
William Evans		
Warner Tucker	8	2208 "
EVANS, Stephen, Junr.	1	1241 "
" Thomas	2	
EZELL, James	1	
EZELL, John		
John Ezell, Junr.	5	300 "
EZELL, Mitchell	1	100 "

Name		Acres
EZELL, William	1	300 Acres
FARMER, Lodowick		
Elijah Baker (Overseer)	4	
FARRAR, Thomas	2	
FLEMING, Col. John	4	
FLOYD, Richard	1	
FLYNN, John	2	181 "
FREEMAN, John	2	
FREEMAN, Joseph		
William Clift	7	820 "
GARNER, Conaway	1	400 "
GOODE, Edward		
Joseph Goode	7	1780 "
GORRE', John (Gorry)	1	
GREEN, Thomas	3	447 "
GREER, Joseph		
Hugh Berry	2	870 "
GREGORY, Lena		
William Gregory	1	100 "
GRIFFITH, Thomas		
John Griffith	2	
HALL, James	3	905 "
HAMMOND, Job	1	200 "
" John	5	200 "
HAMNER, Joseph	3	
HARRIS, William	1	179 "
HARRISON, Moses	1	
HASKINS, Henry	1	200 "
HEOCK, William	2	
HILL, William		1320 "
HOLLOWAY, Bennett	2	177 "
HOWELL, John		
William Darby Organ	5	246 "
HUBBARD, John	2	570 "
HUDSON, Charles	1	200 "
" William	2	100 "
HUMPHREYS, John	4	750 "
HUNT, William	1	136 "
HUTCHINS, Robert		
John Bray (Overseer)	3	550 "
HYDE, John	6	504 "
ISBELL, Henry	4	500 "
JOHNSON, Isaac	1	215 "
" James	1	
" Philemon	1	
JONES, Daniel		
Adam Finch (Overseer)	12	1000 "

KING, Henry		372	Acres
LADD, Gerrard	1	85	"
" William	2	115	"
LARK, Robert	3	449	"
LETT, Francis	1	137	"
LUCAS, Charles	1		
" William	1		
MABRY, Ephraim	2	100	"
MACLIN, Thomas	1	315	"
MALLETT, Stephen (Junr. ?)	1	400	"
MARSHALL, James			
Joseph Medley	4	168	"
MATTHIAS, Charles (Matthews)		404	"
MEALER, William	1		
MERRYMAN, Abraham	1		
MESSERSMITH, Conrad	3	304	"
MIZE, John	1	200	"
MOORE, Joel	1	100	"
MOORE, Mark			
John Doggett	2	200	"
MOORE, William	1		
MOSS, David	1		
MURPHEY, John, Senr,			
Ben Murphey	4	197	"
MURPHEY, John	3	200	"
" William	1	100	"
McCOY, John	1		
" Jane		100	"
McDANIEL, James	2	400	"
McDEARMAN, Michael	1	400	"
McQUIE, Michael (?)			
Isham Malone	4	310	"
NEAL, Thomas	4	100	"
NOBLIN, Thomas	1		
OLIVER, John			
Isaac Oliver	4	190	"
PALMER, Thomas	1	80	"
PARK, James	4	100	"
PETTUS, Thomas	4	404	"
PINKSTONE, Richard	1		
POINDEXTER, Philip			
David Barnhill	7	363	"
PROSISE, Thomas			
George Prosise			
William Prosise	3	100	"
PUCKETT, Isham, Senr.			
Isham Puckett, Junr.	2		

RAGSDALE, John		1	200 Acres
" Joseph		3	217 "
" Richard		3	368 "
RIVES, Isaac		1	100 "
ROBERTSON, John			
Samuel Flowers (Overseer)		3	1650 "
ROBERTSON, John		1	100 "
ROYAL, Sarah		1	265 "
ROYSTER, Joseph		9	
RUFFIN, William		5	300 "
RUSSELL, Jeffrey			
John Russell		3	
SMITH, James		1	404 "
SMITH, John			
Andrew Gregory			
James Gregory		7	400 "
SMITHSON, Micajah		3	
SPEED, John, Senr.			
James Speed			
Lewis Speed			
Drury Collier			
Robert Cunningham		7	767 "
STAFFORD, Labon		1	100 "
STITH, Richard			850 "
TALLEY, Joseph		1	
TANNER, Branch			
Richard Pinkstone (Overseer ?)		13	1397 "
THOMPSON, Wells		3	605 "
TIBBS, William		1	300 "
TIMMS, Amos			
Hollis Timms			
Walter Timms		4	426 "
TISDALE, Edward		1	400 "
TRAYLOR, Joel		1	
TRAYLOR, William			
William Watts		2	400 "
TUCKER, John		1	294 "
TUREMAN, George			200 "
VAUGHAN, Stephen		2	185 "
WADE, Randall		1	100 "
WARD, Wade		1	
WATSON, John		1	100 "
WATSON, Michael			
Robert Drysdale		2	395 "
WEATHERFORD, John		1	200 "
WHITEHEAD, Benjamin		1	1144 "
WHITE, Samuel		1	

WHITTEMORE, Jesse			
Gilbert Evans	2		Acres
WHITWORTH, John	2	240	"
WILKINS, William	1		
WILLIAMS, Henry	4	425	"
" James	1	589	"
" John	1	133	"
" Joseph	1	284	"
WILSON, Henry		1519	"
" James	1	200	"
WITTON, Richard, Senr.			
Richard Witten, Junr.	12	892	"
WOMACK, Alexander		400	"
WOODIN, Robert		445	"

Added to list:

BEDDINGFIELD, Thomas			
John Eaton			
Hugh Killoe			
Cowey Boatswain	12	6161	"

NOTES ON TITHE LISTS FOR 1764

The Order Books for Lunenburg County show that Edmund Taylor, Henry Delony and Richard Witton were appointed to take a list of the tithables in St. James Parish for the year 1764. Since no list taken by Henry Delony has been preserved, or found, it has been assumed that such a list has been lost. While the order books are silent on this point, it is the belief of the compilers that no list was taken by Henry Delony. It is the belief of the compilers that Edmund Taylor not only took the list of the tithables in the area assigned to him, but that he took, also, the list of tithables in the area assigned to Henry Delony.

The tithables of Henry Delony appear on the list that was taken by Edmund Taylor. The two lists returned by Edmund Taylor contain approximately twice as many names as that returned by Richard Witton. This appears to substantiate the belief of the compilers that Henry Delony did not take a list of tithables for 1764. It is believed that the foregoing lists are complete for the year 1764.

The tithe lists for 1764 were the first lists to give the number of acres of land owned by the tithables. A comparison of the tithe list with other records, however, discloses that in some cases the land was apparently not listed. Sherwood Bugg is charged with nine tithes and no land. Richard Fox is charged with twelve tithables, but no land is listed for him. The Brunswick County deed books show that he had purchased 550 acres on the south side of the Roanoke River in 1736 from Charles Kimball.

David Dortch, who had come to the area now Mecklenburg County from Isle of Wight County, was charged with six tithes. No land is listed for him though the land patents show that he had patented land in the area. The extant, but incomplete, land processioning records for the year 1759 discloses that the land of David Dortch was processioned in that year. He left a will which was recorded in 1782 that indicates that he was living on the land processioned in 1759.

The names of slaves have been omitted in the foregoing lists as not being material. With the exception of a few large land owners, the number of slaves owned in 1764 were in most cases small or none at all.

All white males over the age sixteen were tithable or taxable. Those names indented in the lists were chargeable to the preceding name. The tithes for sons between the age sixteen and twenty one were chargeable to the father, or to the mother or guardian as the case might be; and the tithe lists for this reason discloses family relationship in many cases.

John and Thomas Stevens appear on the list returned by Edmund Taylor. They were charged with one tithe, but no land was listed for them. Mary Stevens appears on this list as owning 400 acres of land but with no tithables. John and Thomas Stevens were sons of Mary Stevens. Mary Stevens, a widow, had married (1) Thomas Addaman, and (2) Thomas Stevens. An inventory of the estate of Thomas Addaman was returned to the Brunswick County Court 5 Feb. 1735 by Mary Addaman, administratrix. Thomas Stephens (Stevens) with (stepson) Thomas Addiman (Addaman) is listed in the tithe list for 1748. An inventory of the estate of Thomas Stephens was returned to the Lunenburg County Court on the 2 June 1761. The will of Mary Stevens was recorded in 1791 in Mecklenburg County naming son Thomas Addaman and sons John and Thomas Stevens.

An exception in the foregoing list of father and son relationship is the tithables charged to Abraham Hester. He is charged with the tithe of his brother James Hester.

Abraham and James Hester were living on 816 acres of land owned by their father Robert Hester, Junr., of Louisa County. This is disclosed by the will of Robert Hester recorded in Louisa County. This will was not recorded in Mecklenburg County.

Constables and women were exempted from paying tithes, but were responsible for tithables living with them.

Some examples of family relationship taken from the 1764 tithe lists are as follows: George Baskervill with son John Baskervill; Hutchins Burton with son John Burton; Henry Caviness with sons Thomas and William Caviness; Mary Culbreath with son Joseph Culbreath; Richard Fox with son Jacob Fox; Mary Graves with son Elijah Graves; Samuel Holmes with sons Isaac Holmes, Samuel Holmes, Junr. and William Holmes; John Jeffries with son Swepson Jeffries; Dennis Lark with son John Lark; Nicholas Maynard with son John Maynard; William Norment with son-in-law John Johns; Aaron, John and Thomas Pinson with nephew Moses Grigg; Reuben Vaughan with brother James Vaughan; Elizabeth Bressie with grandson William Bressie; Thomas Eastland with sons Joseph and Will Eastland; Feild Jefferson with sons George, John and Peter Feild Jefferson; William White, Senr. with son John White; Richard Yancey with son Charles Yancey; David Dortch with son Noah Dortch; Thomas Prosise with sons George and William Prosise; John Speed, Senr. with sons James and Lewis Speed; Amos Timms with sons Hollis and Walter Timms; Richard Witton with son Richard Witton.

Richins Brame (Senr.) had acquired land in the area now Mecklenburg County on which he had established quarters in the charge of his son James Brame.

John Camp listed with John Hudson as his overseer was living in Halifax County. Robert Alexander, son of John and Martha Alexander, born January 2, 1733 died in 1784. Joseph Birtchett was a son-in-law of Richard Fox.

The relationship of James Ferrell to Ephraim Ferrell has not been established. Benjamin Harris resided in Brunswick County and never came to Mecklenburg County. Tignal Jones, Senr. and Tignal Jones, Junr. were not father and son but cousins. The Penningtons came to the area from Surry County.

Frederick Cox and John Cox, Junr. were sons of John Cox, Senr. of Finneywood. Bolling Cox, Thomas Cox and John Cox, Junr. were sons of John Cox, Senr. of Bluestone.

Stephen Mallett, Isaac Salle', James Bilbo, John Gorre' and Jacob Michaux were descendants of the French Protestant, or Huguenot, refugees who were settled at Manakin in the year 1700. John Peter Bilbo patented 1626 acres on both sides of Allens Creek in 1750. The will of John Peter Bilbo is recorded in Lunenburg County.

CONSTABLES NAMED IN TITHE LISTS

Marriott Bland, Peter Overby, Nathaniel Robinson, James Blanton, George Brown.

Quarters had been established on land in Mecklenburg County in 1764 by William Black, Richins Brame, John Camp, Benjamin Harris, Col. William Harwood, William Hill, Edward Hogan, Harwood Jones, Peter Jones, Howell Lewis, Robert Ruffin, Richard Russell, Obadiah Smith, Henry Ward, Daniel Jones, Theophilus Feild, Armistead Burwell, Col. Lewis Burwell, Lodowick Farmer, Robert Hutchins, John Robertson and Branch Tanner.

Overseers listed were James Whitlock, James Brame, John Hudson, Isaac Bryant, Henry Street, Evan Owen, Tignal Jones, Junr., Richard Russell, Zachariah Baughan, James Watson, William Martin, Edward Hogan, John Bagwell, John. Oliver, George Tureman, John Westbrook, Thomas Carleton, Hugh Franklin, John Jeffries, Junr., Elijah Baker, John Bray, Adam Finch, Samuel Flowers and Richard Pinkstone.

It should be noted Edward Hogan and Richard Russell are listed as in charge of the quarters of Henry Ward and Peter Jones, respectively, but had acquired land and established quarters while working for others. They were developing their own lands while working as overseers.

NOTES FROM BRISTOL PARISH REGISTER
Prince George County

ADDAMAN   William, son of Thomas and Mary Adaman, born 2 July 1722, baptized 17 February 1723.

Thomas, son of Thomas and Mary Adaman, born 6 October 1724, baptized 12 September 1725.
<u>Page 275</u>

COOK   Richard, son of John and Dihah (Dianna) Cook, born 27 July 1728, baptized 24 January 1729.
<u>Page 297</u>

GREEN   Dorcus, daughter of Henry and Elizabeth Green, born 27 September 1726.   <u>Page 307</u>

Winifred, daughter of Henry and Elizabeth Green, born 17 March 1731, baptized 23 April 1732.
<u>Page 308</u>

HAWKINS   Drury, son of William and Martha Hawkins, born 25 May 1733, baptized 29 July 1733.   <u>Page 316</u>

William, son of William and Martha Hawkins, born 9 March 1734/35, baptized 4 May 1735.
<u>Page 317</u>

GREEN   Mary, daughter of John and Abigail Green, born 9 August 1722, baptized 4 September 1722.   <u>Page 306</u>

Jemima, daughter of John and Abigail Green, born 28 July 1731, baptized 2 January 1732.
<u>Page 308</u>

HUMPHRIES   Catherine, daughter of Robert and Jane Humphris, born 20 July 1730.
<u>Page 315</u>

BLACKSTONE   William, son of John and Mary Blackston, born 9 May 1729, baptized 27 June 1729.   <u>Page 282</u>

Rice, son of Mary and John Blaxton (Blackstone) born 16 September 1732, baptized 5 November 1732.   <u>Page 284</u>

Mary, daughter of John and Mary Blackstone, born 8 November 1734.   <u>Page 287</u>

NOBLES   Mark, son of Robert and Elizabeth Nobles, born 18 May 1727.   <u>Page 346</u>

MORGAN	Philip, son of Philip and Mary Morgan, born 15 December 1729, baptized 10 May 1730. Page 338
	Rhuben (Reuben) son of Philip and Mary Morgan born 11 November 1724, baptized 20 February 1725. Page 336
	John, son of Philip and Mary Morgan, born 30 November 1731, baptized 23 April 1732. Page 339
NIPPER	Martha, daughter of John and Ann Nipper, born 19 November 1726. Page 346
ALEXANDER	Robert, son of John and Martha Alexander, born 2 January 1733, baptized 28 February 1733. Page 275
McNEIL	Catharine, daughter of Malcolm and Catharine McNeil, born 12 February 1741/42, baptized 26 April 1742. Page 341
POOL	Tabitha, daughter of William and Frances Pool, born 13 October 1725, baptized 6 June 1726. Page 351
	Philip, son of William and Frances Pool, born 13 March 1730, baptized 12 September 1731. Page 352
ROTTENBERRY	Martha, daughter of Henry and Martha Rottenbery, born 1 September 1720, baptized 12 October 1720. Page 356
	Richard, son of Henry and Margaret (Martha ?) Rottenberry, born 30 June, 1724, baptized 29 July 1724. Page 357
THOMAS	Peter, son of Peter and Elizabeth Thomas, born 2 December 1734. Page 376
	David, son of Peter and Elizabeth Thomas, born 24 December 1740.

BRUNSWICK COUNTY NOTES

Brunswick County, cut from Prince George County, was established by an Act of the General Assembly on the second day of November 1720. The Act provided that jurisdiction was to remain in the Court of Prince George County until a government for the county was organized. Because of the sparse settlement of the new county, the Act provided that "Inhabitants of the said county are made free of publick levies for ten years from the first of May, 1721".

The first meeting of a court for Brunswick County was not held until 2 May, 1732. It is assumed that deeds, wills and other documents were recorded in Prince George County prior to the meeting of the first court in 1732. Many of these early records have been lost, however, and we find in the area now Mecklenburg County the names of many settlers but with no record of when or how they acquired the land they lived on. It is inferred from an entry on page 99 of Order Book 1 that many deeds were recorded in Prince George County; or that the records, if recorded in Brunswick, had been lost.

Court 3 July 1735

Wilson's Deeds to Bishop & Others

Thomas Wilson came into Court & presented & acknowledged deeds of lease & release to Mason Bishop, Michael C. Young, James Rigby, Richard Ramsey, Charles Golstone, John Fountain, Robert Andrews, Henry Beverly, John Merritt, Samuel Crawley, John Adcock, Henry Morris, Samuel Manning, John Blackstone, Richard York, Thomas Couch, Jr., Benjamin Boing (Bowen), Wm. Couch, James Couch, John Barnes, John Thomason, Richard Watts, Patrick Dorum, Seth Pettypool, Thomas Shelton, John Wilson, Philip Morgan, John Thomason, Jr., James Dockery, Thomas Rawlins, William Douglas, James Arnold, Matthew Creed, Aaron Johnson, John Humphries, Henry Rottenbury, Jr., Wm. Fletcher, Thomas Robertson, Aaron Pinson, Joseph Coleson, Robert Alen (Allen), Francis Rayney, (Rainey), Joseph Dunman, Thomas Haney, John Kilcrease, Thomas Jones, Thomas Moore, Clement Read, John Mealey, Wm. Pennington, Henry Rottenbury, Senr. and William Manning, which at the motion of the said Mason Bishop, Michael Cadet Young and all of the aforenamed persons they are ordered to be recorded.

Order Book 1, Page 99

At a later date, someone in the Clerk's Office wrote on the margin of this page "52 deeds apparently not recorded". No record has been found in the order books to support the hypothesis and it is conjectural, but the compilers believe that a fire had destroyed some of the early records; and that the people listed in this order book entry had come into Court to establish their ownership of land through purchase. Many of those listed in this order book entry resided in the area now Mecklenburg County. No other documentary evidence has been found by the compilers to substantiate these early purchases of land. Later deeds and grants frequently refer to the land deeded or granted as "joining his own land". It is to be assumed, therefore, that some of the early Brunswick County records have been lost or destroyed.

Thomas Wilson was evidently the attorney who had prepared the foregoing deeds. It hardly seems logical that he was the grantor. A comparison of these names with other and with later records indicates that they lived in widely separated sections. Michael C. Young, Richard Ramsey, William Douglas, Henry Morris, John Fountain and Matthew Creed, among others, lived in the area now Brunswick County. Seth Pettypool and the Couchs lived in the area now Lunenburg County. John Blackstone, Richard York, John Thomason, James Dockery, Richard Watts, Patrick Dorum, Thomas Shelton, James Arnold, Thomas Moore, Philip Morgan, John Humphries, Thomas Robertson and Aaron Pinson lived in the area now Mecklenburg County. Francis Rainey, William Pennington and Henry Rottenbury, Junior and Senior, lived along the present Mecklenburg-Brunswick County line. Aaron Pinson lived on the Tewayhomony (now Aarons) Creek.

Many of the early settlers in this area were first generation immigrants as disclosed by the many cases of those who applied for importation rights.

John Scott, Gent. came into Court and made oath that it was now 3 years since his importation from Great Britain, and never before now has he received the benefit from the Act of Assembly which allows 50 acres of land for every person imported from Great Britain.
Court 3 May 1739   Order Book 1, Page 241

Cornelius Keith granted leave to keep a ferry over the Roanoke River from his own landing below the Horseford to Alexander's landing & that he keep for that purpose a good and sufficient Flatt 14½ feet in her bottom & 6 feet upon her beam. He is to receive for his ferriage charges 6 pence for a man, 6 pence for a man & as the law directs for wheel carriages, 2 pence for every hog, 4 pence for each of the cattle kind. He to give bond for same.
                                                Order Book 1, Page 240

Cornelius Keith came into Court and made oath that this is the first time he applied and he never has made up his Importation Right, and he has resided 30 years in this Colony since his importation.
                                                Order Book 1, Page 241

Thomas Avent came into to Court and said he had never yet received his Importation Right and it is now 38 years since his importation which he certified.

Michael Cadet Young came into Court and made oath that he had never received his Importation Right, and that it is now 17 years since his importation.

Marmaduke Johnson, who came from Ireland about 20 years ago, came into Court to claim his Importation Right. Ordered certified.
Court 3 May 1739   Order Book 1, Page 241

SUIT: William Hogan)   William Hogan petitioned the Court
            vs   )   that some time age he sold a
    Richard Russell)   servant woman named Mary Wall to
                            Richard Russell for a small sum.
He now wants to claim the rights & dues as are by the laws of the Colony are due to servants imported.
Court 2 Aug. 1739   Order Book 1, Page 256

John Stephens came into Court and made oath that he had never claimed his Importation Right. He imported himself from Great Britain into this Colony 6 years ago.

Patrick Dempsey came into Court and made oath that this is the first time he has made his Importation Claim although he was imported from Ireland 18 years ago.

John Jackson came into Court and stated that he had not made Importation Claim before although imported into this Colony from Great Britain 3 years ago.
Court 3 May 1739   Order Book 1, Page 242

Petition: Thomas Martin petitioned the Court in behalf of
          his wife Elizabeth setting forth:
"That the said Elizabeth, a native of Great Britain, came into this Colony and was sold as a servant according to the custom of this country & had duly served James Judkins 5 years - the conclusion of time in service". Judkins has refused to release her, and he asks relief from this Court.
Court 5 June 1740   Order Book 1, Page 305

Henry Morris came into Court and declared that he had never made an Importation Claim before although he had been imported from Great Britain 21 years.

William Eaton came into Court and declared that he had never made use of his Importation Right, although he had been imported into the Colony from Great Britain 20 odd years.
Court 3 May 1739   Order Book 1, Page 243

John Watkins is appointed guardian to John Sullivant, orphan of Michael Sullivant. It is ordered that William Reynolds & Joyce his wife, late relict of Sullivant, deliver to Watkins all estate left by will to his son John, son Michael and daughter Honour Sullivant.
Court 6 April 1738   Order Book 1, Page 190

It is ordered that George Tilman take into his care John Tilman, son of John Tilman, deceased, and to take all estate of the orphan into his care.
Court 1 March 1739   Order Book 1, Page 231

Henry Embry, Gent. to pay Major John Wall and Lewis Delony the two undertakers of the Chappels lately built.
Court 3 Nov. 1737   Order Book 1, Page 174

At a Court of Oyer & Terminer held for Brunswick County for trial of Harry a negro man belonging to Lewis Delony of Surry County. Charged with breaking in house of Richard Johnson and taking a gun, and taking a Flat & broadax from John Arnold. Guilty - 39 lashes on bare back.
Court 7 Oct. 1736   Order Book 1, Page 150

John Blackwelder made oath that he imported himself, his sons John Blackwelder and Caleb Blackwelder, his daughters Elizabeth Blackwelder and Margaret Blackwelder and his sister Catherine Blackwelder directly from the Marquiset of Durloch in Germany into the province of Pennsylvania, and from that province into this Colony & this is the first time of proving such Importation, which is ordered to be certified.
Court 3 April 1746   Order Book 3, Page 27

Deeds of Gift from Ambrose Jackson to his son Ambrose Jackson, Junr., and to his son-in-law Samuel Harwell, ordered to be recorded.
Court 3 Sept. 1741   Order Book 2, Page 29

Sarah Baker, widow of William Baker, deceased, came into Court and qualified as administratrix on said estate with James Parrish and Samuel Hudson her securities.
Court 4 Feb. 1741   Order Book 2, Page 71

Ordered that Abraham Cook, Nicholas Moshier and Thomas Robinson appraise the estate of William Baker, deceased, and return appraisal to Court.
Court 4 Feb. 1741   Will Book 2, Page 44

Daniel Nantz (Nance) has surveyed the road from Flatt Creek to the Meherrin River. Ordered that the tithables of John Ezell, Ezekiel Matthews, Edward Hewlin, Anthony Fann, James Hicks, Joseph Hicks, Philip Roberts, William Goff, Daniel Murfey (Murphy), Josiah Floyd, David Nantz (Nance) keep road in repair.   Order Book 2, Page 29

HUMPHRIES, John   Will Book 2, Page 2

    Names: Wife - Mary Humphries
           Sons - William Humphries, John Humphries, Thomas
                 Humphries, Charles Humphries, Richard
                 Humphries
                 Land he now lives on to wife Mary as an
                 absolute inheritance.
                 First four sons named to have a patent
                 entry for 400 acres on Allens Creek.
           Executor: Wife Mary Humphries, but if she should
                    marry again son William Humphries to
                    act as executor.
           Witnesses: William Hagood, Mary (X) Hagood and
                   Clem^t Read
           <u>Dated 17 April 1738</u>   <u>Recorded 1 March 1738</u>

LUCAS, William   Will Book 2, Page 26

    Names: Wife - Martha Lucas
           Sons - Eldest son John Lucas, William Lucas,
               Charles Lucas, Samuel Lucas, David Lucas
           Daughters - Two mentioned in will but not by
                      name
           Grandson - William Lucas
           Bequests - 250 acres of land on south side of
                    Meherrin River to son John Lucas
                    400 acres to son William Lucas
                    400 acres to son Charles Lucas
                    350 acres to son Samuel Lucas
                    200 acres on Miles Creek to son David
                    Lucas
                    All land on south side of Miles Creek
                    to grandson William Lucas
                    Wife Martha home plantation for life
           Executors: Sons Charles and Samuel Lucas
           Witnesses: John Irby, Joseph Chamberlain and
                   Elizabeth (I) Barlow
           <u>Dated 25 Feb. 1739</u>   <u>Recorded 5 March 1740</u>

LUCAS, William   Will Book 2, Page 73

    Names: Brothers - John Lucas, Charles Lucas, Samuel
                    Lucas, youngest brother David Lucas
                    400 acres (left by father) to be
                    divided between brothers Samuel and
                    David Lucas
    Executor: Brother Charles Lucas
    Witnesses: Benj. Seawell, Simon Gale, Tho. Collier
    <u>Dated (no date recorded)</u>   <u>Recorded 2 Feb. 1743</u>

NIPPER, John   Will Book 2, Page 31

    Names: Wife - Anne Nipper
       Sons - John Nipper, James Nipper
       Son-in-law - William Jenkins
    Executor: None named - Wife Ahne qualified on estate
    Witnesses: Cornelius Keith, Thomas (T) Roberts and John
         (M) Nipper, Junr.
    Dated 26 March 1736   Recorded 7 May 1743

Martha, daughter of John and Ann Nipper, born 19 Nov. 1726 *
              Bristol Parish Register, Page 346

CLEMONS, John   Will Book 2, Page 36

    Names: Wife - Jane Clemons
       Sons - John Young Clemons
       Daughters - Susannah Clemons, Hannah Clemons,
           Elizabeth Clemons
       Bequests - Land to all named above
    Executors: Wife Jane Clemons and friend James Mitchell
    Witnesses: John Dodd, Robert Mitchell, Thomas
         Rob(in)son
    Dated 10 Nov. 1740   Recorded 2 April 1741

    Note: James Mitchell refused to qualify as executor.

Will brought into Court by Jane, widow of John Clemons,
who since his death has married William Lidderdale.
Jane Lidderdale granted qualification 4 June 1741.

ROBARDS, Bartholomew   Will Book 2, Page 40

    Names: Wife - Sarah Robards
       Son - William Robards
    Executors: Father-in-law Cornelius Cargill and brother
         George Robards
    Witnesses: John Bowdey, William Bollin and Hugh
         McDowell
    Dated 19 Dec. 1739   Recorded 6 Aug. 1741

    George Hicks, Gent. returned to Court account of
Elizabeth Barlow, orphan of John Barlow, deceased.

    William Smith, guardian of Mary and Sarah Smith, who
are orphans of John Smith, deceased, returned an account to
Court.
Court 3 Sept. 1741   Order Book 2, Page 26

* Since Martha Nipper was only ten years old when the will
  was made, it is inferred that she was a daughter of a second marriage, and that Anne was the second wife of John
  Nipper. The other children were apparently grown.

COOK, John   Will Book 2, Page 53

    Names: Wife - mentioned in will but not by name.
          (Dianna Cook, widow, qualified as executrix)
          Sons - Richard Cook, John Lett Cook, Reuben Cook
              James Cook, Nathaniel Cook
          Daughters - Anne Cook, Sarah Cook, Jane Cook
          Refers to land on Flatt Creek which he patented.
          Land to be divided between sons Richard and John
          Lett Cook.
    Executor: Wife named as executor but not by name.
    Witnesses: William King, Isaac (I) House and George
            Tilman
    Dated 19 April 1743   Recorded 2 June 1743

PARHAM, Frances (Widow) *   Will Book 2, Page 77

    Names: Sons - Matthew Parham, Ephraim Parham, Lewis
            Parham
          Grandson - Ephraim Parham, son of Lewis Parham
          Daughter's children - not named (under age)
          Executor: Son Lewis Parham
          Witnesses: Peter Tatum, William McKnight
    Dated 5 March 1740   Recorded 5 April 1744

* Inferentially Frances Parham was the widow of Ephraim
Parham of Surry County. Lewis Parham is listed in Lunenburg County records as "Lewis Parham, Merchant, of Brunswick County".

HARPER, Newman   Will Book 2, Page 85

    Names: Richard Harper, son of Laselton Harper
          Henry Harper   (Connection not stated)
          Mary Floyd, daughter of my eldest sister Joyce
          Sister Susana's eldest child (Not named)
          Sister Penelopa   - Brother George Harper
    Executor: George Harper
    Witnesses: William Denton, William (X) Whittington
    Dated 5 March 1743/44   Recorded 3 May 1744

JACKSON, Ralph   Will Book 2, Page 100

    Names: Hannah Jackson, daughter of Henry Jackson
          Mary Robertson, daughter of Edward Robertson
          Rest of estate to Edward Robertson
    Executor: Edward Robertson
    Witnesses: John Douglas, Bridget (G) Duke, James (X)
            Rober(t)son
    Dated 15 Jan. 1744   Recorded 4 April 1744

MITCHELL, John   Will Book 2, Page 107

    Names: Wife - Judith Mitchell
           Sons - William Mitchell, John Mitchell
           Daughters - Kersia Mitchell, Sukey (Susanna)
                     Mitchell
           Bequests of land to all named
    Executors: Wife Judy Mitchell, William Maclin, James
           Maclin
    Witnesses: William McKnight, Stephen Moss
    Dated 22 June 1745   Recorded 7 Nov. 1745

JACKSON, Ambrose   Will Book 2, Page 109

    Names: Wife - Anne Jackson
           Sons - Henry Jackson, Ambrose Jackson, John
                Jackson
           Daughters - Anne Harwell, Tabitha Sims
           Bequest - Plantation "where I now live" to my
           wife and at her death to son John Jackson
    Executor: None recorded
    Witnesses: Thomas Lanier, Ralph Jackson, Daniel
              Jackson, John Ogburn
    Dated *   Recorded 5 Dec. 1745

    * Not dated but before 15 Jan. 1744.

    <u>Deeds of Gift</u> - Ambrose Jackson, Senr., to Son Ambrose
Jackson, Junr., and to son-in-law Samuel Harwell.
                                                        Order Book 2, Page 29

WOOD, Richard   Will Book 2, Page 122

    Names: Wife - Mary Wood
           Daughter - Susanna Wood (Under age)
           Bequests: To wife Mary plantation where I now
           live, and land left her by her first husband
           <u>John Humphries.</u>
                          To daughter Susanna 200 acres I
           bought from Thomas Loyd, and 347 acres I have
           patented.
    Executors: Wife Mary Wood and friend Walter Campbell
    Witnesses: Matthew Hubbard, John Ogburn, Tabitha Ogburn
    Dated 28 April 1746   Recorded 4 Sept. 1746

MACLIN, Mary   Will Book 2, Page 129

    (Late relict of William Mattox, deceased)

    Names: Son - William Mattox
           Daughters - Prudence Simmons, Mary House, Sarah
                Loyd
           Sons-in-law John Harrison, Isaac House

  Grandson - William House
  Granddaughters - Tabitha Simmons, Priscilla Loyd,
   Elizabeth Harrison, Blanch Harrison
Executor: Son-in-law Isaac House
Witnesses: John Maclin, Thomas Brooks, M. Cadet Young
Dated 4 Jan. 1745   Recorded 5 Feb. 1746

MITCHELL, Thomas   Will Book 2, Page 134

  Names: Wife - Barbara Mitchell
     Daughter - Kesiah Mitchell
     Bequests to wife and daughter
Executor: Capt. Michael Wall
Witnesses: Mich^l Wall, John Wall, Junr., John (I) Smith
Dated 4 Feb. 1746   Recorded 2 July 1747

COOKE, Robert   Will Book 2, Page 145

  Names: Wife - not named in will and evidently deceased
     Sons - Robert Cook, William Cook, John Cook,
      Reuben Cook, Nicholas Cook, Frederick
      Cook, Berryman Cook
     Daughters - Martha Hawkins, Sarah Blackstone,
      Rebecca Brooks
     Bequests to first three sons named one shilling
     Bequests to three daughters one shilling
     Bequest to son Reuben Cook - 5 pounds to secure
      land in (North) Carolina.
     Balance of estate - real and personal - to be
      divided between sons Reuben, Nicholas, Frederick
      and Berryman Cook.
Executors: Son Reuben Cook and brother Reuben Cook
Witnesses: Randall Bracey, William Hogan, Martha (X)
    Atkins
Dated 4 Dec. 1747   Recorded 4 April 1748

SUIT: John Douglas vs Richard Pepper and Martha, his wife,
  executor of John Alexander, deceased.
Court 2 Feb. 1738   Order Book 2, Page 85

  No will or administration has been found for John
Alexander; and suit briefly listed in the order book was it
is assumed dismissed.

  Martha Alexander appears to have married (2) Richard
Pepper of Brunswick. Richard Pepper does not appear in any
extant records relating to either Lunenburg or Mecklenburg
Counties. No search has been made in Brunswick records for
Richard Pepper.

  The name Alexander does not appear in Lunenburg County
records until Robert Alexander, Richard Fox and William
Davis were ordered to procession land in 1759.

COLONIAL SOLDIERS

AVERY, William

BENTLEY, Samuel
BLANKS, William

CARGILL, Cornelius, Jr.
CHAMBERLAIN, Thomas
COLEMAN, John
COLISON, John
CORN, Robert

EDMONDSON, Samuel
ELAM, Joel
ELLIS, James

FANN, John
FARRAR, Abel
FARRAR, John
FARRAR, William

GRIFFIN, Richard

HALL, John
HAMLIN, Thomas
HATCHELL, Stephen
HAWKINS, Pinkethman
HOLLOWAY, Bennett
HOLLOWAY, William
HOWARD, William
HUDSON, Ephraim
HUNT, William

KIDD, James

LAMBERT, Joseph
LARK, Robert
LETT, James
LETT, John
LETT, Joseph
LIGHTFOOT, Francis

McNEIL, John

MALLETT, Stephen
MANNING, John
MANNING, Thomas
MATTHEWS, Thomas
MITCHELL, John
MITCHELL, William
MONROE, William
MUNDAY, Isaac
MUNFORD, Capt. Robert

NANCE, Robert
NANCE, Thomas
NORRILL, Francis
NORRILL, James

OSBORNE, John
OWEN, James

PARRISH, David
PARRISH, Moses
POOLE, William

ROBINSON, John

SAGE, Henry
SCOTT, Francis
SKELTON, William
SPEED, James

TALLEY, Henry, Jr.
TAYLOR, James
THOMPSON, John
TIBBS, William
TILLMAN, Roger
TOWNSEND, William

VAUGHAN, James

WALKER, William
WATSON, Matthew
WATTS, William
WHITE, William
WORHSAM, John

Many of those listed above received grants of land for participation in the wars against the French and Indians, and for service in the Militia in defence of the frontiers. Many served in the Regiment commanded by Col. William Byrd. A large number of those listed were living in Mecklenburg County at time of enlistment, others moved to the county later.

NOTES ON SOME EARLY SETTLERS

Many of the early settlers in the area now Mecklenburg County are worthy of note, but it has not been the purpose of the compilers to write a history of the county. Nor has it been the purpose of the compilers to present the genealogy of any family. Such genealogical notes as may appear are entirely incidental to the purpose of this work, which has been to present the names of all early settlers and the land owners now to be found in existing records. The notes given are deemed to be of interest, however, to the future historian, the researcher and to all of those who may have ancestry in the county.

These notes have been compiled primarily from the records of Prince George, Brunswick, Lunenburg and Mecklenburg Counties. Some of the notes do not have a direct connection with Mecklenburg County, but have been included for their historic and genealogical interest and value.

John Butcher on the 28th of September, 1728, patented 632 acres of land on the north side of the Roanoke River on Butchers Creek. He sold 300 acres of this land in 1731 to Gabriel Harrison. John Butcher of Brunswick County, Planter sold the remaining 332 acres in 1740 to William Baker of Hanover County. John Butcher does not again appear in records pertaining to Mecklenburg County.

Gabriel Harrison, of Prince George County, sold the 300 acres which he had purchased from John Butcher to Abraham Cook of Hanover County in 1741.

LUNENBURG COUNTY COURT - 4 Aug. 1746

Abraham Cook, Lewis Delony, John Caldwell, Hugh Lawson, John Hall, William Howard, Matthew Talbot, Cornelius Cargill, William Caldwell, John Phelps, Robert Jones and James Mitchell, Gentlemen Justices. *

<u>Order Book 1, Page 35</u>

* Abraham Cook was named in the Commission of the Peace as one of those named to form the first government for Lunenburg County. He was sworn in as a justice on 5 May 1746. At the same court, Abraham Cook was appointed surveyor of the road from Butchers Creek to Bluestone Creek.

LUNENBURG COUNTY COURT - 4 July 1748
"James Cook having Contumaciously and Reproachfully Insulted this Court in forceably and violently taking tearing and Endeavouring to Suppress Cancel and Destroy the last will and Testament of his father Abraham Cook Deceased this Day Exhibited and offered for proof." *

The Court fined James Cook for his outburst which was apparently caused by the terms of his father's will.

It is therefore considered and accordingly ordered that he, the said James Cook, make his fine to our sovereign lord the King - 10 pounds sterling with costs.

Order Book 2, Page 35

* Abraham Cook left his property to his other two sons, Benjamin and Charles Cook. He left one shilling to his son James Cook.

LUNENBURG COUNTY Will Book 1, Page 7

COOK, Abraham
    Names: Wife - Sarah Cook
           Sons - Benjamin, Charles and James Cook
           Daughters - Barbary Hester, Frances Hester
    Executors: Wife Sarah and son Benjamin Cook
    Witnesses: Richard Palmer, Thomas Satterwhite and
           John Fletcher
    Will dated 2 April 1748   Recorded 4 July 1748

Note: Abraham Cook apparently lived in that part of Hanover County which was cut off to form Louisa County in 1742.

Barbara Cook inferentially married Robert Hester, Jr., who by his will recorded in Louisa County 12 March 1770 provided for the use of certain land in Mecklenburg County by his wife Barbary Hester. The 1782 census for Mecklenburg County lists Barbara Hester.

Robert Jones and James Mitchell, named as justices on 4 Aug. 1746, were evidently appointed in the place of Thomas Lanier and William Hill named as justices 5 May 1746.

Abraham Cook, Lewis Delony, William Howard, Cornelius Cargill, Thomas Lanier, William Hill, Robert Jones and James Mitchell lived at the time in the area now Mecklenburg Co.

John Alexander patented 900 acres of land on the south side of the Roanoke River 13 October 1727.

Robert, son of John and Martha Alexander, born 2 Jan'y 1733, baptized 28 Feb'y 1733.

Bristol Parish Register

Martha Alexander petitioned the Brunswick County Court on the 5 March 1741 for a license to keep a ferry from her landing over the River to Cornelius Keith's landing which was granted conditioned on her giving security. Cornelius Keith lived on the north side of the Roanoke River opposite the land patented by John Alexander.

The Vestry of Cumberland Parish on 17 September 1759 ordered Robert Alexander, Richard Fox and William Davis to procession all of the land between the Roanoke River and the County Line (Granville County) up to Cotton Creek.

BRUNSWICK COUNTY   Deed Book 2, Page 18

Robert Humphries of St. Andrews Parish, Brunswick County, to <u>Schertorio De Toriano</u> of the same county and parish ... cons. 20 pounds ... 200 acres on north side of Dan River ... part of a larger tract of land granted to Robert Humphries by patent 11 Feb. 1738 ... adjoining land of Thomas Moon.
Deed dated 4 May 1740   Recorded 5 July 1740

<u>LUNENBURG COUNTY</u> - Court Sept. 1746

Scher Toriano, Peter Toriano and Silvester Gianano came into Court and severally took the usual oaths to His Majesty and Government & subscribed the Test in order to their Naturalization.

Order Book 1, Page 64

Scher Toriani   Sher Torio De Toriano
  for adm. oaths of gov't   10   order thereon   15   25
Pet. Torian
  for adm. oaths of gov't   10   order thereon   15   25
Silvester Gionano
  for adm. oaths of gov't   10   order thereon   15   25

Entries in   Fee Book 1, Page 35

At a period when names were recorded literally as they sounded to the scribe, these Swiss names presented a problem to the Clerks of the Court.

The deed to Schertorio de Toriano was indexed under the letter "D". When the deed was acknowledged in court and ordered recorded, it was entered in the order book as Scher Torio Detorianio. The name Silvester Gianano became Silvester Jouniours in Lunenburg records, and Sylvester Juniel in in Halifax records. The Anglicized name Scher Torian was recorded in Halifax County records as Scare Torian until well into the 1800's. Schertorio de Toriano was the ancestor of the Torian family of Halifax County.

LUNENBURG COUNTY RECORDS

Charles Barnes, last from Shropshire in the Kingdom of Great Britain, came into Court and made oath that he imported himself into this Colony 23 years ago and that this is the first time of claiming his Importation Right. Ordered to be certified.
May Court 1747   Order Book 1, Page 199

James Dockery, last from Bristol in the Kingdom of Great Britain, came into Court and made oath that he had been an inhabitant of this Colony 15 years and that this is the first time of his claiming his Importation Right which is ordered to be certified.
August Court 1746   Order Book 1, Page 50

John Freeman, last of Worcestorshire in the Kingdom of Great Britain, came into Court and made oath that he had been an inhabitant of this Colony 14 years and that this is the first time of his claiming his Importation Right which is ordered to be certified.
August Court 1746   Order Book 1, Page 50

George Ireland, last from Shropshire in the Kingdom of Great Britain, came into Court and made oath that he had been an inhabitant of this Colony 10 years and that this is the first time of his claiming his Importation Right which is ordered to be certified.
August Court 1746   Order Book 1, Page 50

GREEN, Henry   Deed Book 1, Page 477

     Names: Wife - Elizabeth Green
         Sons - John Green, Henry Green, Stephen Green,
             Frederick Green, Richard Green
         Daughter - Dorcas Green
         Abigail Green, relict of brother John Green
     Executors: Brother-in-law Richard Griffin and son John
           Green
     Witnesses: Edward Sizemore, William Jackson and Thomas
           Greenwood
     Dated 15 Oct. 1748   Recorded *

* Date not recorded but before 5 June 1749

GREEN, Henry (Jr)   Will Book 2, Page 8

     Names: Wife mentioned in will but not by name
         Sister - Dorcas Jackson
         John Owen, son of Joseph Owen
         Henry Jackson, son of William Jackson
     Executors: William Sizemore and John Green
     Witnesses: George Moore, Stephen Green and Frederick
           Green
     Dated 23 Feb. 1761   Recorded 5 May 1761

It is inferred from the foregoing wills that Henry Green, Sr., married Elizabeth Griffin; Dorcas Green married William Jackson and that Henry Green, Jr., married a sister of Joseph Owen.
Note: The earliest Lunenburg County wills are recorded in
      Deed Book 1.

Survey made by Robert Bolling, Surveyor, for George Brooks ... 5 Nov. 1724 ... 100 acres on north side of the Nottoway River between the land of Samuel Harrison and Henry Green.

Prince George County Records   Part 5, Page 816

LUNENBURG COUNTY   Will Book 1, Page 8

    RAMBOE, Christopher

        Names: Wife - None named
              Specific bequests to Thomas Pinson, Elonor
              Pinson, John Pinson, Sarah Ann Pinson
              Remainder of estate to Aaron Pinson
              Connection not stated   *
        Executor: William Hancock
        Witnesses: William Hancock and Aaron Pinson
        Dated   Nov. 1747   Recorded 1 Aug. 1748

* Aaron Pinson, in his will dated 26 Dec. 1757, refers to bequests made to Thomas Pinson, John Pinson and Elinor Pinson by their Godfather Christopher Ranbury. He did not name Sarah Ann Pinson in will, but made a bequest to his Grandson Moses Grigg. Moses Grigg is listed in the tithe list for 1764 as living with Thomas Pinson. Sarah Ann Pinson (listed in the will of Christopher Ramboe, or Ranburry), by inference, married a Grigg.

    PINSON, Aaron, Senr.   Will Book 1, Page 223

        Names: Wife - not named in will
              Sons - Aaron Pinson, Thomas Pinson, John
                    Pinson
            Daughter - Elinor Pinson
            Grandson - Moses Grigg
        Executors: Sons Aaron and Thomas Pinson
        Witnesses: Henry Philip Hart, William Royster, and
                  Stephen Wiles
        Dated 26 Dec. 1757   Recorded 7 March 1758

Aaron Pinson was a pioneer settler in the area now Mecklenburg County. Just when he came to the area is not known. The first record found in Brunswick County was the confirmation of a deed in 1735. No record of the recording of the deed has been found.

Aaron Pinson settled on Tewayhomony Creek which is now called Aarons Creek, and is the boundary line between the counties of Mecklenburg and Halifax.

Aaron Pinson, Peter Mitchell and William Hogan were the earliest settlers of record on the western boundary of the area now Mecklenburg County.

BUGG, Samuel   Lunenburg County   Will Book 1, Page 249

Names: Wife - Sarah Bugg
       Sons - Jacob Bugg, Sherwood Bugg, Edmund Bugg,
              Samuel Bugg, Anselm Bugg
       Daughters - Sarah Towler, Agnes Lee (Leigh),
                   Ruth Bugg
       Grandsons - John Bugg, Benjamin Bugg, Jesse
                   Bugg, Sherwood Bugg
Executor: Son Anselm Bugg
Witnesses: Amos Hix, George Freeman, William Cox
Dated 30 Dec. 1756   Recorded 1 May 1759

Agnes Bugg married (1) Walter Leigh, who died in 1771, and (2) Joel Chandler.

Elliott - Early Wills, Pages 55-120

Samuel Bugg (Senr.) left his land to wife Sarah Bugg for life and at her death to son Jacob Bugg. Samuel Bugg of Henrico County purchased 150 acres of land on south side of Roanoke River from John Hyde 16 Jan. 1752. John Hyde sold an additional 195 acres to Samuel Bugg, Senr., 7 Aug. 1753. Samuel Bugg, Senr., does not appear to have moved to Mecklenburg County at once, but his son Edmund Bugg is listed in the tithe list for 1752 and evidently had moved to the land.

Sherwood Bugg purchased 100 acres of land on south side of Roanoke River from William Wood on 7 Jan. 1752; and he is listed with son John Bugg (over 16) in the tithe list for that year.

Samuel Bugg (Junr.) purchased 400 acres of land on the north side of the Roanoke River from Henry Howard 22 May 1752. The deed states Samuel Bugg of Amelia County. Henry Howard, on the same day, sold 400 acres of land on north side of the river adjoining this land to Jacob Bugg of Chesterfield County.

Samuel Bugg, Senr., was, inferentially, the son of Samuel Bugg of New Kent County, and Deborah Bugg his wife.

Deborah Bugg, wife of Samuel Bugg, died 14 December 1715. Samuel Bugg died 10 September 1716.

John Bugg, son of Samuel Bugg, born 5 May 1715; Samuel Bugg, son of Samuel Bugg, born 16 Sept. 1717; Sherwood Bugg, son of Samuel Bugg, born 8 July 1720; Jacob Bugg, son of Samuel Bugg, born 16 Feb. 1722/23; Sarah Bugg, daughter of Samuel Bugg, born 24 Oct. 1725; Edmund Bugg, son of Samuel and Sarah Bugg, born 24 Sept. 1728.

Benjamin, son of John and Frances Bugg, born 24 Nov. 1736. Inferentially grandson Benjamin Bugg named in will of Samuel Bugg.   *Register of St. Peter's Parish*

Henry Delony conveyed 300 acres of land on the south east side of Cox Creek to Isham East by deed dated 18 Feb. 1752 which was witnessed by Feild Jefferson and Julius Nichols. This was recorded in Lunenburg County deed book two on 7 April 1752 at which time Frances Delony, wife of Henry Delony, released her dower right.

Feild Jefferson named daughter Mary Nichols and granddaughter Mary Delony in his will dated 8 June 1762 which was recorded in Mecklenburg County on 10 June 1765. He named Henry Delony as one of his executors.

From these records, it appears, inferentially, that Julius Nichols married Mary Jefferson, and that Henry Delony married Frances Jefferson. Frances (Jefferson) Delony died in 1752. Henry Delony married (2) Rebecca (Broadnax) Walker widow of Alexander Walker in 1753.

<u>Brunswick County, Marriage Bond, 11 May 1753</u>

WRIGHT, John   <u>Lunenburg County   Deed Book 2, Page 138</u>

Deed of Gift: John Wright to his children, slaves and personal property - Son Laban Wright - Daughters: Mary Wright, Alice Wright, Hannah Wright, Edea Wright. Mentions wife Jane Wright.
<u>Dated 3 Oct. 1750</u>   <u>Recorded 3 Oct. 1750</u>

Thomas Clarke of Isle of Wight County purchased from Francis Ellidge 730 acres land on Allens Creek 11 Oct. 1748. Thomas Clarke resided in that part of Isle of Wight County which was cut off to form Southampton County. Under his will recorded in Southampton County 13 Feb. 1752, he gave to son James Clark 400 acres of land on Allens and Laytons Creek.

CLARKE, Thomas   <u>Southampton County Wills</u>

Names: Wife - Sarah Clarke
      Sons - John Clarke, James Clarke, Jesse Clarke,
          Jordan Thomas Clarke, Carter Clarke
      Daughter - Frances Clarke
<u>Will dated 1 Dec. 1750</u>   <u>Recorded 13 Feb. 1752</u>

Notes: Thomas Clarke, son of Thomas and Susannah Clarke, married Sarah Norwood, daughter of Richard and Elizabeth Norwood of Isle of Wight County.

John Clarke married Judith Mallett, daughter of Stephen and Olive Magdalene Mallett.

Carter Clarke married Martha Farrar of Mecklenburg County. Carter Clarke served as an officer in the Mecklenburg County Militia in the Revolutionary War.

Samuel Holmes patented land on both sides of Miles Creek on the 6 July 1741. He, subsequently, patented other tracts of land in the area now Mecklenburg County. He had resided, prior to coming to Mecklenburg County, in Henrico County. He lived in that part of Bristol Parish which lay north of the Appomattox River. This part of Bristol Parish was included in Dale Parish when it was created in the area now Chesterfield County.

Mary, daughter of Samuel and Ann Holmes, born 29 Nov. 1724.
Isaac, son of Samuel and Ann Holmes, born 16 Nov. 1727.
Samuel, son of Samuel and Ann Holmes, born 27 May 1731.

Bristol Parish Register, Pages 314-315

William Holmes, Elizabeth Holmes (?) and Ann Holmes were undoubtedly born in Mecklenburg County as Samuel Holmes had moved to the area in 1732.

BRUNSWICK COUNTY - Court Jan. 1733

Samuel Holmes credited with two wolf heads against his Levy.
Order Book 1, Page 50

Court 7 Oct. 1736
Samuel Holmes appointed overseer of road from Roanoke River near Hogans to the Long Branch instead of Hogan.
Order Book 1, Page 138

Samuel Holmes lived, apparently, near Allens Creek, but there is no extant deed showing purchase of land by Samuel Holmes. The deed was evidently recorded in Prince George County before the formation of the first government for the County of Brunswick. Most of the records of Prince George County for this period have been lost.

The will of Samuel Holmes dated 13 September 1762, naming wife Ann Holmes, children Isaac Holmes, Mary Lark, Samuel Holmes, William Holmes and Ann Holmes, granddaughter Elizabeth Pool, was recorded 14 July 1766 in Will Book 1, at page 18, Mecklenburg County.
Elliott - Early Wills, Page 45

The Henrico Quit Rent Roll for 1704-1705 lists Richard and Thomas Holmes as land owners in Henrico County.

The will of Isaac Holmes was recorded in Mecklenburg County in 1772.
Early Wills, Page 44

LUNENBURG COUNTY RECORDS

HOWARD, Francis   Deed Book 1, Page 479

    Names: Wife - Dianna Howard
           Sons - William Howard, Francis Howard
           Daughters - Elizabeth Howard, eldest daughter,
                 Elenor Howard, Dianna Howard, Hannah
                 Howard
           Children under age
           Cousin - Mary Howard
    Executors: Wife Dianna and brother William Howard
    Witnesses: John Hyde, Henry Delony, William Sandifer
    Dated 6 Feb. 1748   Recorded 5 June 1749

     Dianna Howard, executrix of her husband Francis Howard, has since intermarried with George Farrar.
January Court 1751   Order Book 2, Page 251

     Jacob Miller, for himself and Mary his wife and filia Mary his daughter, last from London in the Kingdom of Great Britain, came into Court and made oath that he imported himself and family into this Colony about 19 years ago and that this is the first time of claiming his and their Importation Rights, and the said Jacob also took the usual oaths to his Majesty's person and Government and subscribed and repeated the teste in order to his naturalization.
June Court 1748   Order Book 2, Page 10

VAUGHAN, James   Deed Book 1, Page 481

    Names: Wife - not named in will and evidently deceased
           Sons - Reuben Vaughan, Stephen Vaughan, James
                Vaughan
           Daughter - Lucy Vaughan
    Executor: Son Reuben Vaughan
    Witnesses: William Andrews, Richard Andrews
    Dated 20 July 1740   Recorded 3 July 1750

     Matthew Talbot, Gent. came into Court and made oath that Charles Talbot was his first son born of the body of Mary Williston his first wife.
August Court 1748   Order Book 2, Page 58

WILDS, Luke (Wiles)   Deed Book 1, Page 493

    Names: Wife - Margaret Wiles
           Sons - Robert Wiles, eldest son, Thomas Wiles,
                Stephen Wiles, Luke Wiles
           Two daughters mentioned but not by name - Under age.
           Land in Goochland County to be sold to pay debts

Land where I live on south side of Roanoke River to be surveyed and divided between four sons.
Executors: Wife Margaret and son Robert Wiles
Witnesses: Josiah Seat, David Embry, Thomas Wiles
Dated 31 May 1749   Recorded 2 June 1750

James Murphey, last from Great Britain, came into Court and made oath that he imported himself and Isabel his wife into this Colony and this is the first time of claiming his Importation Right.
February Court 1749   Order Book 2, Page 106

John Griffith, last from Wales in the Kingdom of Great Britain, came into Court and made oath that he imported himself into this Colony thirty years ago and that this is the time he claimed his Importation Rights.
February Court 1749   Order Book 2, Page 106

BILBO, John Peter   Deed Book 1, Page 496

     Names: Wife - Elizabeth Bilbo
            Sons - James Bilbo, Joseph Bilbo, John Bilbo, Peter Bilbo, William Bilbo
            Daughters - Mary Bilbo, Elizabeth Bilbo, Sarah Bilbo
     Bequest: To Isaac Dutoy - Tract of land in Cumberland County.
     Executors: Wife Elizabeth and Joseph Chandler
     Witnesses: Joseph Green, John Gourd ?, Joseph Chandler and Isaac Dutoy
     Dated 15 Nov. 1750   Recorded 2 April 1751

     Deed Book 3, Page 82

Received of James Coleman, John Williams and Nicholas Major in full proper part of the estate due to my sisters Sarah & Judith Baker and my brothers William & James Baker and myself from my deceased father's estate.
     /s/ Zachariah Baker
Dated 5 Oct. 1752   Recorded 7 Nov. 1752

BROWN, Mary   *   Deed Book 1, Page 188

     I Mary Brown give all my possessions real & personal at my death to Betty Cargill, daughter of Cornelius Cargill ... known also as Betty Brown (Cargill) ... (the reason she is called so is that I the Donor stood for her Godmother), etc.
Witnesses:
     J. Scott   /s/ Mary Brown
     William Irby
Dated 5 May 1747   Recorded 1 June 1747

* Deed of Gift from Mary Brown to Betty Brown Cargill.

Notes: Cornelius Cargill married Elizabeth Daniel before
        2 March 1737.

        Betty Brown Cargill was evidently named for her
        mother Elizabeth and for Mary Brown.

MARRIAGE CONTRACT   Deed Book 3, Page 293

        Marriage contract between Cornelius Cargill and Hannah
Blanks, widow of Joseph Blanks.   Excerpts:

        Cornelius Cargill is to dispose of his estate as he
        sees fit without Hannah Blanks right of dower.
        Hannah Blanks to dispose of her estate with consent
        of Cornelius Cargill as she sees fit.
        Bound by bond for 500 pounds.
        Witnesses: /s/ Cornelius Cargill
            William (X) Roberts   /s/ Hannah (X) Blanks
            Richard Blanks
        Dated 20 March 1753   Recorded 4 July 1753

Note: At the same time, Cornelius Cargill entered into a
        contract of agreement, bound by bond, with Richard
        Blanks and William Blanks, sons and heirs of
        Hannah Blanks, to protect their interest in the
        estate of their mother.

SEAT, Josiah   Will Book 1, Page 338

        Names: Wife - not named and evidently deceased
               Son - Robert Seat
               Daughters - Margaret Gold, Sarah Seat, Elizabeth
                           Seat, Mary Seat.
               Bequests: To son Robert - Land in Halifax County
                         To Margaret Gold - Home plantation
                         To Sarah, Elizabeth and Mary Seat -
                         Land on Buffalo Creek to be divided
                         equally between them.
        Executor: Jacob Royster
        Witnesses: Richard Jones, Robert Jones, John Bray
        Dated 20 Jan. 1750   Recorded 1 Dec. 1761

Notes: Margaret Seat married Daniel Gold, Senr.
        Sarah Seat married William Stovall
        Elizabeth Seat married Thomas Hamlin
        Mary Seat married James Sanderlain
            (Mecklenburg County deeds and other records)

REGISTER OF ALBEMARLE PARISH - Births and Deaths - 1739-1778

Mary Seat died 6 Oct. 1742 - Informant: Robert Seat
                                                    Page 308
Connection inferential

HAWKINS, Thomas   Lunenburg County   Will Book 1, Page 250

    Names: Wife - Mary Hawkins
        Sons - John Hawkins, Nathan Hawkins
        Daughter - Sarah Hawkins
        Brother - Pinkithman Hawkins
    Executors: Wife Mary Hawkins and brother Pinkithman
        Hawkins
    Dated 14 Nov. 1758   Recorded 1 May 1759

Mary Hawkins married (2) John Potter.

    Pinkithman Hawkins, John Potter and Mary his wife, as
    executors of the estate of Thomas Hawkins, deceased,
    conveyed to Richard Stiles 200 acres of land on Beach
    Creek 10 June 1765.
                Mecklenburg County Deed Book 1, Page 81

MITCHELL, John   Lunenburg County   Will Book 1, Page 140

    Names: Wife - Not named in will and evidently deceased
        Sons - James Mitchell, Isaac Mitchell
        Daughter - Catherine Mitchell, wife of Robert
             Mitchell
        Daughter - Mary Mitchell, wife of William
             Yarbrough
        Son-in-law - Jacob Mitchell
        Housekeeper - Elizabeth Sawyer
    Executors: Jacob Mitchell and Isaac Mitchell
    Witnesses: Reuben Searcy, Francis James, Ann James
    Dated 29 Dec. 1753   Recorded 4 Feb. 1754

Note: Judith Mitchell, wife of John Mitchell, released her
    dower right in sale of 400 acres of land to Thomas
    Eastland 3 March 1742.
                Brunswick County Deed Book 2, Page 229

WILKINS, John   Lunenburg County   Deed Book 2, Page 297

    Deed of Gift: John Wilkins for love and affection for
    my daughter Susannah Wilkins and my son Richard Wilkins
    ... gives personal property to son and daughter.
    Dated 8 Sept. 1751   Recorded 1 Oct. 1751

Notes: Other deeds of Gift made by John Wilkins - 10 Oct.
    1747 gift of 100 acres of land to son Thomas Wilkins.

    1 April 1749 gift of 100 acres of land to son William
    Wilkins.

    8 Sept. 1751 gift of 100 acres of land to son James
    Wilkins.
                See: Lunenburg County Deeds

TABOR, Rachel   Deed Book 3, Page 539

    Deed of Gift - Rachel Tabor, widow, to John Tabor, Elizabeth Tabor, William Tabor, Hezekiah Tabor, Zachariah Tabor, Judith Tabor, Susannah Tabor and Mary Tabor, Infants ....
                        for love and affection ....
all of my personal estate to be equally divided among my above named children.
Witnesses: /s/ Rachel (X) Tabor
    None recorded
Dated 7 Aug. 1754   Recorded 7 Aug. 1754

June Court 1752
               Elizabeth Howard, orphan of Francis Howard, being of legal age (to choose her own guardian) came into Court and chose George Farrar for her guardian. George Farrar gave bond as guardian.

               Elinor Howard, orphan of Francis Howard, deceased, she not being of lawful age (to choose her own guardian), George Farrar is appointed guardian to the said orphan.
                                 Order Book 2½-A, Page 58
Lunenburg County Orders - 1752-53

    Jacob Arnest came into Court and took the usual oath to his Majesty's person & Government, and subscribed the Teste in order to his naturalization.
                                   Order Book 2½-A, Page 60

CARGILL, Hannah   Will Book 1, Page 230

    Names: Husband - Cornelius Cargill
          Sons - William Blanks, Richard Blanks
          Grandson - Thomas Blanks, son of William and Judith Blanks
          Goddaughter - Elizabeth Drew
Executors: Sons William and Richard Blanks
Witnesses: William Roberts, John Cargill, Thomas Dendy
Dated 7 Nov. 1757   Recorded 4 April 1758

WILES, Stephen   Will Book 2, Page 10

    Names: Wife - Mary Wiles
          Children - None named
          Brothers - Robert Wiles, Luke Wiles, & Thomas Wiles
    Land left by father to go to brothers
Executors: Thomas Wiles and Joseph Dupree
Witnesses: Neavell Buchanan, Robert Wiles, Luke Wiles, Aaron Pinson
Dated 5 May 1761   Recorded 1 June 1762

RICHMOND COUNTY   Will Book 5, Page 206

   PALMER, Robert

      Names: Wife - Not named in will
            Sons - Parmenas Palmer, Truman Palmer,
                Thomas Palmer, William Palmer,
                Reuben Palmer, George Palmer, Joseph
                Palmer
            Daughters - Prudence Palmer, Elizabeth Webb
            Granddaughter - Sarah Glasscock
      Executor:
      Witnesses: Henry Miskell, Thomas Hightower
      Dated 25 Feb. 1732   Recorded 2 July 1733

LUNENBURG COUNTY   Will Book 2, Page 9

   PALMER, Parmenas

      Names: Wife - Mary Ann Palmer
            Sons - Joshua Palmer, Thomas Palmer,
                William Palmer
            Daughters - Sarah Palmer, Martha Palmer
                Winifred Palmer
      Executors: Wife Mary Ann Palmer, Brother William
            Palmer and Son William Palmer
      Witnesses: Christopher Hudson, Rebecca Palmer
      Dated 24 Aug. 1761   Recorded 6 Oct. 1761

LUNENBURG COUNTY   Deed Book 4, Page 41

   James Tucker to Parmenas Palmer of Amelia County ....
   cons. 35 pounds ... 80 acres on Allens Creek.
   Witnesses:
      Jacob Gibson (Joseph)
      Jacob (X) Coleson   /s/ James Tucker
      Thomas Draper
   Dated 1 Oct. 1754   Recorded 4 Feb. 1755

SURRY COUNTY   Will Book 8, Page 196

   Williamson, John

      Names: Among others
            Daughters - Hannah Fox, wife of Richard Fox
            Susanna Rottenberry, wife of John Rotten-
            berry.
   Will dated 30 Jan. 1731   Recorded 17 May 1732

Some early settlers in the area now Mecklenburg County owned land in both Colonial Granville County in North Carolina and in Lunenburg County in Virginia. Both counties were created in 1746. Granville was formed from Edgecomb and Lunenburg from Brunswick. Among other names appearing as landowners in the area is that of Yancey. The early history of the Yancey family is rather obscure. A number of volumes have been published on the family, but all are at variance in some respects in regard to the early history of the family. All begin with one Charles Yancey listed in the 1704 Quit Rent Roll for King William County. Nearly all are in relative agreement that a Charles Yancey married a Miss Bartlett and had five sons: Robert, Richard, James, Archelaus and Charles.

Nearly all of the published accounts omit, or are mostly silent in regard to two other members of the Yancey family who were in the Mecklenburg-Granville area. They were Jechonias and John Yancey.

Jechonias Yancey appears in the Granville records in 1749 when he was granted 440 acres of land in Granville County by Earl Granville. James Yancey of Hanover County purchased land in Granville County in 1752; and Richard Yancey of Louisa County purchased land in Granville County in 1753. Richard Yancey did not settle in Granville County, however, as he appears in the Vestry records of Cumberland Parish, Lunenburg County, in 1754. He subsequently purchased a part of the land granted to Drury Stith, Henry Morris and Michael Cadet Young in 1753 on Grassy Creek. The inventory of the estate of John Yancey, deceased, was returned to the Court of Lunenburg County in 1761. (Will Book 2, page 108)

PETITION TO DIVIDE COUNTY

Court held for Lunenburg County - April 1755

Present: Cornelius Cargill   John Cox   ) Gent. Justices
         Thomas Bouldin   James Taylor)

A Petition of Sundry Inhabitants of this County praying a division of this county, and for adding a part of Brunswick County to the lower part, is presented.

Petition read and held to be reasonable which is ordered to be certified to the General Assembly.

Order Book 3, Page 335

The western part of Lunenburg County had been cut into Halifax and Bedford Counties in 1752 and 1753, respectively. Action appears to have started in 1755 to further divide Lunenburg County which culminated in the creation of Mecklenburg County in 1765.

SOME MECKLENBURG PEOPLE WHO WENT TO OTHER STATES

NAME	STATE
ADAMS, John	Montgomery County, Tenn.
AKIN, Joseph	Granville County, N. C.
ALLEN, Darling	South Carolina
ALLEN, David	Caswell County, N. C.
ALLEN, Phillip	Clark County, Georgia
ALLGOOD, John	Walton County, Georgia
ALLGOOD, John	Monroe County, Tenn.
ALLGOOD, John	Breckinridge County, Tenn.
ALLGOOD, William	Surry County, N. C.
ANDERSON, James	Bedford County, Tenn.
ANDREWS, Ephraim	Hawkins County, Tenn.
ANDREWS, Ephraim, Sr.	Williamson County, Tenn.
AVERY, John	Columbia County, Georgia
BAILEY, Peter	Montgomery County, Tenn.
BALLARD, Robert	Maryland
BALLARD, William	Halifax County, N. C.
BARBER, Edward	Barren County, Kentucky
BARNES, James	Vigo County, Indiana
BEASLEY, John Pitts	Warren County, N. C.
BEAVERS, John	Barren County, Kentucky
BENNETT, Anthony	Kentucky
BENNETT, Joseph	Davidson County, Tenn.
BERRY, Thomas	Clark County, Kentucky
BEVILL, Edward	Madison County, Alabama
BLACKBOURN, Clement	Madison County, Alabama
BLACKWELL, John	Kentucky
BLANKS, Richard	Trigg County, Kentucky
BOSWELL, David	Williamson County, Tenn.
BOSWELL, John	Granville County, N. C.
BOWEN, Bracey	Rutherford County, N. C.
BOWEN, Charles	Putnam County, Indiana
BOWEN, John	Grainger County, Tenn.
BOWEN, Littleberry	Georgia
BOYD, William	Granville County, N. C.
BRANDON, William	Smith County, Tenn.
BRESSIE, William	Granville County, N. C.
BROOKE, Dudley	Robertson County, Tenn.
BROOKS, Robert	Pike County, Alabama
BROWN, Aries	Spartanburg District, S. C.
BUCHANAN, William W.	Clark County, Georgia
BUGG, John	Georgia
BUGG, William	Georgia
BULLOCK, James	Granville County, N. C.
BURT, William	Warren County, N. C.
BURTE, Moody	Georgia
BURTON, Abraham	Georgia
BURTON, James Minge	Wilson County, Tenn.
BURTON, Robert	Granville County, N. C.

BURTON, Thomas	Georgia
BURWELL, Armistead	Granville County, N. C.
BUSBY, John	Granville County, N. C.
BUTLER, James	Elbert County, Georgia
BUTLER, Patrick	Elbert County, Georgia
BUTLER, Zachariah	Elbert County, Georgia
CARTER, James	Chatham County, N. C.
CARTER, John	Oglethorpe County, Georgia
CAVINESS, William	Chatham County, N. C.
CHANDLER, Joel	Granville County, N. C.
CHANDLER, Jordan	Wilson County, Tenn.
CHANDLER, Robert	Granville County, N. C.
CLARK, James	Mercer County, Kentucky
CLARK, John	Edgefield County, S. C.
COX, Bartley	Georgia
COX, John	Georgia
COX, Samuel	Hopkins County, Kentucky
COX, William	Lawrence County, Kentucky
CRAWFORD, Peter	Rockingham County, N. C.
CROOK, James	Spartanburg District, S. C.
CROWDER, William	Cleveland County, N. C.
CUNNINGHAM, Anselm	Jackson County, Georgia
DAVIS, Edward	Orange County, N. C.
DELONY, William	Georgia
DORTCH, Abel	Franklin County, Illinois
DORTCH, William	Missouri
DUNCAN, John	Granville County, N. C.
DURHAM, Samuel	Green County, Kentucky
EASTLAND, Thomas	Granville County, N. C.
EVANS, Stephen	Georgia
EVANS, William	Georgia
EZELL, Balaam	Trigg County, Kentucky
FANN, Willoughby	North Carolina
FARRAR, Francis	Clark County, Georgia
FLOYD, John	Newberry District, S. C.
FOX, Richard	Bute County, N. C.
FRAZER, James	Orange County, N. C.
GEE, Nevil	Haywood County, Tenn.
GILL, William, Jr.	Granville County, N. C.
GOOCH, Joseph	Granville County, N. C.
GOLD, Daniel, Jr.	Caswell County, N. C.
GOLD, Ephraim	Caswell County, N. C.
GORDON, Charles	North Carolina
GORDON, James	North Carolina
GORDON, Thomas	North Carolina
GUNN, James	Georgia
GUY, William	Granville County, N. C.

HAILEY, William	Elbert County, Georgia
HAMNER, John	Johnson County, Indiana
HARPER, John	Kentucky
HARRISON, James	Overton County, Tenn.
HARRISON, John	Northampton County, N. C.
HASTY, James M.	Richmond County, N. C.
HAWKINS, Philemon	Bute County, N. C.
HAWKINS, Philip	Bute County, N. C.
HAYES, John T.	Christian County, Kentucky
HICKS, Benjamin	Chesterfield District, S. C.
HIX, Daniel	South Carolina
HIX, Nathaniel	Georgia
HOOD, Thomas	North Carolina
HOPKINS, Samuel, Jr.	Christian County, Kentucky
HUNT, Berry	Caswell County, N. C.
HUNT, William	Granville County, N. C.
HUNTER, Henry	North Carolina
INSCO, William	North Carolina
JARROTT, John	North Carolina
JONES, James	Granville County, N. C.
KIDD, James M.	Oglethorpe County, Georgia
KIDD, William	Oglethorpe County, Georgia
KIRKS, William	Orange County, N. C.
LANIER, Thomas	Granville County, N. C.
LEIGH, Anselm	Richmond County, Georgia
LEIGH, Walter	Richmond County, Georgia
McGOWAN, Ebenezer	Rutherford County, Tenn.
McKenney, James	Tennessee
McKINNEY, Charles	Alabama
McNEIL, Michael	Georgia
McQUIE, William	Pike County, Missouri
MALONE, Isham	Granville County, N. C.
MANN, Ephraim	Georgia
MARROW, Daniel	Granville County, N. C.
MABRY, Joshua	Warren County, N. C.
MALONE, John	Bute County, N. C.
MARSHALL, Francis	Sumner County, Tenn.
MARSHALL, Josiah	Tennessee
MITCHELL, Elijah	North Carolina
MITCHELL, James	Granville County, N. C.
MITCHELL, Joab	Mecklenburg County, N. C.
MOODY, Francis	Tuscaloosa County, Alabama
MOODY, Marshall	Haywood County, Tenn.
MOORE, George	Orange County, N. C.
MOORE, Henderson	Trigg County, Kentucky
OSLIN, Henry	Henry County, Georgia

PETTWAY, John	Warren County, N. C.
PETTIFORD, Drury	North Carolina
PHILLIPS, Thomas	Green County, Kentucky
PINSON, Aaron	Granville County, N. C.
POOL, James	Laurens District, S. C.
PUCKETT, John	North Carolina
RANDOLPH, Joseph	South Carolina
RIVES, Thomas	Chatham County, N. C.
ROSE, Howell	Granville County, N. C.
SAGE, John	Rutherford County, Tenn.
SANDIFER, James	Mercer County, Kentucky
SAUNDERS, Jesse	Georgia
SIMS, Leonard	Warren County, N. C.
SIZEMORE, Ephraim	Spartanburg District, S. C.
SKIPWITH, Peyton, Jr.	Georgia
SMITH, Anderson	Granville County, N. C.
SOMERVILLE, John	Granville County, N. C.
SPARROW, Henry	Mercer County, Kentucky
SPEED, Joseph	Haywood County, Tenn.
STROUD, William	Granville County, N. C.
SULLIVANT, Lucas	Kentucky
TANNER, Josiah	Johnson County, Indiana
TAYLOR, David	Jessamine County, Kentucky
TAYLOR, Edmund	Granville County, N. C.
TAYLOR, Jesse	Hamilton County, Illinois
TAYLOR, Richard	Granville County, N. C.
TENCH, John R.	Rutherford County, Tenn.
TILLOTSON, Edward	Montgomery County, Tenn.
TOONE, Argelon	Granville County, N. C.
TRAYLOR, Cary	Bath County, Kentucky
VAUGHAN, Ingram	Alabama
WALKER, Aurelius	Greene County, Georgia
WALKER, Benjamin	South Carolina
WALKER, Matthew	Greene County, Georgia
WALKER, Sylvanus	Greene County, Georgia
WALKER, Tandy	North Carolina
WARREN, Marriott	Richmond County, Georgia
WEATHERFORD, Benjamin	Rutherford County, Tenn.
WELLS, Jesse	Knox County, Tennessee
WESTMORELAND, Jesse	Fentress County, Tenn.
WHITE, John	South Carolina
WHITE, John F.	Trigg County, Kentucky
WHITE, William, Sr.	South Carolina
WILKERSON, Elisha	Franklin County, Georgia
WILKINS, Charles	Rutherford County, N. C.
WILLIAMS, James A.	District 96, S. C.
WILLIAMS, John	District 96, S. C.
WILLIAMS, Washington	District 96, S. C.

WILLIS, John	Surry County, N. C.
WILSON, Archibald	Guilford County, N. C.
WILSON, Caleb	Orange County, N. C.
WILSON, John	Franklin County, Kentucky
WILSON, Miles	Granville County, N. C.
WOOTTON, David C.	Christian County, Kentucky
WRIGHT, Nathan	Lincoln County, Georgia
YANCEY, Lewis	Granville County, N. C.
YANCEY, William	Granville County, N. C.

INDEX

INDEX

Abbott, George 100,161
  Samuel 96
  Watt 100
  William 83,96,100
Adaman, Mary 172
  Thomas 172
  William 172
Adams, David 151
  John 162,200
  Nathaniel 153
  Thomas 100,146,147,148,151
  William 151
Adcock, John 175
Addaman, Mary 170
  Thomas 170
Addiman, Thomas 99,170
Akin, Daniel 100
  John 100
  Joseph 17,97,100,131,134,200
  Lewis 163
  Peter 151
  Thomas 101,158
Alexander, John 6,17,131,171,173
  Martha 7,171,173,183,186
  Robert 12,142,151,161,171,173,183,186
Aliburton, David 149
Allen, Charles 96,100
  Darling 200
  David 77,96,122,124,200
  Drury 114
  John Col. 89
  John 15,17
  Philip 200
  Robert 96,175
  William 118
Allgood, Edward 151
  Ishmael 151
  John 151,200(3)
  William 200
Alling, Mary 92
  Runall 92
Anderson, James 78,129,163,200
  John 6,54,154
  Thomas 11,12,100,143,149,151
Andrews, Eleazar 163
  Ephraim, Sr. 100,110,200
  Ephraim 96,142,163,200
  John 90,100,163
  Richard 96,100,110
  Robert 175
  William 96,100,163
Armistead, John, Jr. 151
Arnest, Jacob 197
Arnold, James, Sr. 163
  James 17,96,100,143,175
  James, Jr. 151
  John 178
  Joseph 163
Ashworth, Leonard 97
Atkins, Martha 183
Atkinson, Roger 9
Austin, Isaac 155
Avent, John 17
  Thomas 17,177,81
  William 17
Avery, Henry 161
  James 100,149,161
  John 91,100,200
  Matthew 162
  Thomas 100,149
  Thomas, Jr. 100
  William 184

Bacon, Lyddall 111,114

Bacon cont.
  Nathaniel 161
Bagwell, John 161,171
Bailey, Henry 100
  Robert 151
  William 100
Baird, Benjamin 11,12,17,96,107,115,146
  John 135
  John Batte 163
Baker, Elijah 165,171
  James 194
  Jerman 17
  John Col. 9,15,61
  Josias 17
  Judith 194
  Samuel 85
  Sarah 178,194
  Thomas 17,117
  William 85,86,178,185,194
  Zachariah 97,100,143,151,194
Ballard, Edmund 163
  John 19,84,87,96,119,138,142,146,163,100
  John, Jr. 12
  Robert 200
  William 19,100,163,200
Banister, John 6,19,131
Barber, Edward 200
Barden, James Thomson 128
Barley, William 151
Barlow, Elizabeth 179
  John 180
Barnes, Charles 187
  Francis 137
  James 137,200
  John 137,138,175
Barnhill, David 166
Baskervill, George 19,125,135,138,142,146,147,151,170
  John 151,170
Bates, Henry 96,100
  John 96,115
Battersby, W. 78,81,84
Baughan, Zachariah 156,171
Beal, John 37
Beale, William 100
Bearfoot, George 90
Beasley, John Pitts 200
Beavers, John 200
Beddingfield, Henry 80,83
  John 19
  Thomas 157,168
Bell, William 100,124,144
Bennett, Absolem 151
  Anthony 200
  Joseph 19,144,163
Bentley, Samuel 184
Berringer, Michael 96
Berry, Hugh 165
  Thomas 200
Beverly, Henry 175
Bevill, Edward 121,148,149,163,200
  Joseph 121
  Luke 163
  William 100,122,130,133
  William, Jr. 121
Biassee, John 96
Biddy, Edward 151
Bilbo, Elizabeth 194
  James 96,100,121,130,161,171
  John 100
  John Peter 19,96,171
  Mary 194
  Peter 194
  Sarah 194
  William 194

Billups, Joseph 19
Bird, Barnaby 97
  William 77
Birtchett, Joseph 147,171
Bishop, Mason 175
Bizwell, Barzilia 100
  Robert 100
  Samuel 100,113,125,130,135
Black, John 100
  William 151,171
Blackbourn, Clement 200
Blackstone, John 20,175,172
  Mary 172
  Rice 172
  Sarah 183
  William 172
Blackwelder, Caleb 96,178
  Catherine 178
  Elizabeth 178
  John 96,178
  Margaret 178
  William 151
Blackwell, John 100,118,200
Blalock, Millington 87,93
  Richard 20,85,86,105,131
Bland, Marriott 151,171
  Theoderick 90
Blanks, Amy 100
  Hannah 100,195
  Harry 100
  Isaac 100
  Joseph 20,195
  Judith 197
  Richard 100,118,195,197
  Thomas 96,197
  William 96,100,195,197
Blanton, George 151
  James 20,161,171
  William 144,145,151
Boatswain, Cowey 168
Bolling, John Col. 20
  John Major 20
  John 20
  John, Jr. 20
  Robert 189
Bolton, Matthew 96
Bond, Richard 163
Booker, Edw. Jr. 118
  Richard 84,148,163
  William 132
Boone, John 104
Booth, George, Jr. 94
Boseman, John 144
Boswell, David 200
  John 200
  Joseph 138,143,148,163
  Samuel 163
Bouldin, Thomas 199
Bowdey, John 180
Bowen, Benjamin 175
  Bracey 200
  Charles 200
  David 96,151
  Drury 21
  Jesse 151
  John 200
  Littleberry 200
  Robert 21,96,100,151
  William 96,100
  William, Jr. 96
Bowers, Francis 96
Bowles, Jeremiah 161
Boyd, Alexander 161
  Patrick 90,136
  William 200
Bracey, Francis 21,96,149
  John 143
  Randall 21
  Randolph 142,147

Bracey cont.
  Thomas 100,125
Bray, John 21,165,171,195
Brame, James 151,170,171
  Richins, Sr. 170
  Richins 151,171
Brandon, Thomas 152
  William 200
Breslar, Anne 106
  Andrew 106,107,125
Bressie, Elizabeth 161,170
  Francis 89,94,100,107,
    111,120,136
  John 133
  Mary 133
  William 161,170,200
Brewer, Reese 151
  William 91
Briggs, Gray 12
Broadnax, Edward 21
  Mrs. Edward 96
  Stephen Edward 21
Brooke, Dudley 200
Brooks, Elisha 151
  George 151,189
  Rebecca 183
  Richard 100,163
  Robert 21,108,145,151,
    200
  Robert, Jr. 100
  Thomas 151,163
  William 96,101
Brown, Abram 163
  Aries 200
  Burrell 86,91
  Charles 152
  Fadias 151
  Frances 81
  George 163,171
  Henry 21,152
  Henry, Jr. 152
  Israel 96
  James 152
  Jane 81
  Jeremiah 89,90
  John 79,81
  John, Jr. 100
  Mary 86,194
  Richard 21,79,81
  Thomas 163
  Valentine 100
  William, Sr. 152
  William 152,158
  William, Jr. 152
Browne, William Jr. 82
Bruce, George 149,150
Bryant, David 100
  Isaac 155,171
  James 104
Buchanan, Nevill 152
  William W. 200
Buckstone, Samuel 82
Bugg, Anselm 21,143,147,
    152,190
  Benjamin 190
  Deborah 190
  Edmund 22,100,124,143,
    147,152,190
  Frances 190
  Jesse 152,161,190
  Agnes 190
  Jacob 127,142,146,147,
    163,190
  John 22,100,152,190,200
  Ruth 190
  Samuel, Sr. 190
  Samuel 12,124,127,132,
    137,138,142,152,190
  Samuel, Jr. 138,190
  Sarah 190
  Sherwood 22,100,124,144,
    145,152,169,190
  William 200
Bullock, David 133,149,163

Bullock cont.
  James 200
Burch, John 92
  Margret 122
  Richard 83
Burgemy, William 100
Burkes, Charles 100,123,
    134,135
  Charles, Jr. 119
Burnett, Richard 100
  Thomas 96,100
Burns, Equator 152
  James 100
Burt, William 200
Burchett, Joseph 100
Burte, Moody 200
Burton, Abram 163
  Abraham 85,200
  Allen 22
  Hutchins 22,122,125,134,
    100,137,147,152,170
  James 100,152
  James Minge 200
  John 152,170
  Josiah 152
  Robert 22,163,200
Burwell, Armistead 8,15,
    16,22,96,100,113,163,
    171,201
  Lewis Col. 148,163,171
  Lewis, Sr. 15,16,22,96
  Lewis, Jr. 16
  Thacker 16
Busby, Henry 152
  John 23,100,201
Bush, John 163
Butcher, John 16,23,77,85,
    185
Butler, George 100
  Hannah 146
  James 201
  Patrick 201
  William 23,96,155
  Zachariah 201
Byrd, Col. William 9,15,16,
    23,90,96,100,112,123

Caden, Redman 80
Cain, William 152
Caldwell, John 185
  William 185
Calliham, David 96,100
  John 96
  Nicholas 96
Calvin, William 103
Camp, John 11,150,152,171
Campbell, James 163
  Robert 24,145
  Walter 88,90,94,107
Cane, George 135
Cannon, William 95
Cardin, John 164
Cardwell, John 24,134
Cargill, Betty Brown 194
  Cornelius 24,79,80,82,
    83,84,85,87,96,100,114,
    137,138,180,185,186,
    194,195,197
  Cornelius, Jr. 100,184
  Elizabeth 80,83,84,195
  Hannah 195,197
  John 100,115,120,197
Carleton, Thomas 100,143,
    148,149,163,164,171
Carmichael, Duncan 152
Carrington, Paul 131
Carroll, Benjamin 93
  Daniel 77,88
  Dennis 152
  Elias 152
  John 93,96
Carter, Edward 135
  James 24,113,121,201
  John 201

Carter cont.
  Timothy 96,100
Cary, James, Jr. 134
Caviness, Henry 152,170
  Thomas 152,160,170
  William 152,170,201
Cely, William 96
Challis, John 96
Chamberlain, Joseph 179
Chamberlayne, Thomas 24,
    152,164
Chambliss, Nathaniel 100
Chamley, Nathaniel 96
Chandler, Elizabeth 194
  James 100,161
  Jesse 154
  Joel 100,161,201
  Joel, Jr. 100
  John 100
  Jordan 201
  Joseph 24,96,100,114
  Robert 201
  Samuel 161
  William, Sr. 101
  William 96,164
  William, Jr. 101
Chassels, William 123
Chavis, George 101
  Jacob 24
Chavous, Henry 152
  Jacob 152
  James 152
Cheatham, James 132
Childress, John 148,152
Chiswell, James 101
Christopher, David 164
  Robert 164
Clack, John 25
  Sterling 112
Claiborne, James 131
  L. Sr. 107,108
  L. Jr. 128
  T. 137
  Thomas 120
Clanch, Jeremiah 96
Clanton, Edward 82
Clark, Archibald 152
  Bolling 25
  Francis 152
  James 152,201
  Jesse 152
  John 25,136,142,152,201
  Joshua 86,89,90
  Robert 89,90
  Samuel 89,90
  Samuel, Jr. 6,79
  Sarah 89,90
Clarke, Carter 191
  Edward 25,96
  Frances 191
  James 25
  Jesse 191
  John 96,191
  Jordan Thomas 191
  Susannah 191
  Thomas 133,191
Claunch, Jeremiah 25,101
  John 101
Cleaton, John 144,152
  William 144,152
  William, Jr. 152
Clements, John 79,82,93
Clemons, Elizabeth 180
  Hannah 180
  Jane 180
  John 105,180
  John Young 180
  Susanna 110
  Susannah 180
Clift, William 165
Clifton, Thomas 111
Coates, Henry 101
Cobbs, Wingfield 96
Cocke, James 147

Cocke cont.
  Richard 96
  Thomas Col. 79
  Thomas 15,25
  William 153
Cockerham, Henry 101
  Philip 101
Cole, John 96,134,135
Coleman, Abner 153
  Ben 153
  Benedict 153
  Christopher 153
  Clary 89,114,122
  Cluverius 148
  James 25,88,89,96,100,
    107,114,122,125,134,
    142,153
  John 26
  Phil 153
  Robert 153
  William 153
Coles, John 84
Coleson, Abraham 102,130
  Jacob 102,130,133
  Joseph 175
  Winney 130,133
Colison, John 184
Colley, Edward 164
Collier, Drury 167
  Howell 142,145,153
  Nathaniel 145
  Thomas 179
  William 26
Colson, Daniel 96
Connell, Robert 101,164
Cook, Abraham 26,86,92,
    185,186
  Anne 181
  Barbara 186
  Benjamin 101,186
  Benjamin Mrs. 96
  Berryman 183
  Charles 186
  Dianna 172
  Dinah 172
  Frances 186
  Frederick 183
  James 101,185,186
  Jane 181
  John 26,172,183
  John Lett 26,101,153,
    181
  Martha 183
  Nathaniel 96,101,113,
    115,146,153
  Nicholas 103
  Rebecca 183
  Reuben 101,151,183
  Richard 172,181
  Robert 183
  Sarah 92,181,183,186
  William 183
Cooper, John McDonald 96
  William 160
Cope, Thomas 153
Cordell, Bryant 147,164
Corn, Robert 152,184
Couch, James 175
  Thomas, Jr. 175
  William 175
Courtney, C. 132
  Clack 26,144,145
Cox, Bartley 201
  Bolling 164,171
  Frederick 95,164,171
  Henry 131,134
  John, Sr. 164,171
  John 8,11,26,27,95,96,
    101,105,108,113,120,
    164,201
  John, Jr. 143,164,171
  Samuel 201
  Thomas 164,171
  William 164,201

Cousens, Charles 137
Cozens, Charles 146
  Robert 147
Crackendale, Henry 83
Craddock, David 100
Craig, Thomas 151
Crawford, Peter 201
Crawley, Robert 27,162
  Samuel 175
Creed, Matthew 175
Crenshaw, Gideon 101,133
  Joseph 101
  Joseph, Jr. 101
Crews, Joseph 153
Crook, James 201
Crowder, Abraham 27,148
  Batt 164
  James 161
  Jeremiah 27,164
  Joshua 153
  Robert 153
  Stephen 161
  William 201
Crump, Stephen 101
Culbreath, Edward 27,153
  John 27,96,101,153
  Joseph 153,170
  Mary 27,153,170
  Peter 27,96,153
  William 96,143,153
  William, Jr. 153
Cunningham, Anselm 201
  James 101,148
  Jonathon 161
  Robert 27,167
  William 153
Currie, John 101
Curry, George 92

Daniel, Chesley 9
  Elizabeth 28,83,195
  Hugh 28
  James 9,28,135
  John 92
  Josiah 9,153
Darden, David 164
Davidson, William 89,93
Davies, Joseph 101
Davis, Baxter 28,81,96,
    101,153
  Baxter, Jr. 153
  Edward 96,100,153,201
  Edward, Jr. 153
  John 28,78,79,80,81,82,
    85,86,87,90,96,101,114,
    120,125,134,153
  William, Capt. 144,153
  William 28,29,96,134,
    101,142
Dean, John 102
Decker, Henry 29,96,101
Delony, Anne 106
  Anne, Junr. 106
  Frances 123,191
  Henry 11,96,101,106,114,
    116,122,123,126,131,
    134,135,137,142,146,
    147,164,169
  Lewis 29,79,96,106,116,
    120,178
  Lewis, Jr. 29,96
  Mary 191
  Rebecca 191
  William 201
Dempsey, Patrick 177
Dendy, Eliza 117
  Martha 117
  Thomas 197
  William 117
Denton, William 181
Dickson, Henry 79
  Thomas 29
Dishman, William 96
Dixon, Judith 153

Dixon cont.
  Thomas 144
Dobyns, William 113
Dockery, James 175,188
Dodd, David 95,97,102,107
  John 86,87
Dodson, Joseph 161
Doggett, John 166
Donald, Alexander 29,153
Donithon, William 149,150
Dortch, Abel 201
  David 29,96,101,118,142,
    145,146,164,169,170
  John 118,119
  John, Jr. 29
  Noah 164,170
  Ruth 119
  William 201
Dorum, Patrick 82,175
Douglas, George 153
  John 30,153
  William 91,96,153,175
Downing, James 101
Dowsing, William 164
Draper, Joshua 153
  Solomon 148
  Thomas 163
Drew, Elizabeth 197
  Hewit 86
  Newer 30
Drysdale, Robert 167
Duggins, Thomas 92
Duke, Bridget 181
  Henry 164
  Jane 89,108
  John 80,81,85,88,96,108
  John Taylor 30,88,96,101,
    108,118,153
  Rejoyce 85
  Rireyel 108
  Taylor 146
Duncan, George 160
  John 101,201
Dunkley, Moses 79,83,90
  Ralph 88
Dunman, James 101
  Joseph 101,164,175
  William 101
Dupree, Joseph 197
  Lewis 30
Durham, Samuel 201
Dutoy, Isaac 194

Earle, John 96,101,125,
    127,147,154
Easley, William 161
East, Isham 101
  Joseph 101,123
Easter, James 164
  John 154
  Robert 149
Eastland, Joseph 96,101,
    142,161,170
  Thomas 30,96,101,161,170
  Will 170
  William 161
Eaton, John 168
  William 177
Edens, William 163
Edloe, John 97
  William 101
Edmonds, Thomas 154
Edmunds, Nicholas 30,79,
    89
Edmondson, Samuel 184
Edmundson, Richard 154
  Thomas 147
Edwards, John 164
  Nathaniel 129,164
  William 30,97,113,148
Eggleston, Thomas 136
Elam, Edward 129
  Joel 164,184

Elam cont.
  William 128
Ellidge, Francis 31,97,
  109,111,116
  Francis (Estate) 101
Ellis, Abraham 101,154
  James 154,184
  Jeremiah 97,101
Embry, David 194
  Henry 178
  John 112,121
  William 121
Eppes, John Jr. 136
Epps, Edward 101,144
  Isaac 101
  John 31
  Peter 101
Erskine, Alexander 31
  Thomas 11,13,164
Estes, Benjamin 164
Evans, Charles 97,101,
  144,161
  Dick 145,154
  Elizabeth 82
  Gilbert 101,168
  Humphry 84
  John 82,101
  Major 101,161
  Morris 129,164
  Richard 129
  Robert 31,164
  Stephen, Sr. 164
  Stephen 31,101,143,149,
  150,201
  Stephen, Jr. 164
  Thomas 97,101,154,164
  William 31,164,201
Ezard, John 32
Ezell, Baalam 201
  George 97
  James 164
  John 95,142,164
  John, Jr. 164
  Michael 97
  Mitchell 164
  William 165

Fain, Joel 153
  John 102,112,153
Fann, Anthony 178
  Jesse 154
  John 184
  William 154
  Willoughby 201
Farmer, Lodowick 165,171
Farrar, Abel 184
  Feild 32,101,127,128,
  154
  Francis 201
  George 97,101,142,161
  John 32,161
  Martha 128,191
  Peter 126
  Thomas 32,101,117,122,
  133,165
  William 122,154,184
Fanquier, Francis 11
Feagin, Edward 154
  Henry 161
Feild, Theophilus 9,32,33,
  79,90,161,171
Ferrell, Ephraim 154,171
  Hubbard 33
  James 129,146,147,154,
  171
  Mary 103
Ferris, Jacob 32
Fifer, Martin 115
Finch, Adam 165,171
Finney, Alexander 33
  Thomas 97
Firth, Daniel 97
Fleming, Col. John 165
Fletcher, Amy 119

Fletcher cont.
  Elizabeth 82
  John 97,119,186
  William 82,175
Flinn, George 101
  James 101,154
Flower, Jesse 109
Flowers, Samuel 101,167,
  171
Floyd, George 97
  John 201
  Josiah 33,112
  Joyce 181
  Mary 181
  Richard 33,97,101,154,
  165
Flynn, John 123,165
Folio, Luke 149
Fontaine, John 7
  Peter, Jr. 7
Forrest, John 97
Fountain, John 175
Fowler, Alexander 161
  Alexander, Jr. 154
  John 33,101,154
  William 161
Fox, Hannah 198
  Jacob 154,170
  Richard 83,97,101,131,
  142,154,169,170,171
  William 154
Frail, John 154
  Patrick 154
Franklin, Hugh 149,163,171
  Owen 33,154
  Thomas 97
Frazer, James 201
Freeman, John 96,106,165,
  188
  Joseph 143,148,165

Gafford, Thomas 101
Gaines, John 154
Gale, Simon 179
Garland, David 33
Garner, Conaway 165
Garrett, Humphry 97
  Thomas 101
Gee, James 101
  Nevil 101,201
  William 101
Gentry, David 101
  Nicholas 109
George, Aaron 151
Gianano, Silvester 187
Gibson, Jacob 198
  Joseph 198
Giles, Edward 154
  John 154
Gileness, John 97
Gill, Henry 101
  Joseph 101,143,148,154
  Peter 148
  William 97,101,154
  William, Jr. 201
Gilliam, John 34,97,101,
  135
  Robert 101
Gionano, Silvester 187
Gish, Benjamin 101
Given, John 108
Gladdin, Richard 97,154
  William 97
Glass, John 101,128,154
  Josiah 157
  Samuel 161
  Thomas 157
  William 157
Glasscock, John 154
  Sarah 198
Glebe, Glebe Land 154
Goff, William 178
Gold, Daniel 154
  Daniel, Jr. 201

Gold cont.
  Ephraim 201
  Margaret 195
Golstone, Charles 175
Gooch, Joseph 201
Goode, Edward 101,143,148,
  165
  Feeby 128,129,137
  John 154
  Joseph 165
  William 117,128,129,136,
  137
Goodrich, Edward 108,121
Gordon, Charles 201
  Gilbert 97,101
  James 201
  John 34,97,101
  Samuel 90
  Thomas 201
Gorre', Daniel 34,101
  John 101,121,165,171
Gourd, John 194
Gowen, John 97,101
  Joseph 101
Graham, Andrew 104
Graves, Elijah 154,170
  Mary 154,170
Gray, Joseph 146,147
Green, Abigail 172,188
  Dorcas 188
  Dorcus 172
  Elizabeth 172,188
  Frederick 154,188
  Gardiner 154
  Henry 34,97,172,188
  Jemima 172
  John 34,97,172,188
  Lewis 97
  Mary 172
  Richard 154,188
  Stephen 154,188
  Thomas 165
  William 35
  Winifred 172
Greenwood, Thomas 188
Greer, Joseph 34,101,136,
  148,165
Gregory, Andrew 167
  Isaac 161
  James 167
  Lena 165
  William 165
Griffin, Elizabeth 188
  Francis 97
  James 34,155
  John 97,102,155
  Ralph 98,110
  Richard, Sr. 97
  Richard 108,184,188
  William 35,97,155
Griffith, John 165,194
  Thomas 165
Grigg, Moses 158,170
Griggs, John 163
Grissell, John 97
Gunn, James 201
  George 35,155
Gunston, George 35,155
Guy, William 201

Hagood, Benjamin 97
  Mary 179
  William 97,108
  William, Jr. 97,102
Hailey, William 202
Haliburton, David 129,138
Halin, Edward 81
Hall, Edmund 35,83,84
  James 165
  John 79,105,117
Halpin, William 96,102
Hamblin, William 98
Hamlin, Elizabeth 195
  Thomas 184,195

Hammond, Job 165
  John 165
  Martin 153
Hamner, James 138,142,146
  John 202
  Joseph 165
Hampton, Andrew 87
Hancock, William 189
Haney, Thomas 175
Hannah, John 98
Hardaway, Thomas, Sr. 109
Harden, Gabriel 102
  William 102
Hargrove, Howell 97
  James 155
Harper, George 181
  Henry 181
  John 202
  Laselton 181
  Newman 181
  Penelopa 181
  Richard 181
  Susanna 181
Harris, Ben 131,134,135
  Benjamin 35,155,171
  Charles 102
  John 81
  John, Jr. 85
  Judith 115
  Samuel 35,40,97,102,113,
    115
  Solomon 97,155
  William 35,36,97,102,
    115,128,143(2),149,
    165
Harrison, Benjamin 90,97,
    102,161
  Blanch 183
  Elizabeth 183
  Gabriel 77,79,85,86,185
  James 202
  John 182,202
  Moses 165
  Samuel 189
  Thomas 102
Hart, Philip 189
Harwell, Anne 182
  James, Sr. 146
  James 36
  James, Jr. 146
  Mark 88,125
  Samuel 36,88,178
Harwood, Col. William
    155,171
Haskins, Henry 165
Hasty, James M. 202
Hatchell, Henry 97
  John 102
  Stephen 102
  William 97,102
  William, Jr. 97
Hatcher, Frederick 36
  Jeremiah 102
  Robert 102
Hatsell, Stephen 155
  William 155
  William, Jr. 36
Hawkins, Drury 172
  John 196
  Martha 172,183
  Mary 196
  Nathan 195
  Philemon 202
  Philip 202
  Pinkethman 97,102,117,
    122,127,130,133
  Rebecca 127
  Sarah 196
  Thomas 36,97,102,105,
    107,117,121,122,124,
    126,134,136,149
  William 37
Hawks, Isaac 155

Hayes, John 155
  John, Jr. 155
  John T. 202
  Mark 93
Haynes, Anthony 37
Hayward, Francis 89
  William 89
Haywood, Francis 37
Hazelrig, Samuel 160
Hazlewood, Daniel 155
Head, William 145,152
Hearn, John 97,102
Hendrick, John 145
Henry, Edward 97,102
Heock, William 165
Herbert, John 37
Hester, Abraham 155,170
  Barbara 186
  Frances 133,186
  James 92,133,155,170
  Robert 92,93,170
  Robert, Jr. 37,170,186
Hewey, Humphry 37,97,144,
    145
  James 155
  John 155
Hewlin, Edward 178
Hewitt, John 37
Hickman, Joseph 132
Hicks, Benjamin 202
  Daniel 77
  George 81
  James, Jr. 112
  John 102
  Joseph 178
  Nathaniel 86
  Robert, Sr. 6,78
  Robert 81,106
  Robert, Jr. 81
  Sarah 77
High, John 109
Hight, John 37
Hightower, John 37,131,147
  Thomas 102,198
Hill, Catherine 115
  James, Sr. 118
  Nicholas 102
  William Major 38
  William 38,97,102,106,
    107,114,123,132,149,
    155,165,171
Hilton, Thomas 97
Hix, Amos 155
  Daniel 202
  George 38
  James 38,97,102,155
  Joseph 97
  Nathaniel 202
  Robert, Sr. 79,88
  Robert 38,88
  Robert, Jr. 39,88
Hobbs, Job 107
  Robert 107
Hobson, John 102
  Nicholas 102
  Philip 132
Hogan, Edward 149,150,
    155,171
  William 97,189
Hogwood, John 102
  William 39,102
Holloway, Bennett 146,
    147,165
  George 39,97,111,154,
    102
  James 154,156
  John 107
  William 155,184
Holmes, Ann 192
  Anne 111
  Elizabeth 192
  George 161
  Isaac 97,107,113,146,
    147,155,170

Holmes cont.
  Mary 192
  Richard 192
  Samuel 39,97,102,111,
    114,146,155,170
  Samuel, Jr. 97,102,155,
    170
  Thomas 192
  William 102,142,146,155
    170
Homes, Charles 155
Hood, Edward 80
  Robert 155
  Thomas 202
Hooper, Obadiah 102
Hopkins, Samuel 11,147,
    148,155
  Samuel, Jr. 202
Hopper, Michael 39
Hopson, John 102
  Richard 102
House, Isaac 181,182
  Lawrence 39,107
  Mary 182
  William 183
Houseman, Stephen 101
Howard, Christopher 39
  Dianna 106
  Elenor 193
  Elinor 197
  Elizabeth 193,197
  Francis 40,97,105,106,
    111,124,148
  Hannah 193
  Henry 40,97,102,122,124,
    127,155
  Mary 193
  Sarah 105
  William 40,97,105,106,
    111,116,148,162
Howell, John 102,110,165
Hownam, James 129,136
Hubbard, John 132,149,165
  Matthew 40
Hudgins, Josiah 162
Hudson, Cary 105
  Charles 165
  Christopher 92,93,97,
    105,109,110,111,116,
    121,143,148,149,155
  Christopher, Jr. 155
  Daniel 102
  Ephraim 144,155,184
  James 102
  John 40,152,171
  Peter 102
  Richard 102,155
  Robert 40,101,144,155
  Robert, Jr. 101
  Samuel 87,90,91
  William 155,165
Huey, Humphry 102
Hughes, Anthony 149
  Edward 40
  Elijah 152
  Samuel 154
Hulen, Edward 89
Humphreys, Charles 40,97,
    109,115,117
  John 40,97,102,109,115,
    116,117,119,121,142,
    148,165
  Marisucar 120
  Mary 110
  Thomas 40,97,109,115,
    117
  William 40,97,109,110,
    115,117
Humphries, John 113,175
  Richard 179
Humphris, Catherine 172
  Jane 172
  Robert 172
Humphry, William

Hunt, Berry 202
　Memucan 40,131
　William 13,115,165,202
Hunter, Henry 202
　James 155
Husky, William 155
Hutchins, Robert 41
Hyde, John 41,97,122,124,
　125,127,131,132,143,
　148,149,165
　Martha 124
　Richard 91

Ingram, John 41
Irby, John 179
　William 194
Ireland, George 188
Insco, William 202
Irvine, Christopher 93
　Mary 93
Isbell, Henry 133,165

Jackson, Ambrose, Sr. 182
　Ambrose 178
　Ambrose, Jr. 178,182
　Anne 182
　Daniel 182
　Hannah 181
　Henry 41,102,155
　John 155,177
　Ralph 181,182
　William 188
James, Ann 196
　Francis 196
Jarrett, Thomas 97
Jarrod, Thomas 82
Jarrott, John 202
Jefferson, Feild 41,97,
　102,105,106,112,122,
　123,134,137,139,147,
　162,170
　Frances 191
　George 147,170
　John 147,162,170
　Mary 191
　Peter Feild 142,162,170
　Thomas 97,112,116
Jeffries, John 149,155,
　170
　John, Jr. 148,163,171
　Swepson 155,170
Jenkins, William 82,180
Johns, John 158,170
Johnson, Aaron 175
　Christopher 41,102,137
　Daniel 148,155
　Isaac 165
　James 165
　John 41,102,156,162
　Marmaduke 177
　Michael 102,156
　Philemon 165
　Philip 41
　Richard 157,178
　William 102
Johnston, John 83,84
　Michael 41
　Peter 41
Jones, Daniel 165,171
　Francis 143
　Frederick 6,42,136
　Harwood 156,171
　Henry 95
　James 79,102,202
　John 42,90,95,136,156
　Peter Capt. 149
　Peter 129,136,156,171
　Richard 54
　Robert 42,156,185
　Robert, Jr. 42,90,91,
　97,102,107,113,116,
　121,125,145
　Samuel 6,42,139
　Stephen 42,156

Jones cont.
　Tabitha 156
　Thomas 90,97,175
　Tignal, Sr. 12,156,171
　Tignal 143
　Tignal, Jr. 156,171
　Vinckler 156,162
　William Capt. 97
　William 43,97,118,129,
　149,156
Jouniours, Silvester 187
Judkins, James 177
Juniel, Sylvester 187
Justice, John 156

Kay, William 137
Keeton, Joseph 43
Keith, Cornelius 6,7,79,
　82,88,106,176
　Elizabeth 88
Kendrick, John 156
Kennon, Robert 43
Kidd, James 43
　James M. 202
　Lewis 156
　William 202
Kilcrease, John 175
Killcrease, Robert 90
Killingsworth, Edward 102
Killoe, Hugh 168
Kimball, Charles 43,78,83,
　85,86,94,169
King, Charles 81,92
　George 43,78,87,89,162
　Henry 162,164,166
　John 43,91,96,101,124,
　130,133,162
　Overby 162
　Peter 44
　Susanna 87
　Thomas 120
　William 44,97,102,162
Kirk, James 156
　Michael 115
　Stephen 156
Kirks, Samuel 102
　William 202
Kitchen, Anthony 164
　John 156
Krug, Andrew 44

Lacks, Henry 162
Ladd, Gerrard 166
　John 156
　Joseph 156
　Thomas 156
　William 153,166
　William, Jr. 44
Lambert, Cleaton 156
　Hugh 156
　James 156
　Jervis 156
　John 156
　Joseph 156
　William 44,156
Langford, Henry 102
　John 97,102,113
Langley, John 91,97
　Robert 44,145
　Thomas 151
Lanier, Benjamin 44,116,
　119
　Bird Thomas 44,78,90,97,
　130
　Elizabeth 132
　John 156
　Nicholas 44
　Thomas 45,88,97,102,106,
　115,132,202
Lankford, George 144
　Henry 156
　John 45,144,156
Lantor, Jacob 155
Lark, Dennis 12,45,95,96,

Lark cont.
　Dennis cont. 102,107,
　115,118,134,135,138,
　142,146,156,170
　John 156,170
　Joseph 97,118
　Mary 192
　Robert 97,102,115,142,
　145,146,166
Larke, Anne 118
Lawrence, William 97
Lawson, Hugh 185
Lax, William 102
Leach, John 153
Lee, Agnes 190
　Walter 156
Leigh, Agnes 190
　Anselm 202
　Walter 190,202
Lett, Amy 92
　Francis 45,92,102,109,
　146,166
　Isham 146
　James, Sr. 146
　James 46,102,107,142,
　146,156
　James, Jr. 146
　John 46,107,115,146,156
　Joseph 184
Lewis, Charles 119
　Edward 102,133,149,150,
　162
　Howell 156,171
　James 46,143,156
Lidderdale, Jane 180
　William 46,97,102,105,
　150
Lightfoot, Francis 184
　John 46
　William Marston 138,139
Lindsey, William 132,147
Locklain, Randolph 162
Long, George 156
　John 109
　Richard 149,156
Love, William 135
Loyd, Priscilla 183
　Sarah 182
　Thomas 91,182
　Thomas, Jr. 46,94
Lucas, Charles 46,166,179
　David 95,179
　John 97,110,179
　Martha 179
　Samuel 46,47,146,179
　William 47,142,145,146,
　157,166,179
Lundy, Richard 97,102,116
Lynch, John 47,157

McAdum, John 102
McCarthy, Edmond 47
McCarty, John 157
McConnell, John 111
McCoy, Elisha 101
　Jane 166
　John 166
McCutcheon, John 164
McDaniel, Edward 47,157
　James 47,102,166
　John 47,102
　Michael 97
McDavid, William 85
McDearman, Michael 166
McDonald, James 102
　James, Jr. 102
　John 98,109
McDowell, Hugh 180
　William 148
McGowan, Daniel 104
　Ebenezer 202
McHarg, Ebenezer 48
McKay, John Noble 102
McKenney, James 102,112,

McKenney cont.
  James cont. 113,202
McKinney, Charles 202
  James 48
  William 95
McKnight, William 92,93
McKoy, John 48
McLin, John 145
  Thomas 145
McMullan, Terence 103
McNabb, Alexander 164
McNeil, Catharine 173
  Daniel 98,128,136,157
  John 184
  Malcolm 48,98,173
  Michael 98,202
McQuie, Michael 102,166
  William 202

Mabry, Ephraim 102,121,
    125,126,130,166
  Joshua 48,139,142,145,
    157,202
  Joshua, Jr. 157
Mack, George 101
Maclin, John 48,49,124,
    135
  Mary 182
  Thomas 102,166
  William 49,83
Major, Mary 111,118
  Nicholas 49,98,102,110,
    118,122,130,133
Mallett, Judith 191
  Olive Magdalene 191
  Stephen, Sr. 102,121,
    130
  Stephen 142,157,171,191
  Stephen, Jr. 102,121,
    130,166
  William 102,130
Malone, Drury 49,84,98,
    102,113,142,144,157
  George 49
  Isham 49,144,157,166,
    202
  John 157,202
  Nathaniel 115
  Phillip 157
  Thomas 49,84,98,102,112,
    113,142,144,157
  William 50
Mangum, John 157
Mann, Ephraim 202
Manning, Henry 98,102
  John 102,145
  Samuel 50,98,102,145,
    157,175
  Samuel, Jr. 102
  Thomas 184
  William 102,175
Marable, Matthew 50,98,
    124,133
  William 50,98,102,133,
    157
Marr, G. (Gideon) 89
Marrow, Daniel 202
Marshall, Francis 202
  James 166
  Josiah 202
  Samuel 51
Martin, Abraham 131
  Elizabeth 177
  John 51,95,102
  Thomas 177
  William 159,171
Mason, John
  Richard 157
Matthews, Anne 78,86
  Ezekiel 178
  Jacob 146
  James 51,78,81,86
  John, Jr. 51
  Thomas 184

Matthias, Charles 166
Mattox, William 182
Maury, James 9
Maxcedan, John 131
Maxey, John 101
Mayes, John 102,116,117,
    150
  Matthew 103
Maynard, John 157,170
  Nicholas 157,170
Mclain, John 125
Mealer, Ann 157
  Matthew 157
  William 166
Mealey, John 175
Medley, Joseph 166
Meriott, William 81
Merritt, John 175
Merryman, Abraham 166
Messersmith, Conrad 166
Michaux, Jacob 171
  Jacob, Jr. 157
Miles, George 162
Miller, Brice 157
  Hugh 9,114,116,135
  Jacob 51
  Joseph 51,93
  Mary 193
Minor, James 103
  Joseph 103,108,111,137
Miskell, Henry 198
Mitchell, Amy 88
  Barbara 183
  Catherine 196
  Daniel 98,162
  David 103
  Elijah 202
  Hannah 138
  Henry 98,157
  Isaac 94,98,103,120,142,
    162
  Jacob 94,98,103,157
  Jacob, Jr. 103
  James 52,80,88,94,98,103,
    108,120,121,123,130,
    202
  James, Jr. 98,103
  Joab 98,134,202
  John 52,87,88,89,103,125
  Josiah 94
  Judith 88
  Kersia 182
  Kesiah 183
  Mary 134,196
  Rebecca 126
  Robert 52,53,78,80,81,
    82,114,120,138
  Susanna 182
  Thomas 53,80,81
  William 53
Mize, Henry 103
  James 82,98,103,110
  James, Jr. 98
  Jeremiah 98,103
  John 98,103,166
  Stephen 98,103
  William 98
Monroe, William 184
Moody, Francis 202
  Marshall 202
Moon, Thomas 13,187
Moore, George 157,188,202
  Henderson 202
  Hugh 98
  Joel 166
  John 53
  Mark 166
  Mary 117,127
  Robert 103
  Seth 53
  Thomas 53,117,122,124,
    127,135,136,157,175
  Thomas, Jr. 157
  William 78,166

Moreman, Andrew 85,89,98,
    106,107,111
  Andrew, Jr. 98,112
  Benjamin 98
  Charles 98
Morgan, John 103,139,173
  Mary 173
  Philip 53,78,79,81,82,
    83,84,85,92,98,103,
    106,116,145,163,173,
    175,176
  Reuben 98,145,147,157,
    103,173
  William 162
Morris, Henry 7,8,64,65,
    112,123,175
  William 53
Morrison, James 156
Morrow, John 103
Morson, Alexander 152
Moshier, Nicholas 178
Moss, David 166
  Stephen 182
Mullen, Pat. 121
  Valentine 98
Mullins, Richard 157
  Valentine 103,105,149,
    150,157
Munday, Isaac 184
Munford, Edward 6,128,129
  James 53,90
  Mary 6,128,129
  Robert Capt. 184
  Robert 6,11,12,13,15,
    54,77,82,89,92,129,
    150,157
  William 54
Munroe, John 162
Murphey, Benn 166
  Benjamin 103
  James 194
  John, Sr. 166
  John 166
  William 157,166
  William, Jr. 157
Murphy, Daniel 178
  Drury 54
  John 113
  William 98,103
Murray, James 54
  John 150
Musampe, George 157
  William 157
Myrick, Owen 55,98,103,
    135

Nance, Daniel 112,113,144
  David 178
  Elizabeth 112
  John 119
  Robert 184
  Thomas 144,184
  William 55,144
Napier, John 55
Nash, Thomas 116,131
Neal, Thomas 166
Nelson, Thomas 11
Newman, Richard 137,147
Newsom, Amos 103
Newton, Henry 157
  John, Sr. 157
  John, Jr. 157
  Robin 157
  William 158
Nichols, Julius 96,103,
    105,110,111,114,118,
    121,123,130,132
  Mary 134,191
  William 103,134
Nicholson, Joshua 55
Nipper, Alexander 98
  Ann 173
  Anne 180
  James 98,180

Nipper cont.
  John 77,87,180
  John, Jr. 158
  Martha 173,180
Nobles, Elizabeth 172
  Mark 172
  Robert 55,172
Noblin, Thomas 166
Norment, William 158,170
Norrell, Mary 158
  Thomas 158
Norrill, Francis 184
  Hugh 55,103
  James 184
  Thomas 103
Northington, Jabez 55
Norton, Stephen 103
Norvell, Hugh 142
Norwood, Elizabeth 191
  Sarah 191
  Richard 191
Nott, James 98

Ogburn, John 182
  Tabitha 182
Oldham, Samuel 160
Oliver, Isaac 166
  James 56
  John 163,166,171
O'Neal, Hugh 85
Orchard, Matthew 100
Orgain, Matthew 103
Organ, William Darby 165
O'Reily, Philip 79,80
Osborne, John 184
Reps 98,128,129
Oslin, Henry 202
Overby, Nicholas 98,103,
  143,158
  Obadiah 158
  Peter, Sr. 98,103
  Peter 143,158,171
  Peter, Jr. 98,203
Owen, Edward 98
  Evan 155,171
  James 184
  John 188
  Joseph 98,188

Paisley, John 133
Palmer, George 198
  Joseph 198
  Joshua 198
  Martha 198
  Mary Ann 198
  Parmenas 198
  Pirmenas 149
  Prudence 198
  Rebecca 198
  Reuben 198
  Richard 98,103,105,110,
    134,143,149,150
  Robert 198
  Thomas 166,198
  Truman 198
  William 198
  William, Jr. 163
  Winifred 198
Palmore, Edward 158
  John 162
Pankey, John
  Stephen 162
Parham, Ephraim 56,83,87
  James 82
  Lewis 9,56,78,84,91,112,
    116,123,128
  Matthew 181
  Sarah 124
  William 144
Parish, James 78
Park, James 166
Parker, John 56,103,108
  Samuel 103
  William 98,103

Parnell, John 98
Parrish, David 184
  Henry 128,132
  James 56,84,89,113,117,
    121
  John, Jr. 84
  Moses 184
  Peter 103,147
Patrick, John 98,134,144,
    145,158
Peasley, Rev. William 158
Peebles, Jehu 85
  John 89
Pemberton, Richard 18
Pennell, William 142
Pennington, George
  James 56,158
  John 142
  John George 98,103,158
  Sack (Isaac) 56
  William 56,87,175,176
Pepper, Martha 183
  Richard 183
Peringer, Michael 103
Perrin, Joseph 92
Perry, Nathaniel 91
  William 158
Person, Thomas 89
Peters, Edward 102
Pettiford, Drury 203
Pettus, Thomas 120,166
Pettway, John 203
Petty, Francis Moor(e) 119
Pettypool, John 98
  Peter 98
  Seth 98,175
  Seth, Jr. 98
Phelps, John 93,185
Phifer, Martin 57,98,114,
    125,130
Phillips, Thomas 158,203
Pinkstone, Richard 166,167,
    171
Pinson, Aaron 57,98,103,
    108,158,170,175,203
  Aaron, Jr. 98,108,189
  Elinor 189
  Elonor 189
  John 158,170,189
  Sarah Ann 189
  Thomas 158,170,189
Piron, Charles 151
Pleasant, John 148
Poindexter, Philip 57,103,
    166
Pool, Adam 57,145,158
  Elizabeth 130,192
  Frances 173
  James 203
  Philip 173
  Tabitha 173
  Thomas 100
  William, Sr. 145
  William 57,58,158
  William, Jr. 158
Poole, Adam 103
  Robert 98,103,125,130
  W. 82
  William 84,87,89,95,98,
    103,124,125,129,130,
    184
  William, Jr. 103,125,130
Pope, John 162
Potter, Daniel 98
  John 11,12,13,161,196
  Mary 196
Pouncey, Anthony 105
Powell, Ed 136
  John 158
  Richard 158
Presley, Andrew 92
Price, John 103
  Rice 93
Prosise, George 166,170

Prosise cont.
  Lewis 170
  Thomas 166,170
  William 166,170
Puckett, Isham, Sr. 166
  Isham, Jr. 166
  John 203
Pulliam, Benjamin 149,150,
    157,158
  Patterson 58
  William 58
Pully, Spettle 147,162
Purger, John 150
  Peter 150
Puryear, John 158
  John, Jr. 158
  Peter 58,110,136
Pyland, Hannah 111
  Thomas 111
Pyle, Andrew 97

Rabourn, John 58
Ragsdale, Benjamin 135
  John, Sr 103
  John 167
  Joseph 121,167
  Peter 58
  Richard 167
  William 158
Rainey, Francis 58,158
  William 157
Ramboe, Christopher 189
Ramsey, John 163
  Richard 175
Ranburry, Christopher 189
Randle, John 91
  Josias 58,79,89,116
  William 91
Randolph, Joseph 203
Ravenscroft, John 58
  Robert 59
  Thomas 59,136
Rawlins, Thomas 175
Ray, Francis 98,110,118,
    137
  Rachel 110,118
Rayley, Miles 77
Rayney, Francis 144,175
Read, Clem 81,83
  Clement 88,106,107,116,
    175
Reily, Charles 103
  Charles, Jr. 103
Renn, William 161
Reynolds, Joyce 178
  Sherwood 98
  William 178
Richards, Jonathon 103
Richardson, Richard 59
  William 103,158
Riddle, William 132
Ridley, George 59
Rigby, James 175
Riggby, James 83
Rivers, William 98
Rives, Isaac 167
  Thomas 91,203
Robards, Bartholomew 180
  George 180
  Sarah 180
  William 180
Roberts, James 98,158
  John 59
  Philip 59,87,125
  Thomas 59,98,103,125,
    135
  Thomas, Jr. 158
  William 103,117,129
Robertson, Abraham 103
  David 103
  Edward 103
  Henry 59,103,136
  Isaac 59
  John, Sr. 120

Robertson cont.
  John 60,103,122,124,136,
    145,154,167,171
  John, Jr. 60,103
  Mark 103
  Mary 93,124,181
  Matthew 60,126
  Nathaniel 103,143
  Nicholas 60,103
  Richard 124,127,136,158
  Robert 103
  Sarah 127
  Thomas 83,93,105,164,
    175
  William 60,103
Robinson, Abraham 60,98
  Edward 98
  Henry 158
  John 60,97,98,130,158,
    161,184
  John, Jr. 98
  Mark 98
  Mary 130
  Matthew 98
  Nathaniel 60,98,158,171
  William 158
Rockett, Richard 158
Roffe, William 61
  Richard W. 103,139
Roper, John 107
Rose, Howell 203
  Thomas 98
  William 98
Rottenberry, Henry Sr.
    175,176
  Henry 61,98,103
  Henry, Jr. 175
  John 98,103,145,158
  Margaret 173
  Martha 173
  Richard 173
  Samuel 145,158
  Susanna 198
  William 144
Rowland, Robert 162
Royal, John 149,158
  Joseph 61,98,122
  Sarah 149,167
Royster, Jacob 12,100,135,
    159
  Joseph 167
  William 61,100,135,143,
    159
Rudd, Joseph 127,159
Ruffin, John Col. 9,15,61
  John 147
  Robert 61,147,159,171
  William 167
Russell, Elizabeth 121,
    122,123
  Jeffrey 98,103,122,123,
    167
  Jeremiah 156
  John 85,167
  Philemon 101,123
  Philip 103,121,122
  Richard 118,149,156,
    159,171
  Thomas 152
Saffold, William 103,132
Sage, Henry 98,103,184
  John 203
Salle', Isaac 159,171
Samuel, John 157
Sandefer, William 61
Sanderlain, James 195
  Mary 195
Sandford, John 98
Sandifer, Elizabeth 134,
    159
  James 159,203
  Philip 159
  William 98,103,111,134,
    159

Sandifer cont.
  William, Jr. 159
Santhorpe, Thomas 103
Sargent, John 145,159
Satterwhite, Bartlett 159
  John 103,119,125,133
  Michael 103,119,125,131,
    137,138
  Thomas 62,98,103,105,109,
    110,119,125,133,150,
    159
Saunders, Jesse 203
  Meriwether 159
  Thomas 103
Sawyer, Elizabeth 196
Scarborough, Lewis 103
Scogin, John 81
Scott, Benjamin 102
  Elias 154
  Francis 184
  George 62
  Grissell 138
  J. 91
  James 62,118,120,138
  John 84,90,176
  Joseph 84
  Robert 62,159
  William 102
Searcy, Abraham 157
  Reuben 103,130,137,138
Seat, Elizabeth 195
  John 62
  Josiah 62
  Mary 195
  Robert 62
  Sarah 195
Seaton, William 159
Seawell, Benj. 179
Seeley, William 105,107
Seward, Henry 118
Shearman, John 106,107
  Katherine 106,107
Shelley, Amos Timms 62,63,
    135
Shelton, Thomas 175
Shepherd, John 104
Shockley, David 159
Shotwell, John 63
Shuffly, James 153
Simmons, Prudence 182
  Susanna 109
  Tabitha 183
Sims, Charles 93
  George 93
  Leonard 203
  Tabitha 182
Sisson, Thomas 85
  William 85
Sizemore, Edward 98,188
  Ephraim 98,203
  Henry 98
  James 98
  John 159
  William 98,159,188
Skelton, William 184
Skipwith, Peyton Sir 16
  Peyton, Jr. 203
Smith, Abraham 131
  Anderson 203
  Charles 63,98,100
  Cuthbert 91,92
  Drury 157
  Elizabeth 92
  Guy 143,159
  James 63,103,167
  John 62,103,167
  Luke, Sr. 108
  Luke, Jr. 98,108,137,138
  Martha 108
  Mary 180
  Obadiah 159,171
  Sarah 180
  Thomas 135
  Timothy 63

Smith cont.
  William 63,78,85,86
Smithson, Micajah 167
Solomon, William 151
Somerville, John 203
Sparrow, Henry 203
  James 63
  John 98
Spears, Augustine 103
Speed, Henry 164
  James 161,167,170,184
  John, Sr. 167,170
  John 11,63,89,99,103,
    106,107,110,116,119,
    122,126,135,139,142,
    146,147
  John, Jr. 11,159
  Joseph 203
  Lewis 167
Spencer, John 91
Spradley, John 101
Stafford, Labon 167
Stagner, John 103
Stanfield, Robert 131
Stanley, James 128,129
Stark, James 135
Starke, William 64,90,136
Steed, John 81
Stembridge, John 164
Stephens, Charles 99
  James 99
  John 177
  Mary 148
  Thomas 99,135
Stevens, John 159,170
  Mary 159,170
  Richard 162
  Thomas 94,103,159,170
Stewart, Anne 112
  Charles 64,112,123,134
  James 99
  John 64
Stith, Buckner 64,107
  Drury 7,64,65,83,94,112,
    123,132
  Richard 114,116,125,149,
    167
  Thomas 116
Stokes, Robert 128
Stone, William 103
Stovall, Bartholomew 100
  Sarah 195
  William 195
Strange, Mitchell 162
Street, Henry 155,171
  Richard 155
Stroud, William 65,78,203
Sullivan, Honour 178
  John 99,178
  Lucas 203
  Michael 178
  Owen 99
Sumerford, Jeffery 79
Swepson, Richard 11,13,
    103,148,149,159

Tabb, John 11,12
Tabor, Elizabeth 197
  Hezekiah 197
  John 103,131,197
  Judith 197
  Mary 197
  Rachel 197
  Riah 149,150
  Susannah 197
  William 92,93,99,105,
    131,150,197
  Zachariah 197
Talbert, William 153
Talbot, Charles 108,134,
    193
  Matthew 185
  Matthew, Jr. 113
Talley, Abraham 148

Talley cont.
  David 104,162
  Henry 65,99,127,137,139,
    147,148
  Henry, Jr. 184
  John 104
  Joseph 104,167
  Judith 137
Tanner, Branch 129,167,
    171
  Josiah 203
  Lewis 65,99,104,125,
    139,159
  Lucias 99,104,125,145
  Matthew 104,117,121,
    134,149,150,159
  Thomas 65,99,104,125,
    145,159
Tapley, Adam 88,89,125,
    130
  Hosea 82
Tarry, Samuel 162
Tate, Jesse 65
  Nathaniel 99
  Thomas 104,125
  William 99,150,159
  William, Jr. 150
Tatum, Peter 181
Taylor, David 203
  Edmund 11,12,65,66,159,
    169,203
  Ethread 91
  Goodwyn 159
  Henry 91
  James 137,159,184
  Jesse 203
  John 92,159
  Joseph 12
  Patience 91
  Philip 12
  Richard 203
  Samuel 98,138
  Thomas, Sr. 144,145
  Thomas 66,118,159
  Thomas, Jr. 145,159
  William 12,103,158,159
Tench, John R. 203
Thomas, David 173
  Elizabeth 173
  John 100
  Peter 153,173
Thomason, James 99,104,
    159
  John 78,159,175
  John, Jr. 175
  Mary 120
  William Turner 120
Thomerson, William 66
Thompson, John 66,97,99,
    104,112,143,148,159,
    164,184
  John Farley 159
  Michael 151
  Richard 104,122,159
  Wells 66,167
  William 66
Thomson, Mary 123
Thornton, John 129
Throughten, Andrew 135
Tibbs, William 66,167,184
Tillman, Roger 184
Tillotson, Edward 203
Tilman, George 91,178
  John 178
  William 91
Timms, Amos 66,99,125,
    145,167,170
  Amos, Jr. 99,125,142
  Hollis 167,170
  Walter 167,170
Tisdale, Edward 167
Toms, Margaret 82
  William 78,79,82,83,105
Tomson, John 66,119,122,123

Toney, James 159
Toone, Argelon 203
Torian, Pet. 187
  Scare 187
  Scher 187
Toriani, Scher 187
Toriano, Peter 187
  Scher 187
  Schertorio de 187
Towler, Sarah 190
Townsend, William 162,184
Traylor, Cary 203
  Joel 167
  Samuel 151
  William 99,132,167
Tucker, Elizabeth 77
  Francis 99
  Gardiner 159
  Isham 162
  James, Sr. 121
  James 67,104,121,122,
    133,149,159
  James, Jr. 121
  John 167
  Robert 95
Warner 104,119,121,122,
    164
  William 77,94,99,104
Tune, James 67
Tureman, George 104,163,
    167,171
  Joseph 13
Turner, James 91
Twitty, John 67,85,105,108,
    109,110,114,117,120,
    136,138
  Mary 118
  Thomas 83,89,106,118

Upton, Henry 99

Vaughan, George 99,142,160
  Ingram 203
  James 87,99,160,170,184
  John 160
  Lucy 193
  Reuben 67,104,143,160,
    170
  Stephen 67,167
  William 67,160
Vincent, James 96

Wade, Charles 104
  Hampton 111
  Henry 138
  John 99
  Randall 167
  Robert 104,111,131,136,
    137
  Robert, Jr. 123,136
  Stephen 102
Wagstaff, Basil 150,160
  Francis 138
Walke, Anthony 129
Walker, Alexander 191
  Aurelius 203
  Benjamin 203
  David 67,77,85,128
  Matthew 203
  Rebecca Broadnax 191
  Sylvanus 203
  Tandy 203
  William 184
Wall, John Major 178
  John 90
  John, Jr. 183
  Mary 177
  Michael Capt. 183
  Michael 84
Wallace, John 104
  William 104
Waller, John 99
Walton, George 68,108,119,
    124,128

Ward, Henry 131,150,160,
    171
  John 87
  Richard 95
  Wade 68,104,146,167
Warren, John 68
  Marriott 203
  Thomas 104
Washington, Richard 80
Watkins, John 178
Watson, Burwell 160
  George 160
  Henry 160
  James 171
  John 68,87,99,104,109,
    113,115,145,146,167
  John, Jr. 104,146
  Matthew 184
  Michael 167
  Rebecca 87,109
  William 104,160
Watts, Richard 175
  Thomas 99
  William 167,184
Weatherford, Benjamin 203
  Charles 99,104,139
  John 104,139,148,167
  Richard 68
  Temperance 132,133
  William 99,104,132,148
Webb, Elizabeth 198
Weekes, Michael 99
  Thomas 99
Wells, Barnaby 119
  Jesse 203
  John 99,104,115,118
  John, Jr. 99,104,135
  Lewis 135
  Susannah 135
  Thomas 98,104,118,135
Westbrook, John 163,171
  William 69
Westcott, Thomas 104
Westmoreland, Jesse 203
  John 69
Wheeler, Samuel 69,104
Whisell, Matthew 69
White, George 160
  James 160
  John 149,162,170,203(2)
  John F. 203
  Samuel 167
  William, Sr. 162,170,203
  William 104,116,117,118,
    138,184
Whitehead, Benjamin 69,167
Whitlock, James 151,171
Whitlow, Henry 69
Whitt, Edward 99
  John 104
  Richard 104
Whittemore, Abraham 146,
    160
  Jesse 168
  John 69,146,160
  William 104,146
Whittington, William 181
Whitworth, John 168
Wilbourn, John 69,99,104
Wildman, Elias 154
Wiles, Luke 69,99,197
  Margaret 194
  Mary 197
  Robert 99,104,131,160
  Stephen 30,104,197
  Thomas 99,104,143,160,
    197
Wilkerson, Elisha 203
Wilkins, Charles 203
  Hannah 119,126
  James 104,119,125,149,
    150,160,196
  John 70,84,92,93,104,
    105,108,109,110,119,

Wilkins cont.
  John cont. 150,196
  Mary 93,105
  Mary Ann 150
  Richard 101,196
  Susannah 196
  Thomas 99,104,105,109,
    125,133
  William 99,110,168,196
Williams, Benjamin 70,89
  David 70
  Henry 168
  James 70,99,109,110,
    111,120,168
  James A. 203
  John 99,118,168,203
  Joseph 124,168
  Matthew 104
  Peter 162
  Susanna 89
  Thomas 70
  Washington 203
  William 99,104,115,134,
    146,147
Williamson, John 160,198
  Martha Jones 129
  Thomas 129,133
Willie, William 9,107,125
Willis, Edward 104
  John 204
  Richard 160
  William 162
Williston, Mary 193
Wills, Matthew 160
  Richard 160
  Thomas 115
Wilson, Archibald 204
  Caleb 204
  Edward 104
  Elimileck 160
  Henry 104,168
  James 168
  John 175,204
  Nathaniel 70
  Robert 104
  Samuel 104,160
  Thomas 9,175
  William 99,104,160
Winders, Adam 104
Winfield, Joel 144
Witton, Richard, Sr. 168
  Richard 11,12,71,104,
    169,170
  Richard, Jr. 168,170
Womack, Alexander 168
  William 71,116
Wood, John 71
  Mary 182
  Penuel 124
  Richard 71,160
  Richard, Jr. 160
  Susanna 182
  William 99,106,124,132
Woodin, Robert 168
Wooding, Robert 7,104,119,
    123,128,129
Woodward, William 160
Wooten, Samuel 160
Wootton, David C. 204
Worsham, John 184
Wray, Francis 71,124
  John 91
Wright, Alice 191
  Edea 191
  Hannah 191
  Jane 191
  John 71,72,99,104,191
  Labon 144,145,160
  Mary 191
  Nathan 204
  Solomon 99,104
  Thomas 104
Wynne, William 83

Yancey, Archelaus 199
  Charles 162,170
  Charles, Jr. 199
  James 199
  Jechonias 199
  John 199
  Lewis 204
  Richard 143,162,170
  Robert 199
  William 204
Yarbrough, John 91
  William 196
Yates, William 160
York, David 102
  Mary 94
  Richard 72,94,175
  William 99
Young, John 98
  Lemuel 99,104
  Michael C. 78,88,175
  Michael Cadet 7,8,64,65,
    79,83,86,112,123
  Samuel 103,127,134,142,
    160

ERRATA

Anderson, Thomas 16
Banister, John 15
Blanks, Richard 200
Bolling, Major John 15
  John, Jr. 15
Brown, John 21
Burton, Thomas 201
Carleton, Thomas 16
Cheatham, Leonard 132
Cook, Abraham 178
Eastland, Thomas 201
Erskine, Alexander 15
Feild, Theophilus 15
Fox, Richard 201
Franklin, Hugh 16
Hunt, Memucan 15
Jeffries, John Jr. 16
Johnston, Peter 15
Jones, Peter 15
Langley, Robert 15
Morris, Henry 15
Munford, James 15
  William 15
Oliver, John 16
Pinson, Aaron, Sr. 189
  Aaron 15
Pool, Thomas 16
Ravenscroft, John 15
  Robert 15
  Thomas 15
Royster, Jacob 15
  William 16
Smith, William 16
Starke, William 15
Stith, Drury 15
Tureman, George 16
Walton, George 15
Wells, George 119
Westbrook, John 16
Young, Michael Cadet 15

www.ingramcontent.com/pod-product-compliance
Lightning Source LLC
Chambersburg PA
CBHW020649300426
44112CB00007B/297